Table of Contents

A Word from the Author, Donald H. Harrison vii

Torah Rebirth Sparks Spirit of "Ani Ma'amin":
    Awe and Joy Mingle in Tears of Worshipers 1

Courts of Honor 7

Salk Institute: Bringing Light to Science .19

The Vision of Jonas Salk 30

Welcome to Mount Rebbe 35

Drawing the Line against Hate: Abe Foxman Visits the Border . . .40

Saga of a Scroll: A Torah's Odyssey from Roudnice to
    San Diego 45

Giving Peace a Chance: Jewish Woman Directs New Peace
    Center at University of San Diego 61

Judaism under the Shade of a Torrey Pine:
    Adat Yeshurun Builds a New Home in La Jolla 73

"Sneak Preview" of the New Beth Israel .77

Carter, at USD Peace Center, Hits Bush Tribunals 80

Orthodox Girls School Finds a Happy Home on
    Reform Campus 83

What Swallowed Jonah? Sea World Educators Identify
    the Prime Suspects 86

Elephants in the Garden 91

Soille's Headmaster Passes on His Passion to a New Generation . . 94

San Diego Names Bayside Circle after Louis Rose,
    its First Jewish Settler 105

San Diego Jewish Academy: A Quarter Century of Teaching . . . 110

Many Farseeing Visions behind Ratner Children's Eye Center . . . 114

Rock Formations and Belief Systems
    Co-mingle in San Diego's Mission Trails Regional Park 120

Zion Avenue in San Diego: An American Street with Just a
    Bit of Jewish Flavoring 125

Stopping at San Diego's Airport for a Little
    Hometown Sightseeing. 132

Restoration of Casa de Bandini Wins Support from Religious,
    Ethnic Groups 136

A Star of David Button Is Intriguing Find at Presidio
    Golf Course 143

Here's Something on which Two Jews Can Agree:
    Torrey Pines State Reserve Is Uniquely Beautiful 147

"Any Hotel that Would Have Groucho as a Guest"
    Prompts Other La Valencia Stories 151

San Diego Mesa College Librarian Jack Forman a
    Connoisseur of Jewish Books 154

New Americans Museum Celebrates Some of This Country's
    Richest Blessings 158

Tibor Rubin, Jewish Recipient of Medal of Honor, Heads
    for San Diego Exhibit 165

A Conversation with Andrew Viterbi, National Medal
    of Science Laureate 170

But How Do the Fish Like Tashlich?........................178

UCSD Colleagues Recall Former Israel President Ephraim
  Katzir's Hideaway Life in La Jolla 180

Mingei International Museum 185

Model Railroad Museum, Balboa Park 189

Three Generations of Commanding Officers Probe
  Star Trek's Popularity.................................193

"Liberation Moment" at Miramar National Cemetery
  Honors American Ex-POWs...........................196

A Visit to the House of Israel.............................200

New Americans Museum Debuts Again 203

JFS Dedicates its Jacobs Family Campus 206

Israeli Rain Barrel System on Trial at 3 Schools 210

Gravitating to the Familiar at the Fleet 214

San Diego Schools Salute Conductor David Amos 218

Jewish Community Day with the Padres....................221

La Jolla Walkway Named for Walter Munk, 100..............223

Tifereth Israel Prayer Space Named for Aaron Gold 227

Community Says Farewell to Gussie Zaks, z"l 232

JFS, Looking Back a Century, Recalls Rose Neumann.........239

Sea World Encounters on World Penguin Day...............247

Lag B'Omer at Kumeyaay Lake Campground................253

Evangelical Christian Directs StandWithUs in San Diego 257

Curator Tells of LGBTQ+ History, Struggles, Triumphs........271

Survivor Ruth G. Sax Impresses Comic-Con Audience.........282

Plaque Recalling First Roseville Hotel Unveiled. 287

Crafts, Art, Books Featured at Temple Emanu-El Fair. 290

Christina de Jesus Is a Jewish Song Leader 295

Variety of Form, Materials in SDMA Outdoor Sculptures 302

Jews of the U.S. Military Honored at Veterans Museum 310

"Escape the Nat" Diversifies the Museum Experience. 314

Immigrant Stories Told at New Americans Museum. 319

Sightseeing Review: Seal Tours. 323

Sightseeing Review: "Living with Animals" Exhibit 327

Intermarried Couple Honors Each Other's Beliefs. 331

Sightseeing: Adventure Hornblower Whale Watching 338

The Fleet and "The Nat" Teach about Water 342

Sightseeing Review: Birch Aquarium 350

Weinberger v. Taft in Arizona Statehood Battle 354

Community Mourns Rabbi Leonard Rosenthal 357

The Charity We Need Now: The Bus Station Project
    Serves Migrant Families at the Border. 363

Index 369

A Word from the Author, Donald H. Harrison

Most Jewish residents of San Diego County are unaware of how rich a history and how varied an experience Jews have had in this southwestern corner of the continental United States. This is not their fault. Most have moved to San Diego County from other parts of the United States or from other countries. My hope for this first book in a two-volume set is that it can fill in some of the blanks for both the Jewish and Gentile communities, while providing source material for local historians and journalists who wish to treat local Jewish history more extensively.

I have been a journalist since 1962 when I joined the staff of the UCLA *Daily Bruin* and went on to write freelance stories for the *Los Angeles Times* and the *Los Angeles Herald Examiner* before becoming a fulltime reporter and editor for the Associated Press, working in the Los Angeles, Sacramento, and New York Foreign Desk bureaus. In 1972, I came to San Diego as a politics writer for *The San Diego Union*, remaining in that position until 1980, when I began work in the field of public relations. I served as communications director for San Diego's Acting Mayor Bill Cleator, supervised local coverage of the visit to San Diego in 1983 of Queen Elizabeth II, and then branched into tourism, serving as the executive director of the San Diego Cruise Industry Consortium, and as one of the founders and first general manager of Old Town Trolley Tours of San Diego.

Missing reporting, even as I continued to earn my living in tourist-related public relations, I began volunteering as a writer for the *San Diego Jewish Press Heritage*, eventually working my way up to its editorship. When publisher Herb Brin, for financial reasons, had to close the Heritage newspapers in Los Angeles, Orange County, and Central California, Norman Greene and I decided to try to save the San Diego edition. We co-published it for another two years, through the end of 2003, before we had to fold it because of insufficient revenue. Thereafter, I continued in my role as the chronicler of San Diego's Jewish community by writing a column for the *San Diego Jewish Times,* which had been a friendly rival to the Heritage. But that newspaper also had to fold.

Next, with encouragement from the former staffs of the *Heritage* and the *Jewish Times,* I converted a website I had named jewishsightseeing.com to one called *San Diego Jewish World*, which since then has been offering a daily diet of feature stories, arts reviews, op-ed pieces, travelogues, and San Diego-based, Jewish-themed news coverage. Approximately 50 writers have been regularly contributing on various frequencies to *San Diego Jewish World*.

Along the way, I also have written four Jewish-themed books, in addition to these present two volumes. The first was *Louis Rose: San Diego's First Jewish Settler and Entrepreneur* (2005), which was both a biography and a history of San Diego's first 38 years as an American city, from 1850 to 1888. I had found that, up to the time I undertook the project, general histories of San Diego seemed to take little notice of the growth of the Jewish community, while Jewish histories about the area often did not integrate the Jewish experience into the overall story of the city's development. Because Louis Rose was an active, engaged civic and political leader in San Diego, I was able to weave both the general and Jewish histories of San Diego together.

The biography was well received, eventually leading to my appointment to the editorial board of the *Journal of San Diego History*, and to a contributing editorship and later editorship of *Western States Jewish History*. I also wrote extensively in other publications about San Diego's Jewish community, including the centennial book of Tifereth Israel Synagogue, and a history of the Wax family and Waxie Sanitary Supply. The theme of *San Diego Jewish World* is "There is a Jewish Story Everywhere," and pursuing that approach, I also wrote two Jewish-themed travel books. The first was *Schlepping Through the American West: There Is a Jewish Story Everywhere*, and the second was *77 Miles of Jewish Stories: History, Anecdotes & Tales of Travel Along I-8*.

This current effort, *Schlepping and Schmoozing Through San Diego County*, is a city by city, town by town, collection of Jewish stories (with a few exceptions) that I have covered in the county over the years. Some stories are about places, others are about interesting individuals who have had an impact in our area, and all are Jewish-themed.

No book is ever a solo effort. This one has been a family enterprise. Nancy, my wife since 1968, has filled a role analogous to that of a television producer, lining up appointments for interviews and tours. My daughter, Sandi Masori, who makes a living coordinating the production and marketing of books, is a never-failing source of good advice. My grandson, Shor Masori, an accomplished photographer, often accompanies on assignments. John Finley, not related by blood but nevertheless a member of our extended family, proofread and critiqued stories.

In addition to these relatives and friends, I would like to thank the San Diego Jewish community, which has been a continuing source of inspiration, amusement, and fulfillment. I hope you, the readers, will enjoy getting to know the community's institutions and personalities.

— San Diego, 2019

Torah Rebirth Sparks Spirit of "Ani Ma'amin": Awe and Joy Mingle in Tears of Worshipers

San Diego Jewish Press Heritage,
January 2, 1987

After touching his prayer book to the Holocaust Memorial Torah, and then to his lips, one member of Tifereth Israel Synagogue had to tuck his book under his left arm. His right hand was needed to rub the tears from his eyes. On that Friday night, December 19, it was thus with so many members of the Conservative congregation. But with their tears there were smiles.

Multiple emotions were reflected on the faces of the people who were selected to escort this very special Torah in the procession. The man who had the honor of carrying it, Gary Pollak, had an expression of mixed pride and awe.

What a moment it was for him! He was the father of the *bat mitzvah*—Tanya Pollak—in whose name his family had decided to underwrite the cost of making this Torah once again kosher for ceremonial Jewish use.

Indeed, Pollak also was the son of Bernard Pollak who had survived numerous concentration camps, including Auschwitz, and the son-in-law of Henrietta Revel, who had spent her childhood in hiding from the Nazis.

And now these forebearers, whose will to survive had enabled Gary to reach this moment, were walking just behind Pollak, along with his wife Brigitte, and his children, Tanya and Jeffrey.

In this ceremony celebrating the recovery for Judaism of a Torah that the Nazis had planned to make a museum piece, the Pollak family was followed by some 40 members and dependents of San Diego's New Life Club—the club of Holocaust survivors who had made new lives for themselves in San Diego County.

In their faces, too, one could observe the bitter sweetness of this moment. Here, one was smiling, joyfully shaking hands and wishing "Good Shabbos" to his friends in the congregation.

Here was another in whose throat the lump was so visible, it made one want to cry for him. And here was a third whose expression was a mystery, whose eyes seemed to be looking inward, dwelling on who knows what memories.

The procession was accompanied by the singing by the choir of "Ani Ma'amin"—"I believe"—the song which through time has become the anthem of the Six Million Jews who perished at the hands of the Nazis.

Its words come from the 13 principles of faith enunciated by Maimonides: "I believe in the coming of the Messiah, and even when he tarries, still I believe." Words echoing that sentiment were found on a wall of a cellar in Cologne, Germany, where some Jews hid from the Nazis. In translation, their poem said:

> *I believe in the Sun even when it is not shining.*
> *I believe in love even when not feeling it.*
> *I believe in God even when He is silent.*

"Ani Ma'amin" were the words that Dr. Jacqueline Jacobs, a pediatrician and textile artist, chose to put on the top of the Torah mantle that she had been commissioned to design for this Holocaust Memorial Torah.

At its bottom, the Torah mantle depicted the darkness of the concentration camp, with jagged threading graphically portraying the barbed wire of the camp. Some butterflies are caught on the barbed wire, but others have managed to soar to the light above.

From dark to light. From the horror of the Nazis to the free practice of the Jewish religion today. Like the survivors of the Holocaust, the very Torah which the mantle now covered had gone from the darkness to the light.

How exquisite of Dr. Jacobs, attuned in her medical practice to bringing care and comfort to ailing children, to remember in her artistic practice a portion of that heart-rending poem of Pavel Friedmann, one of the thousands of youths sent from the Terezin concentration camp to be murdered by the Nazis at Auschwitz.

For seven weeks I've lived here
Penned up inside this ghetto
But I have found my people here.
The dandelions call to me
And the white chestnut candles in the court.
Only I never saw another butterfly.

"Here, Pavel, here are your butterflies!" the congregation seemed to be saying as the procession ended and the Torah was placed in a compartment in Holocaust case at the side of the sanctuary. "On Saturday, when Tanya becomes a *bat mitzvah,* she'll read from this Torah, and Pavel, she'll see your beloved butterflies!"

3

Once this Torah had been used in the central synagogue of Prague, Czechoslovakia—the synagogue that once boasted the most famous rabbi in his time in Central Europe, Judah Loew ben Bezalel, known popularly as the Maharal.

The Maharal had lived in the late 16th and early 17th Centuries, and had been one of the leading commentators on the Torah in his day.

Among his numerous publications, ironically, was a work whose title became the name of the synagogue where the Torah dedication was now taking place: "Tifereth Israel," the glory of Israel.

According to the folk legends of both the Jews and the Czechs, the Maharal once had fashioned from clay a monstrous man, called a golem, and had been able to bring the golem to life by pronouncing the sacred name of God. The golem, according to the legend, defended Prague's Jewish and Gentile inhabitants from outside attack.

While just a folk legend, the story of the Maharal and his golem had become so popular in Czechoslovakia that during this century when the authorities wished to commemorate the early history of Prague, they built outside the Town Hall two statues: one of an ancient medieval knight; the other, of the Maharal. The Maharal's statue still is standing in the remnants of what once had been Prague's self-governing Jewish community.

Alas, there was no golem to protect either the synagogue or the rest of Prague against the Nazis. Czech Jews were rounded up and sent to the nearby Terezin concentration camp *en route* to the death camps.

The Torahs and other ceremonial religious objects were seized by the Nazis and sent to the Jewish Museum, where Jewish inmates were forced to catalogue them for a museum the Nazis planned to build in celebration of the extinction of Judaism.

Those Jewish archivists did their work meticulously hoping that by keeping exact records some day in the future when the madness subsided, these objects could be returned to their owners or to their heirs.

It was because of their work that the exact origin of the Holocaust Memorial Torah would become known to the authorities who safeguarded it and hundreds of scrolls like it following World War II.

The Holocaust Torah had been stored by the Czech government in the collection that one day was to become the source for the Precious Legacy exhibition that recently toured the United States.

But well before the Precious Legacy was put together, the Czechoslovakian government in 1964 agreed to turn over 1,564 scrolls to the Westminster Synagogue in London for repair and distribution to Jewish congregations around the world.

Rabbi Aaron Gold, spiritual leader of Tifereth Israel Synagogue and himself the son of a Polish Chasidic rabbi, visited Europe in 1968 and stood on the *bima* where the Maharal once had served his congregation.

Little did he dream that the London authorities to whom he later applied for the Torah would make available to his congregation exactly 10 years later in 1978 a Torah from the actual Czech synagogue he had visited.

While the Torah had been on exhibit as a museum piece since its arrival at Tifereth Israel in 1978, it could be used in regular worship only after Rabbi Gold had it taken to a scribe in Los Angeles, Rabbi Shmuel Zadok, who made certain that every letter of the Torah conformed to Holy Scripture.

In between 1880 and World War II in Prague, this Torah had been part of the same culture as such famous Czech Jews as Franz Kafka, Sigmund Freud, Albert Einstein, and the parents of United States Supreme Court Justice Louis Brandeis.

How many more Kafkas, Brandeises, Einsteins, or Jonas Salks were wiped out by the Nazi Holocaust? demanded Rabbi Gold during his sermon. In those Six Million was there the founder of the cure for cancer? For AIDS? The one who could have brought world peace?

Rabbi Gold noted in his sermon that this ceremony of dedication fell just a week before the first day of Chanukah. How rich the parallel.

Even as the Maccabees reclaimed the ancient Temple for Jewish life after withstanding another attempt to extinguish Judaism, so too, today, had the Jews of San Diego witnessed the reclaiming for Jewish life of a Holy Torah by a family who had withstood and survived the Nazi scheme to exterminate the Jewish people.

Courts of Honor

San Diego Jewish Press Heritage,
April 29, 1994

There are two federal courthouses in San Diego. The older one was named in 1988 for a well-loved Jewish judge, who had died 14 years before. The newer one may soon be named for another Jewish judge, still living, who is equally revered by his judicial colleagues.

The House of Representatives, with one dissenting vote, approved legislation April 12, sponsored by Rep. Lynn Schenk (D-San Diego) to name the newer building the Edward J. Schwartz Courthouse and Federal Building.

As the legislation, H.R. 3770, was being prepared by House clerks to be sent to the Senate for consideration, Rep. Schenk called Schwartz to tell him of the honor she and his fellow jurists had cooked up for him. "But I'm not dead yet!" exclaimed Schwartz, utterly surprised.

Exactly 10 days later, on April 22, federal judges and other dignitaries gathered at 325 W. F Street to dedicate the Jacob Weinberger United States Courthouse, which had been vacant since 1976, when the new federal court building at 940 Front Street was opened.

The older courthouse had been renamed in honor of Weinberger in 1988 in anticipation that someday it would house the federal bankruptcy court—which now is in the process of moving into the refurbished Spanish colonial building.

For the rededication ceremony, a Marine Corps band played patriotic airs; red, white, and blue bunting was wrapped around the bases of the courthouse's 10, three-story-high columns, and the United States and California flags were raised ceremoniously atop the courthouse's two bastions.

The top step of the courthouse was used as a dais, and there the national and state flags were joined by a third flag—that of our neighboring state of Arizona.

In 1910, Weinberger had served as an elected member of the convention which drafted Arizona's state constitution. Fifty years later, he was honored by that state as the last surviving member of the 52 constitutional framers.

The federal judge who served as emcee for last Friday's ceremonies was John Rhoades, who had been a leader in the campaign to have the building physically renovated, then restored to use as a courthouse instead of as a catch-all adjunct federal building housing a variety of agencies.

"It looks like a courthouse; it smells like a courthouse; it says 'courthouse' on the front; it should be a courthouse," Rhoades had often been quoted as saying.

The ceremony over which Rhoades presided provided skillfully blended elements of the life of Weinberger, who immigrated to the United States from Hungary as a boy.

In his career as a federal judge, Weinberger had naturalized more than 16,000 new American citizens, telling them: "It isn't a fairy tale; it's true. America will give back thrice-fold what you give to her. She did it for me, and she can do it for you."

Reflecting that aspect of Weinberger's life was a presentation of some of the flags of the world by representatives of Balboa Park's House of Pacific Relations, most of whom wore traditional dress.

Ironically, though invited, no representative of the Cottage of Israel was present. The cottage's president, Morris Showel, later told *Heritage* he wanted to participate in the ceremony but was unable to do so because of the recent amputation of his malignant right thumb.

During Friday's ceremony, Joyce Ling-Yaiin Liou, a San Diego High School student who immigrated from Burma, recalled to the audience that, when she took the oath of citizenship in 1986, "I could feel a light breeze against my skin. The sound of waves crashing against the shore and seagulls flying above . . . seemed like an orchestra playing in the background."

A sculpture in the courthouse's lobby area provided a more permanent reminder of the special place the naturalization process had in Weinberger's heart. T.J. Dixon and James Nelson's piece shows a father, mother, and child—"a family that has come to this country to seek their dreams," Rhoades said.

The sculpture, a plaque, and furnishings inside the building were paid for by the Jacob Weinberger Foundation.

Between the time that Weinberger helped draft the Arizona Constitution in 1910 and when he was appointed a federal judge in 1946 by President Harry S. Truman, he had become deeply involved in both civic and Jewish affairs in San Diego, to which he had moved in 1911.

A member of Congregation Beth Israel, Weinberger was the founder in 1937 of the United Jewish Fund, the forerunner organization of today's United Jewish Federation. Under Weinberger, the United Jewish Fund strived to "help Jews caught in the web of the Hitler debacle" and to foster Jewish settlements in Palestine.

The family's dedication is reflected in in the local Weinberger-Breitbard Lodge of B'nai B'rith being partially named for Jacob's brother, Henry Weinberger.

From 1918 to 1939, Jacob Weinberger had been a member of the San Diego Board of Education—a role that was remembered by his successors when they named the Weinberger Elementary School after him. Later, when various schools were consolidated, he shared the honor with San Diego Zoo curator Belle Benchley in the combined name of the Benchley-Weinberger School.

Rhoades introduced Erin Chambers, a pupil of Benchley-Weinberger School, who led the audience in the salute to the flag.

Rhoades credited Judge Richard Chambers with the following version of Weinberger's wedding in Arizona Territory in 1907 to the former Blanche Solomon.

"The ice cream not arriving . . . and a Mormon lady saving the day. The rabbi's train being stopped by a trestle being washed out and the wild ride by stagecoach to the ceremony . . . And the need to open up the general store to find shoes for the waiters who had arrived for the wedding dinner barefoot.

"All of these yarns were pulled with the special detail of a Swiss watch, and of course with a Chambers' twist to the account . . . It turns out that Judge Chambers viewed the festivities from a baby basket, he was but a few months old at the time."

Rhoades also said that Chambers, former chief justice of the U.S. Circuit Court of Appeals, was responsible for leading the campaign to fund $13 million for the refurbishment of the 51,500-square-foot building erected in 1913.

"San Diego has precious few buildings that reflect our history, our heritage—buildings that give us a link to the past . . . I am sure that you will agree that it is worth every penny put into it," Rhoades said. Harry C. Hallenbeck of Hallenbeck, Chamorro & Associates was the architect for the project.

Judge James Meyers, chief judge of the U.S. Bankruptcy Court, said the five judges and 74 employees of the bankruptcy court "now will have a home we can call our own" instead of being spread out over two buildings.

Meyers said that when he was a young Assistant United States Attorney, he was impressed by Judge Weinberger's "natural politeness." Meyer pledged that the bankruptcy courts would continue the "Weinberger tradition of civility."

Judge Schwartz was introduced by Rhoades, without any reference being made to the fact that Rhoades is planning to emcee a similar ceremony at the new courthouse as soon as the legislation is enacted naming it for Schwartz.

At one point, Rhoades and his fellow judges had planned to surprise Schwartz at this ceremony with the news of the naming— but because passage of the bill had been televised over C-SPAN, Congressman Schenk and Judge Judith Keep, chief judge of the U.S. District Court, decided Schwartz should be notified before he heard the news from anyone else.

Schwartz's role at this ceremony was to summarize some of the high points of Weinberger's 92 years of life—and in doing so, he referred to Weinberger often as "Jake."

First, however, he explained that although some people consider the name "Jake" not so dignified as "Jacob," that Weinberger himself signed personal messages with the nickname.

The explanation probably told the audience more about Schwartz than about Weinberger; like his predecessor, Schwartz is considered by his colleagues to be a model of civility. He wouldn't dream of playing light with a man's feelings, not even a *dead* man's.

Schwartz said that "Jake" was one of 10 children and that his family first had settled in Colorado. As a boy, Weinberger saw an accused murderer taken from a jail and lynched, an event which may have planted Weinberger's devotion to due process.

From high school, Weinberger went straight to law school, graduating in 1904, and moving a year later to Globe, Arizona, where in the space of six years he served as a deputy district attorney, and as an elected representative to the Arizona constitutional convention.

In San Diego, Weinberger founded the law firm that today is one of San Diego's best known: Higgs, Fletcher & Mack. At one point, his name was listed first on the law firm's letterhead, but it was removed when he was appointed a Superior Court judge in 1946. He held a position for only a brief time before losing it in an election. President Truman promptly appointed him to the federal bench.

At first, Weinberger was based as a judge in Los Angeles, headquarters for the judicial district which included San Diego. But in 1949, San Diego became the headquarters for a new federal court district, and Weinberger became its first resident federal judge.

Schwartz said that when he was appointed to the federal bench in 1968 by President Lyndon B. Johnson, Weinberger became his mentor.

At the time "my knowledge of federal law and procedure was minimal," Schwartz said. "Jake's kindness helped me become a reasonable facsimile of a federal judge."

He said that Weinberger "avoided contentiousness and turmoil" and, unlike the motto of President Theodore Roosevelt, he "spoke softly and carried a silken wand."

There was a final, special touch in the ceremony honoring Weinberger. His great-grandson, Jacob Weinberger Weil, a fifth-grade student who lives in the Central California town of Springville, joined Judge Meyers in symbolically opening the doors of the courthouse.

Young Jake's mother, Gay Weinberger Weil (a granddaughter of Judge Weinberger) was prevented by illness from traveling down for the ceremony. But there was no shortage of family present to cheer on the young, pre-bar mitzvah boy.

The audience included the judge's son, Richard, who is young Jakes's grandfather. Also present were three other granddaughters of the judge: Jeri Hafter, Jill Rigoli, and Wendy Bowers, all of San Diego.

How does it feel to open a courthouse named for a great grand-father? "Pretty neat," young Weil commented later to *Heritage.*

Mickey Fredman and Jim Hall, both of whom attained prominence of their own in civic affairs, remember the Weinberger era well.

Fredman once served as a commissioner of the San Diego Unified Port District and Hall once was head of the California Business and Transportation Agency under Ronald Reagan's governorship.

Shortly after becoming a lawyer at the state level, "I didn't know what to do with myself, so I walked into the federal court to watch the proceedings there," Fredman recalled.

"A fellow was charged with smuggling aliens, and the judge (Weinberger) asked him if he needed an attorney. He looked out and saw me, and said, 'Mr. Fredman, I appoint you. Are you a member of this court?' When I said I wasn't, he instructed me to raise my right hand and swore me in on the spot, charging me the fee of $5.

"Through an interpreter, I started talking to my client and found out that he wanted a carton of cigarettes. That cost me another $1.50 . . . so in the space of a few minutes, I was out $6.50."

In another case, Fredman said, "We were finishing our witnesses—it was getting close to 5 p.m.—and Weinberger asked, 'Are you ready for my decision?' I said, 'I haven't closed yet,' and he said, 'Well, it is 5 o'clock and I've made up my mind.' P.S. I lost."

Hall recalled arguing a case before Weinberger around the time that the judge was 80. "He knew exactly what I was going to say before I was going to say it," Hall said.

"He was never aggressive or bombastic, but he could be very direct," Hall said. "He required you to keep a hand on the podium—to maintain physical contact at all times—so you wouldn't stray as you presented. You observed all the rules of procedure in his courtroom."

* * *

Although federal judges are given life-long appointments, some choose to retire outright when they get on in years. However, even though he is 82 years old, Judge Ed Schwartz leads a very active life.

He has the posture and stamina of a much younger man, and anyone who doubts that might want to challenge him to a round of tennis or to a bike ride around Lake Miramar—two of his regular exercises.

True, he has slowed down a little. At his request, he no longer serves as chief judge of the U.S. District Court, a post he occupied for 13 of his 26 years on the federal bench.

Today, he is a senior judge, meaning he can determine which cases he wants to hear and which he doesn't. Those that fall in the latter category are assigned by present Chief Judge Judith Keep to the other district judges.

Judge Keep has respected Schwartz for a long time; after all, it was Schwartz who swore both her and Congresswoman Schenk in as lawyers in the first place. Today, Schwartz chooses to hear quite a few civil law cases, explaining in an interview with *Heritage* that he feels fit and that his wife, Gertrude, needs no help in running the house.

Judge Rudi Brewster said the 12 judges of the Southern District of California, the formal name for the courts of San Diego and Imperial Counties, are "very, very close with a high level of collegiality and camaraderie, and a great bond of mutual respect."

Every Monday they have lunch together to discuss the calendar.

Because criminal cases often are "pleaded out" before they get to court, as many as six to eight criminal cases will be put on a single judge's calendar for the same day, and only one still will be pending by the time that day arrives, Brewster said.

However, sometimes two or more cases still will be pending, and then the judges will see if any of their colleagues have the time to hear them instead. "Someone will say, 'flip me one,' and the judge will try the case, and keep our calendar moving along," Brewster said.

"The tradition for this attitude among us is attributable to Ed Schwartz; that's the way he ran the court when he was chief," Brewster told *Heritage*. "When he was chief, he inculcated in the newcomers the recognition that this is a cooperative and mutually respectful court."

"The attitude and traditions are very strong," Brewster continued. "It's almost as if we are all law partners, yet none of us selected each other. We all were appointed by presidents—and four or five of them, Republicans and Democrats, are represented on this court."

"Today, Ed basically tries civil cases, but three weeks ago I had two criminal cases to try," Brewster said. "He had just settled a civil case, so he was clear. He told me he'd be happy to try the criminal case, and he tried it in two days. Boom, and it was over."

Brewster, Keep, and Rhoades all told *Heritage* that they voted to ask Rep. Schenk to sponsor a bill naming the new courthouse for Schwartz based on the fact that he fought for a design that would enhance—rather than detract—from judicial business.

Originally the design proposed by the federal government was for "Tom Thumb courtrooms—not big enough for what we needed," Rhoades said. "He appeared before he Congress, stuck to his guns, and deserves the recognition."

"We handle so many matters which involve many, many people that we literally fill up our courtrooms, Brewster said. "A high percentage of the time we need all the room we've got."

Courtrooms measuring 28 feet by 40 feet with 10-foot high ceilings had been proposed; Schwartz persuaded Congress that they should be 44 feet by 45 feet with the traditional 12-foot ceilings. Previously courtrooms had measured 40 by 60 feet, so once again Schwartz had engineered a satisfactory settlement.

The idea to name the building for him "was very spontaneous among the judges," Judge Keep said. "It came up because one of the courthouses in Orange County has been named after Ronald Reagan (who is still alive) and we said, "Wouldn't it be wonderful if we could name ours after Ed Schwartz?"

"We thought it would be a wonderful surprise, a golden cap for a wonderful career," the chief judge said. "He rates among the best of the legal profession. He is very courtly, very calm, never loses his temper; he is fair, well-respected by other judges; he has an incredible temperament."

Beyond that, she said, "He had to fight enormous battles to get this building built; he had to fight to get it in Congress . . . and then he and his wife supervised everything from blueprints to construction. It was a labor of love for him."

Judge Keep said the judges also wanted the building named for Schwartz while he was alive so he could know "how honored he is by the judges who have served with him and by the Bar."

Congresswoman Schenk said she had no difficulty moving the bill through the House, except for the fact that Rep. Scott McInnis (R-Colorado) "put in his voting card and pressed the wrong button," thereby representing a lone nay vote against the bill. "He called later to apologize, saying that, if he could have withdrawn his 'no' vote, he would have."

When Rep. Schenk telephoned Schwartz, she called "to confess there is a conspiracy going on behind your back to name the courthouse after you." When he protested that he wasn't dead yet, the congresswoman said she replied, "That's the whole point; we wanted to do it while you were alive."

"Aren't you taking a chance?" Schwartz next asked. "I might do something to embarrass you."

"I don't think you'll do anything to tarnish your name," Rep. Schenk replied.

Among members of the bar who remember Schwartz fondly are Alec Cory who was his law partner in a firm that also included Sol Price and Frank Knotbusch.

After World War II, Cory said, "office space was kind of hard to find, but one space was available in the San Diego Trust and Savings Building. Ed and I got there at the same time and met each other. Since there was only one space, we decided we would divide it, and formed the partnership of Cory and Schwartz.

"Next door to our office was another firm, which had been there a few years, called Price and Knotbusch. After a little while, we just got together and merged the two."

Price went on to become a merchandiser, first running Fed-Mart and later founding the Price Club. Knotbusch became a municipal court judge. Only Cory remained in the firm, although he, too, received recognition when he was appointed a state college trustee. Today the firm which Schwartz helped found is called Procopio, Cory, Hargreaves & Savitch.

"Ed was a very quiet, conservative, capable, honorable guy," Cory said. "You couldn't have a better partner."

Schwartz has lived in San Diego since he was three; he sold newspapers here as a "child of the Depression" and worked constantly.

He is a member of Congregation Beth Israel and a supporter of the United Jewish Federation. He has a son, Stephen, who is a tile and marble contractor in Encinitas, and two daughters, Suzanne Friestedt, a public relations practitioner, and Eileen Boniecka, a graphics designer.

Schwartz left Cory's firm in 1959 when he was appointed a municipal court judge by Governor Edmund G. "Pat" Brown, who later elevated him to the Superior Court in 1964.

Attorney Frederick "Pat" Crowell said he always enjoyed trying a case before Schwartz because "he has a great sense of fairness, is a good guy, and a damn good judge."

"He didn't put on a lot of airs about running the court; I thought he did a great job," Crowell added. Not a bad compliment considering that Crowell "tried my very first lawsuit before Ed, and lost it."

Attorney Mike Poynor says Schwartz wears "the brightest color ties, always full of energy and good will, and is fair to people."

For his own part, Schwartz says, "When I was a lawyer, I always wanted a judge to sit there patiently and hear me out."

Practicing before the federal court, he said, "is the spectrum of lawyers—some great and some in the middle range—and a judge has the obligation of moving cases. So, I do it, but I try not to be offensive."

Salk Institute: Bringing Light to Science

San Diego Jewish Press Heritage,
September 9, 1994

Before the Salk Institute was built, in a collaboration between Dr. Jonas Salk and architect Louis I. Kahn, the two men energized each other by speculating how basic features of the environment—air, light, water, views—could stimulate humans to make great leaps of creativity.

The two men's conclusions found material shape in 1965 when the Salk Institute for Biological Studies was opened on a site in La Jolla overlooking a bluff where hang gliding enthusiasts strap on wings and soar on wind currents to the beach below in a daily expression of human poetry.

The man who succeeded Salk as president of the Institute, Dr. Renato Dulbecco, won a Nobel Prize in 1975 for basic research into the processes of cancer—research that he said was favorably influenced by the environment which Salk and Kahn had created for him to labor within.

Now under the leadership of a third president, the epidemiologist Dr. Brian Henderson, the Salk Institute is reaping even more dividends from the interaction of great minds working in an environment conductive to their creativity.

Recently, the Institute for Scientific Information culled research papers published in various learned journals, counting each instance when a scientist cited the work of a colleague. In its prestigious publication, *Science Watch,* it ranked the top 25 institutions based on the average number of times their research was cited in a minimum of 200 papers. Salk Institute was rated first both in molecular biology/genetics and in neuroscience.

Obviously, something must be working well. But the prevalent feeling on the beautiful campus is that much remains to be done. Conceptually, architecturally, scientifically, the Salk Institute is what artists like to call "a work in progress."

* * *

I had the chance to meet Jonas Salk, founding director of the Salk Institute, in his office overlooking the bluff. I didn't have the opportunity to interview him for the record, but he did show to me a sketch of the institute as he envisions it in the future. He also gave me plenty of reading material to take home with me.

Imagine a diver a moment after he has leaped into the air, his head is tucked in; his arms are stretched out parallel in front of him. The current buildings of the Salk Institute occupy the head and body of the campus, but Salk envisions twin ridges jutting into the Pacific with centers for lodgings for the great thinkers of the arts and the human sciences.

As he will turn 80 in October., Salk's planning reminds me of the *midrash* about the elderly man who plants a fig tree-obviously not for his own benefit but for that of future generations.

It was on the beach between these two ridges that Salk's friend and original fellow at the institute, the late Jacob Bronowski, narrated several portions of the PBS television series *The Ascent of Man,* in which he suggested that we can trace man's development by his great leaps of imagination as represented in the works he left behind.

Copernicus, the astronomer who first suggested that maybe the Earth revolves around the Sun, and not vice versa, had to have such a leap of faith. Imagine him standing still and extending his arms out horizontally like the familiar Leonardo da Vinci drawing, and then slowly turning himself around, picturing his head as the Sun and his hands as orbiting planets. Could such a leap of imagination have been inspired by the famous da Vinci drawing? Could art profoundly have influenced the course of science?

In one of his books which is entitled *Man Unfolding* in English, but is called in French *Metaphor Biologique* (Biological Metaphor), Salk suggests that the discoveries made by the biological sciences such as how a cell is formed, how it deals with environmental factors, what causes it to become cancerous, and so forth, may be of great value to practitioners of what he calls the "human sciences," such as philosophers, sociologists, political scientists, psychologists, and authors, as they try to understand human behaviors and societies.

"The potential for nobility, as well as for brutality, must be biologically endowed and therefore is present at birth," he also speculated in that 1972 work. "There must be a time in life when man's nobility could be evoked and then strengthened . . . ."

"If school is a part of life itself, and not merely preparation for life, then should we not expect nobility there to serve as an example?" Salk continued. "Can nobility be taught, just as reading, writing, arithmetic, and biology are taught?"

Perhaps drawing upon his experience of successfully introducing a polio vaccine made from a "killed" virus, at a time when orthodox scientists believed only a weakened "live" virus would do the trick, Salk switched to an inoculation metaphor to pursue his speculation further.

"Perhaps," he wrote, "we should seek a preventive against the human disease which we might call 'brutality.' What could we 'inject' to induce a positive effect, how can it be done, and when?"

21

As Salk unrolled for me old plans for the extension of the campus, I tried to imagine "biological" scientists and "human" scientists engaged in a great symposium, discussing in free-form style, brutality preventatives and other subjects.

Would not a poet enjoy such a rap session with Dr. Francis Crick, the Nobel Prize-winning co-discoverer of DNA, who was among the original faculty of the Salk Institute?

Don't think scientists care only for dry formulas and pungent test tubes. C.P. Snow, the physicist turned novelist, was an original trustee of the Institute. And Crick, just for the fun of speculating, once proposed that life on Earth could have started when alien beings sprinkled seed spores all over the Earth.

Outside Salk's window, another hang glider enjoyed the view reserved for those with the courage to leap.

* * *

Dr. Walter Eckhart is the director of the Salk Institute's Armand Hammer Center for Cancer Research, so named because the Los Angeles industrialist and oil man was a major donor.

I asked Eckhart how many separate research projects are occurring simultaneously at the Salk Institute, figuring he would tell me a specific number which might help me develop my interview. But I found his answer far more instructive.

"One way of estimating that is to say that each principal investigator, or each faculty member, would have his or her own research project," he said. "Those might be related to each other, but they would certainly be distinct, not identical, so you could say as a first approximation there are about 50 kinds of research corresponding to one per faculty member."

Given the fact that there are three faculty members pursuing separate lines of inquiry into AIDS, one could identify AIDS as a superproject, in which case it could be said that there are about a dozen superprojects. "Then," said Eckhart, "if you really wanted to boil it down, you could say that there are only two—molecular biology and neuroscience."

"Within molecular biology would be such projects as AIDS, cancer, developmental biology, plant biology, and so on," Eckhart said.

The scientist said one of the most interesting and exciting projects within his own cancer research center is the study of how the cell cycle is controlled.

"What causes a cell to divide?" he asked. (Thankfully, he did not pause for me to answer.) "When a cell gets a signal that it should go ahead and divide, it goes through a defined cycle of processes, including multiplying its genes and then dividing itself in two—pulling its genes apart."

"A lot is becoming known about the control of that cycle," Eckhart continued. "We have one person who works on controlling yeast and we have other people working with human cells, controlling the cell cycle, but the mechanisms by which that is all occurring is beginning to become clear quite rapidly now.

"These mechanisms are among the ones that are perturbed in cancer cells, so we are beginning to see what genes are involved in cell cycle control; how some of those genes are altered to cancer cells, and what you might try to overcome that."

A man who apparently enjoys explaining scientific concepts to lay people, Dr. Eckhart said when a cell becomes cancerous, basically there has been a change in the operation of its genes.

"What makes one cell different from another in our body is not that it has different genes but that different sets of genes are turned on and turned off," he said.

"So, we try to study how those sets of genes are turned on and turned off because that is the fundamental defect in cancer cells, that lots of times they will have the wrong genes switched on and the wrong genes switched off."

I wondered aloud how the Salk Institute's plant biologist fit into the research scheme for molecular biology.

"They work, for example, on how plant cells respond to light," Eckhart replied. "Light is very important to plants, so they have ways of responding to it and regulating their responses."

Another area of concern for the plant biologists is how the plant responds to pathogens in the environment.

"Just as we have an immune system that protects us from intruders, the plants have a whole set of mechanisms that protect them from intruders," Eckhart said.

"Because they can't run away, they have to sit there and deal with the intruder as it happens. Since all of life's processes have a similar chemical setup, a lot of things about how plants respond, how they switch their genes on and off, may apply to how our cells and our bodies respond as well."

To help me develop an overview of the Salk Institute, Eckhart turned to "the other half of the institute, which is neuroscience."

"It spans a very broad range," he said. One study focuses on how nerves and muscles interact; another on "how nerves transmit impulses from one nerve to another using neurotransmitters, chemical transmitters, and that has importance for diseases of the nervous system like Alzheimer's Disease . . . ."

"Then we also have a big group studying endocrinology—hormones and how they communicate from one part of the body to another—because we are beginning to realize that a lot of fundamental processes of the body are controlled ultimately from the brain," Eckhart said. "The brain makes chemicals which release hormones that subsequently control things like stress and social development and a lot of the other things that happens in our bodies, so we study those hormones and how they work."

The neuroscience field includes "a large group of people studying cognition," Eckhart said. "That is a process by which we see the external world and organize it into some way that we can deal with it. So there is a group working on vision, for example; how we see things and how that picture that is taken by our eyes is processed by the brain . . . ."

Later, as I stood on the plaza of the Salk Institute, watching the Sun play off the water and a raven fly to the rooftop of one of the buildings, I wondered if the Salk Institute's two great areas of research—neuroscience and molecular biology—might be further reduced to the study of change in living beings.

* * *

Sherry Root is co-president with Ettie Delawie of the Salk Institute Association. I recalled that the group had been founded in 1962 as a women's auxiliary by Sally Cohn, the wife of Rabbi Morton Cohn. I knew that Rabbi and Mrs. Cohn (may they both rest in peace!) had been very proud of Salk and Kahn, believing that the Jewish scientist and the Jewish architect had personified the Hebrew concept of *tikkun olam*—repair of the world.

I asked Ms. Root, who is Christian, whether many Jews still were active today in the Salk Institute Association. "About "two thirds of our membership," she informed me. "My co-president is Jewish."

We began our tour in the courtyard between two facing buildings. A small channel of water pointed like an arrow to the Pacific horizon before recycling itself through a series of pools.

Like an artist or a writer, a scientist "needs an aesthetic contemplative environment," Ms. Root told our small tour group. Salk and Kahn wanted "to take the idea of the scientist working in a little dark laboratory and to replace it with scientists in an aesthetic environment where light was dominant and where they could come out and feel an inspiration from the sea and from the sky."

Salk expressed his idea to Kahn by saying he wanted a place where even Picasso could be inspired—apparently never dreaming that someday his second wife would be artist Francoise Gilot, who had been artist Pablo Picasso's soulmate. Some of her paintings hang in Salk's office today; another example of how art can inspire science?

Ms. Root said Kahn "felt that a building should really reflect what goes on in that building. There are 29 different units here, so it is sort of like cell biology, which is studied at the Salk Institute. . . .

"The way he has cut out the stairwells and the window wells and so forth, when the Sun shines, it casts these rather mysterious shadows across the courtyard and gives a sense of mystery, almost ancient mystery. . . .

"Science is rooted in the past; you cannot proceed without that past knowledge. And this building has that kind of feelings of the great Roman and Greek structures, yet the lines of the buildings reach out to the Pacific Ocean or reach toward the future."

The landscape architect Luis Barragan was consulted about putting eucalyptus trees between the two facing buildings—to fashion a grove for contemplation—but Barragan rejected the idea.

"He said that this should be a great piazza, and the focus of your attention should be the Pacific Ocean," Ms. Root said. "So, to identify that more clearly, Louis Kahn designed the waterway down the center of the courtyard area and he calls that "the stream of life."

Ms. Root directed our attention to the buildings themselves, which she said are composed of four materials: travertine from Italy, concrete molded on site, lead to plug the holes in the concrete, and teakwood.

"Kahn left the stipulation that no paints, no varnish, no artificial materials should be used," she said. "Over 30 years, there has been scarcely a repair on the building. They occasionally clean and oil the teak, but never any polish."

The teakwood outlines cubicles that jut from the building, each cubicle being an office for the faculty members who guide the research in connecting laboratories. With 50 faculty, and an assortment of researchers and administrative staff, 550 people are employed at the facility.

We left the courtyard area and walked up a stairwell. Ms. Root smiled as she motioned to a wall covered with slate. "This is a touch of Kahn," she said. "The myth behind it is that before fax machines and computers, scientists would come out here and put a formula on the chalk board so that it could be shared with other members of the institute. I don't know!"

I tried to imagine the biological sciences' equivalent of an Albert Einstein running out to the stairwell, and calling out, "Jonas! Francis! Jacob! Renato! Come out here for a minute!" and then writing on the slate board, $E=MC^3$," then standing back, suddenly blushing, and saying, "Wait a minute, that's not right." Then he would wipe the slate with a corner of his lab coat, and rewrite the formula, $E=MC^2$. "Bravo! Bravo! Albert," they'd all say, "Relatively speaking, that is . . . ."

Ms. Root led us to the Sam and Freda Davis Library, where I noted a plaque had been mounted for Bronowski, who had been a resident fellow of the Institute from its conceptual state in 1961 to his death in 1974.

Our guide took hold of a wooden panel and slid it easily, revealing a picture window behind it. "Light is such an important element of creativity for Salk that even the shutters are placed inside so that everything can be open to the light," she said.

"Notice that at the edges of the building, shafts of light come in; he did that to permit the maximum light possible," she said.

The main work of the Salk Institute is done in the laboratories, not in its offices; and here, too, Kahn and Salk were innovative. Kahn conceptualized buildings in terms of "servant" space and "served" space. Laboratories need to be served with flexible infrastructure. Can you imagine a scientist unable to carry on his work because the architect failed to put in sufficient electrical outlets?

Rather than making the experiments fit the structure, Kahn and Salk decided the structure would have to fit the experiments—whatever they might be. To do that, they decided to build separate floors above each laboratory floor through which they could run conduits for water, gas, electricity, waste removal, and venting. These utilities are brought down through the ceiling of the laboratory in any configuration the scientist desires.

"It is wonderful," Ms. Root told us, as we viewed one of the utility floors. "It means they can come in here and repair the equipment without any disturbance to the science below. They can also update the equipment." The approach has caught on. "I've had hospital administrators come and say, "We are doing this in our hospital now," Ms. Rose reported.

In addition to being served by utilities, even laboratories on the basement level, are illuminated partially by natural light provided through light wells, Ms. Root said. Even the furnace room has windows, conforming to Kahn's belief that every building—let alone every human being—must have light.

* * *

One of the articles that Dr. Salk gave to me was a reprint of a piece that he wrote in the December 1990, edition of *Arts and Antiques,* a magazine Francoise Gilot served as a contributing editor. One quotation in particular told much about both the man, Salk, and the institute that he founded.

"Whether from the west or from the east, when one is in the space created by two structures bound by the sky and the sea, one becomes possessed by a sense of order, a sense of orientation that looks to the future, to the horizon of the setting Sun," he wrote.

"The court evokes a sense of peace, a place for reflection for those who enter it to find an inspiration that comes from within. That is what great art can do . . . ."

The Vision of Jonas Salk

San Diego Jewish Press Heritage,
July 7, 1995

As he requested on that day less than a year ago, I kept my tape recorder off and stashed inside the front pocket of my camera case. Dr. Jonas Salk, the discoverer of the polio vaccine, had said he did not want to be quoted directly on anything. He explained that any controversy his words inadvertently might engender could divert him from important work.

To my everlasting astonishment and gratification, Salk had asked to meet with me after he had learned from his public relations assistant, Anita Weld, that I was researching a story for *Heritage* about the Salk Institute for Biological Studies in La Jolla. That feature ran last September, a three-page spread.

Salk wanted to make sure that you, the *Heritage* readers, understood his vision of the Salk Institute, and in the course of imparting his thoughts on the Institute's development, he graciously agreed to answer my questions about other topics as well.

When our interview was over and I was safely in my car, I recapitulated as much as I could remember into my tape recorder.

Alas, Salk no longer needs to fear being diverted from his work; he died June 23 at the age of 80. Sadly, I now may share that interview with you.

I had asked him if it were true that he had encountered anti-Semitism from La Jolla residents in 1960 when the topic of building the institute was first breached.

He did indeed, he said. One resident demanded to know "how many Hebrews" he would be bringing to La Jolla with him. Another suggested, with no flattery intended, that the institute would be a branch of Tel Aviv University.

Old animosities, Salk sighed. No use raking over that, he added. But history is important, I countered.

We were in the cafeteria in the building facing the one in which he kept his office. Before Salk could reply—if he intended to at all—a young man who had just started a job in the cafeteria unknowingly interrupted, telling Salk how delighted he was to meet him in person.

The young man said that Salk had saved his father's life—a reference apparently to the scientist's discovery of the polio vaccine. Salk looked positively embarrassed. "I didn't know that," he half-stammered to the young man.

Public adulation given to Salk unstintingly by cafeteria workers and newspaper columnists like me, as well as by statesmen and politicians beyond numbering, had been both a blessing and a curse for the medical researcher.

As awards and medals for Salk from the lay world were heaped one atop the other, a kind of jealous scorn settled over the scientific world. Salk, in some of his colleagues' view, was a showboater—someone who played to the public, not a serious scientist.

The man whose vaccine in fact may have saved the cafeteria worker's father and whose work erased the general public's fear of polio, never was accorded a Nobel Prize.

On the other hand, the institute bearing his honored name received funding as it might never have otherwise—and today the Salk Institute is acknowledged as one of the top basic research institutes in the world.

I asked Salk if there was anything to be reported on the progress of his research into AIDS. It was the kind of question that I, as a reporter, felt duty-bound to ask, all the while knowing that Salk was unlikely to break a big important story like *that* with me.

He was kind enough to let me off graciously. When and if he has something to say, he replied, he will have to issue a very carefully worded paper. Otherwise, whatever he said could get overblown and become counterproductive. He had bitter experience with what happened when his words were taken by others out of their context.

Throughout the interview, Salk was very patient with me, taking time to elucidate concepts with which I as a layman was unfamiliar. When he answered a question, he did so carefully, measuring each word not only for the information it conveyed but for its possible impact.

Wanting to sketch Salk the Jew for this Jewish newspaper, I asked him about his religious beliefs. He said the great Jewish tradition of *tikkun olam*, helping to repair the world, motivated him in his work. But as to the question of his religiosity, he said, he departed from standard Jewish belief. "God is evolution, evolution is God," he declared.

In English, one of his books was entitled *Man Unfolding*, but in his view the French had a much better title, *Metaphor Biologique* (Biological Metaphor). Cells have within them genes which respond to changes in the environment. Once triggered, they prompt a metamorphosis. Social structures, too, are influenced and transformed by the environment.

We had arrived in the conference room in his office suite. He unrolled some blueprints and showed me what he hoped the Salk Institute would look like in the future—a place which not only performs award-winning basic scientific research, but also a place where great minds from the arts and the humanities would meet in ongoing dialogue with scientists.

In his vision, people of intellect would sit down and say, "What is the issue?" and discuss it not just from the standpoint of their own disciplines but by bringing their minds and thoughts together.

"This so far has been a dream still to be realized," he said. "I hope that it can still be accomplished."

On land between the institute and the Pacific, he had envisioned building a conference center where intellectual giants from diverse fields could hold such freewheeling brainstorming sessions.

There also would be on-campus housing so the gatherings could go deep into the night or into the next morning, as long as the ideas flowed.

There was an air of wistfulness about Salk as he told me about the plans; I had heard that the other scientists on the faculty were not nearly so enthusiastic as he.

Scientific research is a competitive world, with grants to be applied for, research to do, results to be tabulated and analyzed. While the faculty hadn't completely dismissed the institute's founder's idea of bringing together the great intellects of the sciences and the humanities, Salk knew few shared his passion.

As we spoke, Salk suddenly realized that he had left some papers at his house that needed to be faxed somewhere. He invited me to accompany him in his car the few blocks from the campus to his La Jolla home.

As we continued our conversation, I had the sense that Salk was frustrated and disappointed by his inability to translate his vision into reality, but willing to do whatever it might take to push the idea along in the popular mind.

As he drove into the carport, he said he would just be a second, and dashed inside his house to fetch the material while I waited in the front passenger seat, wishing he had invited me to follow him inside. But he was only a moment, and soon we were back on campus.

This time, we went not to the conference room but to his office, which I found cluttered with his papers and brightened with the artworks of his wife, Francoise Gilot.

Art and science are part of the same fabric, he told me. He liked his late colleague Jacob Bronowski's conceptualization of how Copernicus might have made the leap of imagination that was necessary to conclude that the Earth revolved around the Sun and not vice versa.

Perhaps, Copernicus stood like the man in the famous Leonardo da Vinci drawing, *Vitruvian Man,* with his arms fully extended to the sides. Perhaps Copernicus closed his eyes and turned in a circle, imagining his head as the Sun, and his outstretched fingers as points along the Earth's orbit.

Salk delighted in the notion that Copernicus even may have been inspired by the da Vinci drawing in the first place.

Now that Salk is gone, I find myself dwelling on his unfulfilled wish for a marriage between the humanities and the sciences.

If modern Copernicus is too preoccupied to become so engaged, perhaps such a proposal shall have to be fashioned by a modern da Vinci.

Welcome to Mount Rebbe

San Diego Jewish Press Heritage,
November 29, 1996

L a Jolla has its Mount Soledad, La Mesa has its Mount Helix. And now the Scripps Ranch neighborhood of San Diego has its Mount Rabbi Schneerson.

Twenty-seven acres of high ground about a mile east of Interstate 15 was so named by Rabbi Shlomo Cunin and Rabbi Yonah Fradkin, respectively the West Coast and San Diego regional directors of Chabad Lubavitch, in honor of the late Lubavitcher Rebbe during ceremonies dedicating the Chasidic organization's Scripps Ranch Center on Sunday, November 24.

Unlike Mounts Soledad and Helix which have large crosses erected on them, even though they are public land, the privately owned Mount Rabbi Schneerson has a 32-foot menorah sculpted by Jack Winer.

The menorah is planned as the first of 50 monumental sculptures in a garden that is to depict Jewish history, according to Winer. The sculpture garden is one component of a complex that will include a school, synagogue, teen center, library, community center, and gymnasium.

"Chabad is here for only one reason: the Lubavitcher Rebbe had his dream of sending people to go into the world and to make the world a better place," commented Fradkin, who emceed the ceremonies. Organizers said the dedication and an ensuing outdoor carnival drew approximately 1,000 attendees.

Cunin told the audience that he and Fradkin "looked at the mountains and looked at the trees and looked at the faces of the beautiful children here and we decided to call this mountain 'Mount Rabbi [Menachem] Schneerson,' the mountain of the Lubavitcher Rebbe."

Recognized throughout the United States as the man who annually hosts Chabad's fundraising telethon, Cunin didn't stray far from that role.

He told the crowd gathered in a large tent for the ceremony: "Everybody worries about the future. They make committees and commissions—what is going to be the future. The little *kindele,* that is the future and you have to make it happen . . . . All you have to do is write a little check."

Rabbi Moshe Bogomilsky, dean of the Lubavitch Yeshiva in New York, recalled that when the Lubavitcher Rebbe died two years ago, "many people began to wonder what is going to be the future of Chabad and there were many who predicted that Chabad will begin to decline, that little by little, it will go out of existence."

"I must say . . . as I see what has taken place in a short time, how Chabad has bulldozed a wilderness and is building an edifice, I am sorry for all those predictors of gloom who thought that Chabad was over," the yeshiva dean said. "I see that Chabad will grow and grow and that the spirit of the Rebbe is with us."

George McNeil, the non-Jewish principal of Chabad's secular school, said the school has "very high academic standards and the children meet those standards, but please don't feel that academic superiority is our only goal."

"As the Rebbe instructed, we educate through love," he added. "He stated that without love, education is at best incomplete and at worst destructive. We are developing well-rounded, caring Jewish children who have an in-depth knowledge of their religion and their culture."

During the ceremonies, Barbara and Maury Steiman, who made a major gift for construction of the Scripps Ranch Center, were called to the dais and Maury Steiman was moved to tears. "To see this wonderful sight," he said in choking voice. "If you came here six months ago, you would have seen nothing but trees, but with your help we will make this look like a beautiful palace— Amen!"

His daughter, Nancy Steiman Krasnoff, then announced that she and Steiman's other children had decided to carry on a family tradition. They said their grandfather had helped to build the Winnipeg, Canada, Lubavitch Center and had dedicated the cornerstone to his father, their great-grandfather. About 20 years ago, their father had helped to build the new facility for Beth Jacob Congregation in San Diego, dedicating a cornerstone in memory of his parents.

"And now, mom and dad, like you, with great pride, we would like to dedicate the cornerstone of the Chabad Scripps Ranch Center in honor of you because we know that this is important to you and we want to follow in your footsteps," she said, her voice breaking with emotion.

Another emotional moment came when in the midst of the celebration, Rabbi Fradkin said he wanted to introduce a subject of great solemnity: the fact that Chanah Abrams, a former art teacher at Chabad Day School, was lying very ill following a five-year battle against cancer. He said that Jewish leaders from throughout the city came on very short notice to a special, unscheduled prayer service for her on the evening before the dedication.

The mother of two young children, Abrams was the author of a recent article in the *Heritage* in which she told how moved she was when a Simchat Torah procession went from the Chabad center to her house so she could gaze upon the Torah from her window.

Fradkin appealed to people to contribute funds to help defray the Abrams' family's medical costs, and a friend, Miriam Schraer, distributed a letter urging people to "please pray every day for Chana Chaya Sura bas Sura"—Abrams' Hebrew name—and to contribute funds earmarked for the Chana Abrams Medical Fund to the Chabad House.

Commenting on the spirit of unity that brought together Jews of different backgrounds to pray for Abrams' health, Fradkin said, "With God's help, when each of us, Jew and Gentile, Jew and Jew, Satmar, Lubavitcher, Chasidic, Mitnagdic, wherever we come from, whatever background we are, when we can all learn to appreciate, love, and forget about the rest of our differences, then we know miracles are happening."

Rabbi Avram Bogopulsky, spiritual leader of Beth Jacob Congregation —which belongs to the non-Chasidic branch of Orthodoxy—referred to Steiman's contribution, then said he was "honored to be the rabbi of a congregation where we have such great people who contribute and give such terrific moral support for all types of communities and activities that go on in San Diego."

Bogopulsky added: "The bottom line is that we have to be together because no one else is going to be with us, so we need to be together."

San Diego City Councilwoman Barbara Warden, in whose district Chabad's Scripps Ranch Center is located, brought with her the congratulations of Mayor Susan Golding, whom she said was kept away from the ceremony by an unspecified illness.

Warden said that before she became a councilwoman, and before she was the publisher of a community newspaper in Rancho

Bernardo, and even before she and her husband Dick had two sons, "I was a teacher and it was the toughest job I had."

"But today you have dedicated teachers, a wonderful principal, and you are moving forward again to enlarge your facility—it is a glorious day for all of us here."

Jerry Goldberg, vice president of the United Jewish Federation, told the assembly that 20 years ago, anyone would have thought a miracle would be needed for a large Jewish center to arise on a hilltop in Scripps Ranch.

"As we know, we make our own miracles and this tent is filled with miracle makers," he said.

Drawing the Line against Hate: Abe Foxman Visits the Border

San Diego Jewish Press Heritage,
December 27, 1996

After touring the rugged terrain of the U.S.-Mexico border in an off-road vehicle, Abraham Foxman, national director of the Anti-Defamation League, watched an illegal immigrant from Acapulco, Mexico, place his index finger on a machine that would beam an image of his fingerprint to FBI headquarters.

It was hard to tell whether the man's eyes were more frightened or sad, as an officer also took his photograph.

By this computerized identification process, the Immigration and Naturalization Service can distinguish impoverished job-seekers from hardened criminals.

As it turned out, the Acapulco man's fingerprints indicated that he had no criminal record, and that he had told the truth about this being the first time he had been apprehended trying to enter the United States illegally. He would be repatriated to Mexico, his dreams of earning more money for his family dashed, at least temporarily.

As Foxman watched the procedure, what did he see in the man's eyes? Was it a vision of himself as a 6-year-old, when his parents illegally crossed Eastern European frontiers in 1946 to get to the post-World War II American sector? They would later legally immigrate to the United States.

Or, given the Mexican's age, did Foxman perhaps see the eyes of his parents, who had managed to survive the Holocaust while he lived as a "hidden child" in the home of a Christian family in Vilna, Lithuania?

Foxman himself could not say exactly what images had been invoked as a result of seeing the man from Acapulco, but he acknowledged in an interview, "It was very distressing."

"We saw an individual," he added. "I don't know what happens when the place [processing center] is filled. You talk to one individual in a more tactful manner and you treat him with more humanity. I don't know what happens if there are hundreds or thousands (to be processed), but even so, it was a painful moment."

Foxman's tour of the border December 17 had been arranged by Morris Casuto, the Anti-Defamation League's regional director in San Diego, through the offices of U.S. Attorney Alan Bersin. As Foxman and an entourage were conducted through the border gullies and hillsides between the ocean and Interstate 5, running commentaries were supplied by Marco Ramirez, a senior Border Patrol agent, and Amalia L. Meza, a deputy to the U.S. Attorney.

Asked by *Heritage* for background on ADL's interest in the border, Foxman replied that although immigration policy is a subject merely tangential to ADL's main interests, the fact that "bigotry, racism, and discrimination" have entered the debate "puts it on our agenda."

"Therefore, a better understanding of what this means, how it operates, what are the tensions, what are the potential exposures in terms of issues of bigotry and racism, is something that is important to us."

41

The tour had begun at Border Patrol headquarters, where Ramirez showed Foxman maps of the border, emphasizing that most of the illegal crossings occur in the 14-mile stretch between the ocean and Otay Mountain—an area that is relatively flat and offers immediate access to metropolitan San Diego.

As a result of Operation Gatekeeper, the government increased the number of Border Patrol agents; it built new patrol roads; it installed high fences, stadium lights, and electronic sensors along the border, Ramirez said.

Additionally, he said, Border Patrol agents received more off-road vehicles, sophisticated mobile radios, infrared night-viewing scopes, and the computerized fingerprint identification system.

Ramirez, who recently hosted Israeli Border Patrol guards and later paid a reciprocal visit to Israel, told Foxman that Israeli security guards greatly admired some of the U.S. agents' equipment.

Foxman asked Ramirez whether, as a Mexican-American, he experienced criticism from other Latinos for working as a Border Patrol agent.

Indeed, Ramirez replied, he has experienced such criticism— as have many other Mexican-Americans who are Border Patrol agents. However, he said, he had spent considerable time in the Middle West of the United States, and had seen factories where illegal immigrants had taken jobs that otherwise would have been filled by Americans.

He said he concluded that it is a myth that illegal immigrants take only those jobs which Americans don't want and which otherwise would go unfilled. As a result, he said, he decided that—sad as it might be in human terms—to help his country, he must do what he can to stop the flow of undocumented workers.

At the same time, he told Foxman, he is cognizant that "99.8 percent of the people who come across are good people," looking only for work and meaning no harm to anyone. He said he believes he performs a valuable role as a public information officer in helping to sensitize the public to that fact.

Meza, the special deputy in the U.S. attorney's office, told Foxman that her office conceptualizes a double role for itself: to enforce U.S. immigration policy and at the same time vigorously enforce civil rights.

She said a program developed in the local district now is being implemented in all other districts along the U.S.-Mexican border by order of Attorney General Janet Reno.

The program involves having civil-rights enforcement training and expedited review. "And if there is any complaint that has any merit, it is investigated aggressively by the FBI and the Office of the Inspector General (OIG) and we prosecute them," she said.

"I personally, along with the FBI and OIG, train every single Border Patrol agent that we get in this district," she said. "This is an issue that is near and dear to my heart, and yet at the same time I recognize that we can't say we are not going to have immigration enforcement."

Notices in Spanish tacked up at processing centers advise immigrants that they have rights, and that they get in touch with officials of the Mexican consulate if they believe those rights have been violated.

Meza said there is a close liaison between Mexican and U.S. officials on the issue of civil rights. "But what they [Mexican officials] will not do," she said, "is prevent their people from entering the United States illegally. That violates their constitution. So they will not intervene in that respect, but they do have laws that now make it a crime for smugglers to smuggle people into the United States."

She said efforts on both sides of the border have helped reduce the instances of immigrants being abused, "but it really is a sad, sad situation."

"When I first joined the U.S. Attorney's office and I went on the border tour, I tell you, my heart broke to see all those people waiting for night, to come across with all their belongings on their back," Meza said.

"You think, 'These poor people. It is a modern-day *Grapes of Wrath.*'"

Foxman told *Heritage* later that in examining the terms "racism" and "opposition to illegal immigration," one needs to pick one's way carefully.

"It is very difficult to separate out, because if you are talking about illegals and the illegals are in fact people of color, one could say that is racism, yet it isn't," he said. "I think a lot depends on the words you use, the messages you send, and the disclaimers you make."

The ADL director said he believed that California Governor Pete Wilson, who led the fight for Proposition 187, the voter-approved, court-stalled initiative that would deny California benefits to illegal aliens, had made appropriate disclaimers differentiating his position from racism.

He suggested the ADL should enter the immigration discussion "when bigotry and racism enter . . . . It is not an up-front issue, but it can become more up-front if it is in fact taken over by those who espouse racism."

Additionally, he said, "We may want to offer to the Border Patrol and some of its staff some sensitivity training in diversity. I don't think it can hurt. They are in a crisis situation. It is very taxing emotionally, and I think it might help if they had a little more exposure."

Saga of a Scroll: A Torah's Odyssey from Roudnice to San Diego

San Diego Jewish Press Heritage,
June 25, 1999

Detectives have a saying in criminal investigations: "Follow the money." But this inquiry deals with how love developed between two Jewish communities widely separated in time and in place. The key to this investigation is to "follow the Torah."

We begin our tale in 1983, shortly after a new Conservative Congregation Beth Am was established in a former tire store in Solana Beach, California.

Rabbi Wayne Dosick, who was the congregation's spiritual leader, learned that Westminster Synagogue in England had approved Beth Am's application to receive one of the Holocaust Torahs held in trust for the Jewish people.

Following the defeat of Nazi Germany in World War II, Westminster Synagogue became the custodian of 1,564 Torahs which had been looted from the synagogues of central Europe. These precious legacies had been stored in Prague with the intention of someday creating a museum to an extinct people—an exhibit the Nazis had hoped would justify the genocide they committed against the Jews.

After Czechoslovakia was reestablished as an independent country, agreement was reached for the Torahs—all carefully numbered by the Nazi looters—to be turned over to Westminster Synagogue and from there to be returned, one by one, into the active service of the Jewish people.

Congregation Beth Am was not the first synagogue in San Diego County to obtain a Holocaust Torah, nor would it be the last. But nowhere to date has a Holocaust Torah weaved a more wondrous spell than it did with this congregation.

There were certain fees and shipping costs associated with transporting this Holocaust Torah from the Westminster Synagogue to the United States. Dosick, today leader of the Elijah Minyan in Carlsbad and a successful author of numerous Jewish-themed books, recalled that the total was somewhere between $1,500 and $2,000, money that simply was not within the new congregation's budget.

"I called up a person immediately whom I knew bringing a Holocaust Torah would mean the most to—Lynn Schenk—because her parents (Sidney and Elsa Schenk) were survivors," Dosick recalled. "I told her the story and there was a check on my desk the next day."

At the time, Schenk was working as an attorney. She later gained civic recognition as a commissioner for the San Diego Unified Port District, and later as a Democratic member of Congress. Today she serves as the chief of staff for California Gov. Gray Davis. Both she and her brother, attorney Fred Schenk, along with their families, belong to Congregation Beth Am.

At dedication ceremonies on Sunday, June 13, for Congregation Beth Am's new synagogue complex in the Carmel Valley section of San Diego, Schenk told a large audience that when Rabbi Dosick asked her and her husband, Hugh Friedman, to make the special donation, the, rabbi in fact, had conferred upon them "a rare privilege."

"Our Torah in many ways became the foundation of all that was to come," she said. "It organized us as a congregation and became the symbolic link to our collective roots."

Dosick recalled that when the Torah arrived at the U.S. Customs facility at San Diego's Lindbergh Field, "It came in a long, narrow box, and there I was. I had more hair and more beard in those days, and the guy [an inspector] thought—I'm sure—that we must have been trying to smuggle drugs or something, because he made me open the entire box, then the entire Torah and roll it out, so he could see indeed that it was a sacred scroll."

While giving the Torah such a close inspection, Dosick noticed the number 747 on it. Being at an airport, one might have associated this number with Boeing-747s, the large jumbo aircraft. But this was the Nazi catalogue number. And there was a bittersweet irony to that number—747. For if you add the three integers, 7, 4, and 7, they total 18—the number associated with the Hebrew word, chai, meaning "life."

(Before the use of Arabic numerals became commonplace around the world, Hebrew speakers used their alphabet as numbers. Alef was 1, Bet was 2, Gimel was 3, and so forth. One could add the value of each letter to obtain the value of the word. The word chai is spelled Chet-Yud. Chet has the value of 8. Yud has the value of 10.)

So here was a Torah, once bound for a museum of extinction, now headed for a new life in the United States!

Along with the catalogue number was a notation that the Torah once had been housed in the synagogue of Roudnice, Czechoslovakia, a town lying on the River Labem (known in German as the River Elbe), about 25 miles north of Prague.

"Roudnice" is pronounced "Rude-Nietzsche," which is a coincidental, but perhaps apt, description of the philosophy of German philosopher Frederic Nietzsche, who believed power was the chief motivating force of societies and people.

After returning from the airport, Dosick went to his *Encyclopaedia Judaica* to learn more about Roudnice. It reported that 23 Jewish families were known to have lived there in 1570, but that the Jewish community must have existed there before. The entry went on to say that the original homes and cemetery were abandoned to make room for a monastery, and that in 1631, the Jewish community (which had moved elsewhere in the town) "saved the town from destruction by the Saxons by paying a large sum of money."

There was a massacre of some Jews in Roudnice in 1744, at the same time that Jews were expelled from Prague. A new synagogue was built in 1853, and another cemetery established in 1896. In 1930, the community numbered about 136 Jews or about 1.7 percent of the population.

Then the entry in the *Encyclopaedia Judaica* reported: "When the community was liquidated by the Nazis in 1942, its synagogue equipment was sent to the central Jewish Museum in Prague. No congregation was reestablished after World War II. Richard Feder served as rabbi of Roudnice."

So, the Torah had been out of service since 1942, and in 1983 it was coming back. Like Moses and the Israelites, it had been in the desert for some 40 years!

The *Encyclopaedia Judaica* also sketched the life of Rabbi Feder, who was born in 1875 and who was graduated from a rabbinical seminary in Vienna. Feder was an author. In 1919, he wrote a book titled *Jews and Christians,* and in 1923, he developed a textbook on the Hebrew language.

He was based in the town of Kojetin, but also conducted regular services in the nearby villages of Roudnice, Kolin, and Louny, before Nazis arrested him and sent him to the concentration camp at Theresienstadt, where he continued to serve as a rabbi. He survived the war and eventually resettled in Brno, where he was designated as chief rabbi of the Czech province of Moravia.

In 1961, he added to his portfolio service as the chief rabbi of the province of Bohemia, in which Roudnice is located.

Feder went on to write in 1947, *Jewish Tragedy,* one of the first books published on the Holocaust. He several times updated *Jewish Tales,* a collection of stories for children. In 1955, he published *Jews and Judaism,* and in 1955 wrote *Sinai,* a textbook of religious instruction. In 1965, the communist government of Czechoslovakia gave Feder a medal for his "uncompromising stand in the fight against fascism" and for his efforts in behalf of peace. The rabbi died in 1970 at the age of 95—a full life.

Dosick designed a mantle to dress the Torah in—one which is hauntingly beautiful in its starkness. The mantle, still used today, is of pure black with a yellow cloth star—similar to the stars that the Nazis had forced their Jewish victims to wear as identification on their clothing.

On Yom Kippur Day, 1983, the Torah ceremonially was brought under a chuppah into the synagogue, in what Lynn Schenk later would describe as an "electrifying High Holy Day service."

"There under the chuppah: one survivor, my father, clutching another survivor, our Torah," Schenk recalled, as the emotion crept back in her voice. "It was a moment that I don't think anyone will ever forget who had the privilege of sharing that. Each person who was gripped with emotion, young or old, we thought our own thoughts of family, of heritage, of six million lost."

Dosick recalled that Schenk told him following that High Holy Day procession "that while we were standing there waiting to come in, her father told her for the first time in her life that his job in the camps was to make the yellow star." The mantle had triggered his memory, "So, for the first time in her whole life, she learned from her father, *that* had been his job in the concentration camp."

After the service, Dosick remembered, he was approached by congregant Nellie Katsell, who told of being born to survivors after liberation, and living in Czechoslovakia. Rabbi Feder travelled throughout Czechoslovakia after the war and often had stayed with her parents when he visited their community, she told the rabbi. So, here was a connection: "Not only did we have a picture of the man [Feder] who had read from the Torah, we had a live witness to his life and work," Dosick exulted.

After the ceremony, Dosick decided that the Torah should not simply be put into a ceremonial case in the synagogue, nor its use limited to special occasions like the annual Yom HaShoah observance.

Halacha, or Jewish law, dictates that every word of the Torah be perfectly legible, and that the scroll be repaired of all blemishes, because the Torah is the word of God. Only a perfect copy of the Torah is considered eligible for reading. Damaged Torahs either are buried like a human being or kept for exhibits.

"That it could be a living memorial and not a museum piece, I had to make a really serious halachic decision," Dosick said. "The Torah was nowhere near a kosher Torah, and it would have taken many thousands of dollars, probably $10,000 - $15,000, to make it kosher again. Even then, a sofer who looked at it wasn't quite sure it could be done without harming it.

"I had to make a decision that I thought God would rather have the bar/bat mitzvah child read from a not-quite-kosher Torah, but make it a living memorial," Dosick said.

"I have written more than once that we Jews are good at saying *kaddish,* but not so good at saying *hallel*—that we are good at crying but not so good at rejoicing," the rabbi-author said. "I wanted us to have both messages: 'We do not forget those children who didn't live to stand at the Torah', and at the same time, 'We celebrate that a new generation of Jewish children is standing at the Torah and is celebrating bar/bat mitzvah and is triumphing over evil and serving God.'"

And so, Dosick began Congregation Beth Am's tradition of having every bar/bat mitzvah child read at the ceremony from the Holocaust Torah. "I always said that they not only came to the Torah for themselves but also for one of the little children of Roudnice who would have liked to have come to Torah for his bar mitzvah but whose life ended instead in a puff of smoke from a crematorium chimney."

He repeated that lesson week after week, year after year, until he left Congregation Beth Am in 1991, and "After a certain time, the kids began to tease me about it, as they will, because if you hear something 30 times a year, sometimes it becomes a parody of itself," Dosick said.

Nevertheless, the message had staying power. One example was when "One of the families from the shul went back to Illinois and asked me a few years later to officiate there at their kid's bar mitzvah, and even though they did not have a Holocaust Torah, they asked me to tell that story."

* * *

Other congregants who remembered the story were Carol Davidson Baird, who in 1989, was president of the San Diego Jewish Genealogical Society; her husband, Dr. Stephen Baird; their children, Daniel and Geoffrey Baird, and her parents, Ernest and Eva Davidson, who were Holocaust survivors.

The Bairds and Davidsons decided to go on a genealogical trip to trace their roots—a trip which took them to the Davidsons' native Germany and also to Poland, Czechoslovakia, and Hungary.

After the families arrived in two rental cars in Czechoslovakia, they had intended to spend a day sightseeing in Prague, but political unrest there—associated with protests against the state during the dusk of the Communist system—persuaded them to head instead for the Theresienstadt Concentration Camp, also known in the Czech language as Terezin.

"Wayne Dosick was always talking about the Torah in human terms, so we decided to go see the town where it came from" *en route* to Theresienstadt, Carol Baird recalled.

Using her training as a genealogist, Baird suggested to her German-speaking mother that they stop in the center of Roudnice and "find the oldest person, who probably would speak German, and ask where the synagogue was.

"So, we did that," Baird related. "Mom talked to this old lady in German, who gave her very interesting directions, which we followed up the street, and there was nothing there, just a vacant lot. I figured maybe that was where the synagogue was destroyed. Across the street my husband said, 'Look at that building; it is now a school, but it sure looks like all the other synagogues that we have seen in Europe.' So, we took pictures of it as well."

Not being certain that was the synagogue, the family kept walking down the street and eventually came to a police station. These were the Communist times and officialdom was none too friendly to Americans. "But we went into the police station and asked two of the policemen if they knew where the synagogue was. They just laughed, really snidely, at us, and said 'Synagogue Kaput!' We left thinking we were very lucky to be able to leave."

Nevertheless, the family continued to walk around the town, and just as they were ready to leave, they saw a woman admiring one of their German rental cars. They asked her about the synagogue, and she replied that although she didn't know where it was, perhaps some of the ladies in the nearby beauty parlor might. She went in and conferred and "All of a sudden, a gaggle of old women came out, all talking and pointing in different directions where the old synagogue was," Baird said.

The lady reported what the consensus was, and then offered to accompany the American strangers to the site. She gave her purse to her husband before climbing into the car with the Davidsons, who drove in front as the Bairds followed. They drove out of town and stopped momentarily at a Catholic cemetery where men were seated on a bench surrounding a tree. The woman got out to confer with the men, while the Davidsons and the Bairds, misunderstanding what was happening, started to explain that they were looking for a Jewish cemetery, not a Catholic one. The woman said she understood but just wanted to ascertain the directions. The men told her to follow the dirt road.

"We continue further until the road ends and there is no place to go," Baird related. "On one side is an open field, on the left side is an enormous forest. We all get out of the car and she points to go through the forest. There is a broken wall. We climb over that . . . .

"We ducked under the branch of a tree and it was the most extraordinary sensation. We all got goose bumps. There was a building with a big Jewish star, which we thought was the destroyed synagogue. We went out and started tracing (putting a piece of paper over inscriptions and penciling over the paper to copy the impression)."

Meanwhile the Bairds' two sons started exploring the dome roof that had fallen into the center of the burned structure. "Geoffrey found a burnt timber from the roof, and Danny found a block from the wall itself where the stucco had come off," Carol Baird said. "We kept that, and I started taking pictures of the other buildings—the attached buildings that had Hebrew writing on the walls."

After returning to the United States, the Bairds learned through research that the building that they thought had been the synagogue in actuality was a ceremonial building located adjacent to a Jewish cemetery on the outskirts of town. The inscriptions were psalms said for the dead. In this building, bodies had been watched and washed before burial.

The Davidsons and Bairds reunited the lady with her husband (and her purse), and "drove out of town feeling very satisfied

53

that we had accomplished our mission," Baird said. "That was an incredibly friendly and wonderful thing for her to do."

The next adventure was getting the pieces of wood and stone from Czechoslovakia to the United States. There was the possibility that unfriendly Czech authorities might consider the wood and stone to be valuable historic items—rather than simply sentimental ones—and accuse the Americans of attempting to steal treasures. Son Geoffrey wrapped the souvenirs in his dirty laundry and put them in the bottom of the suitcase. "When we left Czechoslovakia, they did search a lot of stuff, but they didn't bother with that," Baird said.

Upon return to the United States, Baird had her photograph of the ceremonial building printed and framed. She presented it to the synagogue, along with the wood and stone, which Dosick had mounted in a shadow box. The photograph and the shadow box were dedicated on Yom Kippur of 1989 and given a place on the wall alongside the *bima* of the shul in Solana Beach.

The congregation hired its present spiritual leader, Rabbi Arthur Zuckerman, in 1992, a year in which he recalled there were eight b'nai mitzvah students who read from the Holocaust Torah.

The congregation has grown so dramatically that 55 b'nai mitzvah students will read from it this year, "and next year, God willing, 70 students will be bar and bat mitzvah and they each will have a chance to read from it," Zuckerman said.

The congregation's current president, Candice Fagan, quoted Baird at the recent dedication ceremonies: "Torahs are not just pieces of parchment wrapped in velvet. Aside from the words that they contain, they have a history and a story to tell.

"Certainly our Holocaust Torah could tell us of Shabbos mornings in Roudnice when congregants fondly kissed it and children read their *maftir* from it. The Torah could also tell us of vicious abductions by the Nazis and its loneliness sitting catalogued in a dark warehouse until the end of World War II . . . . Our Torah had a life-long age. It was lost, and then found, and reborn in our synagogue. We give life to the Torah and it in turn gives us words to live by."

Fagan noted that the photograph and effects brought back by the Baird and Davidson families inspired architect Michael Witkin "to make his own excursion to Roudnice and he came back very inspired to create this beautiful synagogue."

"One of the features of our new home is the Wall of Remembrance," Fagan said. "Our architect painstakingly recreated this wall from what he found of what remained of a once flourishing Jewish community. When our generation and future generations view this wall, we will be reconnected to the past and thrust forward to our responsibility as Jews in the future."

✷ ✷ ✷

The Wall of Remembrance replicates the facade of the ceremonial house that the Davidsons and Bairds found that day in the woods. It still was being designed by Witkin last year when Milos Pojar, a former ambassador of the new Czech Republic to Israel, visited San Diego with other Eastern Europeans on a study tour sponsored by the American Jewish Committee. Pojar (pronounced Po-yar) today is director for education and culture of the Jewish Museum in Prague.

One of the advantages of being a journalist is the occasional ability to help make connections between the people that you meet in the course of gathering stories. After sitting in on the AJC conference on border problems, I told Pojar about several Holocaust Torahs that were located in our community, including the one at Congregation Beth Am. I also told him that Congregation Beth Am, inspired by the origins of its Torah, had in fact developed an architectural design invoking Roudnice.

A meeting was arranged among Pojar, Rabbi Zuckerman, and the architect Witkin at the Holiday Inn at Mission Valley, where the AJC conference had been held.

Witkin told Pojar that after he found the ritual hall, he made architectural sketches and also took molds of the building. He explained then that the re-creation of the ritual hall's facade would provide an entranceway to the new Beth Am complex. Some of the architectural elements of the ritual hall, especially its columns, would be repeated in the design of the overall synagogue, which would occupy 25,000 square feet.

The architect also told Pojar that his own son recently had read from the Holocaust Torah for his bar mitzvah. "That is really what we are doing, honoring children and connecting us to our past," Witkin said.

Pojar's own father had been forced by the Nazis to work in the Prague museum cataloguing Jewish ceremonial objects looted from the synagogues. His father specialized in examining and classifying textiles, but it is possible he could have come into contact with the very same Torah.

When Pojar returned to the Czech Republic, he did some research on Roudnice—research he shared with members of Congregation Beth Am during the dedication ceremonies, so that they could know more about the original home of their Torah.

In the 14th Century, the town was considered quite important, because it was where the Roman Catholic Archbishop Arnost of Pardubice made his headquarters. This archbishop, who had responsibility for all of Bohemia, was a close friend of Charles IV, emperor of the Holy Roman Empire, which included Bohemia. Charles IV often visited his friend the archbishop in Roudnice.

Another visitor was the Italian poet Petrarca.

Jews were "relatively well protected" during Charles IV's time when they were advisors to the emperor, Pojar said. But after he died, there was a pogrom in the Prague Ghetto, which may also have affected the Jews of Roudnice.

In the 17th Century, he reported, Czech Catholics became rulers of the town and all the farms, forests, and lands around. The leader of this family, Polyxena of Lobkovic, "ordered Jews to remove from their ghetto, from the Jewish quarter and go close to the river, close to the bridge, to set up a new ghetto there. On the spot where the [first] Jewish quarter was, and the first synagogue and the first cemetery were, everything was demolished." A monastery was built in the ghetto's place.

It was in the new ghetto, founded in 1630-1640, that there were "approximately 15-20 small houses around one street, with some yards, where Jews lived until the beginning of the Second World War," Pojar reported. "And in this street is located, in fact, the third synagogue which was founded in 1822 and which exists, but which is closed, which is empty. In 1952, it was transformed into an apartment house and afterwards to a school." Apparently, it was the building the Bairds and Davidsons had seen when they first arrived in Roudnice, but had not recognized as a synagogue.

There are today, two Jewish cemeteries in Roudnice. The older one was established when the ghetto was moved in the 17th Century. Apparently, some tombstones had been transferred there from the original cemetery, because at least one bore the date of 1611, Pojar said. "This cemetery was closed in 1890 and now there is a new wall constructed around, and no one can go in, and all the tombstones, all the gravestones are intact. . . . Only there are a lot of trees and bushes and grass; it is almost not possible to see anything there. But, nevertheless, it is only a question of cleaning it and it would be a nice cemetery."

The third cemetery—or the second one still existing—was built around 1890, and this is the one where the Davidsons and Bairds found the burial hall in ruins and which inspired Witkin's design.

"The walls around are also in ruins and the same with the tombs," said Pojar. "It is very sad. It happened partially during the Nazi time, partially during the Communist time, partially because of some vandalism."

Pojar noted that the Jews of Roudnice, along with 80,000 other Jews from Bohemia, Moravia, and Silesia, died in the Holocaust. Among the Czech victims was Pojar's grandmother Berta Popperova, who was sent first to Theresienstadt and later to Treblinka in Poland, where she was murdered.

In his research, Pojar located the names of 78 Jewish men and women from Roudnice who died in various Nazi concentration camps, including some whom he memorialized by setting down small stones at Treblinka.

The Treblinka victims from Roudnice were Berta and Gisela Freund, Eleanora Sabat, Salomon Schreiber, and Oskar Taussig, he said. They too might have read from the Torah or touched it with their prayer books.

* * *

The Holocaust Torah is now in a new Ark, in a new sanctuary which people reach by walking through a courtyard featuring the Roudnice-inspired Wall of Remembrance.

But much of the story woven around the Holocaust Torah remains to be learned and told. Stan Schwartz, owner of Schwartz Judaica and president of the Jewish Historical Society of San Diego, is researching which of Rabbi Feder's books are still in print. He reported that the libraries at the University of California at Berkeley and the Jewish Theological Seminary of New York each have at least one of Feder's works.

And Alberto Attia, a San Diego sofer to whom the Holocaust Torah recently was taken for inspection and some minor repairs (the major repairs still need to be done), still is pondering an amazing mystery.

At the same time that he was examining the Holocaust Torah, he also was examining another Torah that was owned by Congregation Beth Tefilah, which since then has merged with Adat Ami Synagogue to become Ohr Shalom Synagogue.

Attia was amazed that the very distinctive handwriting that formed the Hebrew letters of the Holocaust Torah seemed to be the same handwriting that also formed the letters of the Torah owned now by Ohr Shalom.

Whereas the Holocaust Torah had come to Congregation Beth Am via Westminster Synagogue, the provenance of Ohr Shalom's Torah is unknown. Shelly Berman, a past president of Beth Tefilah, believes it may have been purchased from a dealer in New York, but where the dealer obtained it is unknown.

Attia is certain that the two Torahs were written by the same unknown person. "The sofer had a very distinct writing style," he said. "You can tell the signature of a sofer by his writing style. Like in English, there are no two people who write alike—even if it is a square block print letter. It was very distinct, the way in which he wrote."

Pojar made two suggestions for continuing the Saga of the Holocaust Torah during his speech at the synagogue building's dedication: "Jews in Roudnice are unfortunately forgotten, not here, but in the Czech Republic," he told the congregants.

Pojar said that the present-day Count Lobkovic is an American citizen, with whom the Czech Republic has restored the castle after its confiscation by the Nazis and the Communists. He suggested that Congregation Beth Am in cooperation with Prague's Jewish Museum, the Terezin Foundation and Lobkovic help to establish in the castle a museum, with "one or two rooms commemorating Jews in Roudnice, keeping their past in the memory and to show the Czech population that [Jews] contributed for generations, for centuries, to the grooming of the city, crafts, industry, agriculture, and so on."

The Czech visitor also told the congregation that Tana Fiser and Milos Dobias are Czech citizens who created a music and poetry program based on poems of children who perished in Terezin.

The musicians will be bringing their program to the United States in the fall and "you might think of inviting them to your congregation," he said. Fiser, who is Jewish, is a close friend of the Czech Republic's President Vaclav Havel, he added, while Dobias is a "famous musician and composer."

Former Congresswoman Schenk, who followed Pojar to the podium, commented "thank you for bringing to us this wonderful challenge, which I am confident that my fellow congregants are going to meet." Zuckerman later also endorsed the ideas.

And so the saga of the Holocaust Torah continues.

Giving Peace a Chance: Jewish Woman Directs New Peace Center at University of San Diego

San Diego Jewish Press Heritage,
December 8, 2000

The Catholic-sponsored University of San Diego is building a new peace center directed by a Jewish woman who helped former U.S. President Jimmy Carter negotiate a ceasefire in Bosnia in 1994 and the restoration of diplomatic relations between skirmishing Uganda and the Sudan in 1999.

The exact mission of the Joan B. Kroc Institute for Peace and Justice is being mulled even as steel girders are beginning to reveal the imposing outlines of the on-campus building in which the center will host conferences and scholars' offices.

The executive director is Joyce Neu, who spent eight-and-a-half years at the former president's peace center in Atlanta, Georgia, before accepting the job in San Diego. A California native, whose parents still reside in the Los Angeles area, Neu recently told *Heritage* that the combination of returning to her home state and being able to fashion a peace program from scratch made for an irresistible opportunity.

While some peace centers focus on specific geographic regions of the world, others adopt thematic approaches to building peace, Neu said. As she develops recommendations for what niche the IPJ—Institute for Peace and Justice—should seek to occupy, Neu is weighing some intellectually exciting options.

One possibility, she said, would be to concentrate on how to build peace after two warring sides stop shooting at each other. "Once a war is over, people have to come together and rebuild, and nobody knows really how to do that; in many cases it is very ad hoc," Neu said.

"Everyone agrees that five years after signing the Dayton Peace Agreement, for example, Bosnia is not a real stable society. And Bosnia is just one example. Look at Angola, which despite its agreement, never had peace, went back to war almost immediately. Similar things have happened with Haiti and Cambodia; it has been very difficult to stabilize the situations."

Neu said one possible focus for the Kroc Center could be to concentrate its resources on developing answers to the questions "How do you build peace? What goes into peace-building? What would a good model of peace-building look like? What works? How do you get sustainable agreements? How do you get justice with peace?"

Another thematic possibility for the IPJ might be to focus on border issues. "There are a lot of border issues that cause conflict," she said. "So, there isn't any reason why we couldn't look at border issues in terms of our own [U.S.-Mexico] border and other borders that have caused conflict and look at why, and how does one address these?"

Such an approach might delve into questions like "Where should the border be?"

"Countries have to agree on where the border is, and that is not always clear," Neu said. "In many countries, there are problems because the actual geographic or political border is not the real border in terms of the people. You can often have a border that cuts across ethnic groups who belong together."

An example of this, she said, is the Kurdish nation. "I believe there are 40 million Kurds," Neu said. "There are so many countries, so many states, that don't have 40 million people in them, and yet here are a people of 40 million without a state." Another issue is that "You have a lot of different groups who are within states who believe they should be their own state. That is what we have with Kosovo, and it looks like the U.S. government is changing its policy for Kosovo. It may in fact become its own state."

A third possible niche "that has a lot of appeal, especially given what is happening in the Middle East right now, is the link between the grass roots and the leadership. How do you create a culture of peace with the grassroots to the extent that they do not allow violence to recur?"

Neu posited that "a sustainable peace requires people from all levels of society to stop demonizing the other." She said Israelis and Palestinians made such efforts but obviously they were insufficient to prevent the onset and continuation of the second intifada.

"What usually happens is an outbreak of violence is followed by a rejection of that violence by all sides and a recommitment to the peace process, but in this case, that didn't happen right away," Neu said.

Among the methods for transforming a conflict from violence to peace is to attempt to develop a consensus on a variety of topics. For example, "You have historians from the two sides meet with historians from outside the region to talk about the textbooks. 'What are we teaching the kids? How do we create one text? How do we create one history for our region, which all view as fair?' That is a process that has been gone through in many societies . . . . You can't educate youth to believe that the people who live across the street from them, or who are their neighbors, are dangerous."

Neu said such efforts were made in Estonia and other parts of the former Soviet Union, and are now occurring in Bosnia. "It is not something that is real common yet, but it is something that is acknowledged as a real need."

Psychologists are another group of people who should be brought together in peace-making, Neu continued. Psychologists from both sides, or the several sides in cases of multi-party conflicts, can be brought together "to talk about trauma. 'How do we get our people through this?' You have a country basically that is unable to make decisions because the people are traumatized by the conflict. One of the symptoms of trauma is the inability to make rational decisions."

Neu said in conflict areas throughout the world, "You have leaders who have witnessed atrocities, who have had people close to them killed. Therefore, are they making decisions in the best interest of their people, or are they making decisions out of hatred for the other?"

Whichever niche the IPJ settles upon will help to determine what kind of "scholar-practitioners" it will seek for its faculty, Neu said. "The institute is not going to be an ivory tower," she said. "My vision for this institute is that we will have people who are scholars and really very fine researchers but who are interested in applying their research skills to practical problems."

So, for example, if IPJ chose "borders" as its focus, it would try to attract specialists in that field, who could not only teach a class, but who could help arbitrate border disputes. Similarly, if it chose "peace building," scholars with that expertise would be sought.

"The institute will basically have three basic branches or components," Neu said. "There will be an education program. We will offer a master's degree in peace and justice studies, and that will begin in Fall 2002. The educational program will most likely also provide other kinds of educational outreach. A possible example may be working with the military here in San Diego to provide conflict-resolution training, or basic understanding of human rights, especially for military forces involved in peacekeeping efforts."

Research in peace studies will be the second component.

The third component will be to provide the IPJ building as a center for actual peacemaking and conflict resolution. "The institute is being designed with the notion that we would bring in high-level people" from nations experiencing conflict, Neu said. "We would be inviting people to come to what is a very peaceful, lovely environment to be able to speak honestly and outside the media's gaze, because San Diego is not a Washington or a New York . . . . I view the institute as helping to provide a safe space for dialogue."

Philanthropist Joan Kroc donated $25 million for construction of the 90,000-square-foot IPJ building, which will include "an auditorium that will seat 300-350 people, and have break-out rooms for smaller groups," Neu said.

"It will have state-of-the-art conference rooms, like a board room area which will seat 30-40 people. The technology through the entire building will be sophisticated. It means that there won't be any wires visible, the tables will all be wired (for sound and electricity). As far as I know we will have a production studio at the institute, so we can do live satellite broadcasts. We will also have booths for simultaneous interpretation."

Neu said the IPJ also will maintain a residence that could house three or four visiting dignitaries. "If delegations came in, we would put them up at a hotel."

In addition to the IPJ, various USD academic departments which are now short of space will also be housed in the center's building. Neu doesn't anticipate that the IPJ will need too much space for its own faculty's offices. "Probably in the first three years, if we get up to 10 people (including support staff) it would be wonderful," she said. Part of her job will be to raise funds for operating expenses. The Kroc grant was for physical infrastructure.

* * *

Although Neu's residence while growing up was Redondo Beach, where her parents had helped to found Temple Menorah, the family also lived in other cities. In 1960, when she was nine, the family moved to Brussels for two years because her father, a consulting chemical engineer, was retained to develop an agent for filtering beer. "Belgium was the largest beer drinking country per capita in the world."

While many American diplomats and military personnel in Belgium stuck together as part of an American colony, "we weren't part of that group . . . Business people were completely excluded," Neu recalled. "I think my parents were not included in any of the social activities of the Americans overseas." The pattern was reflected in the American school, where Neu felt like such an outsider she asked her parents to let her attend a regular Belgian school, even though she didn't yet know how to speak French. "No one in our school spoke English . . . . It was a good experience because my friends were Belgian kids, except for one Danish girl."

After graduating with a major in French and English literature from the University of Colorado at Boulder, Neu volunteered for the Peace Corps. She was sent in 1972 to Senegal, a French-speaking country in West Africa, where she taught English as a second language in the northern city of St. Louis.

"While I was there, there were three Senegalese professors who were physically dragged off and put into jail with no charges brought," she recalled. "I visited one because he taught English like I did . . . . He was in there for three months without charges brought. We were all terribly distressed at the injustice of all this, but none of us had a clue what to do. We didn't know how to take action.

"So that was one incident, and then there were instances of injustice with the students. They weren't getting the money; there was corruption. We were tremendously aware of how U.S. foreign aid was being wasted.

"You would go to a market place and you would find huge sacks of grain that would say 'Gift of the people of the United States of America' and the market ladies would be selling them," Neu recalled. "They had cut open the bags and were scooping out grain and they would sell it to you. I doubt that they knew it wasn't supposed to have been for sale; it was a gift. But somebody at the docks got hold of it and sold it to somebody else."

There were also many positive experiences. In particular, she recalls her transfer to the Senegalese capital of Dakar and going to a market place and asking a woman sitting on the corner how much the tomatoes were. The woman did not answer her at first, instead saying pointedly, "Hello!"

"They would teach you that they weren't going to sell you anything until you went through the greetings. In the Wolof language, the greetings are quite elaborate. You don't know these people, but you would ask about their family, and afterwards you could ask them how much the tomatoes were. Once you would go through that, people would know you and it would be a lot of fun."

Neu drew from that experience the lesson that "negotiation wasn't only about the money; it was also about 'I am a person, acknowledge me. Don't just come to buy my tomato or cloth. Let's have some kind of exchange here.'"

Following Peace Corps, Neu worked for six years in the United States, including at an employment agency which placed workers in a variety of blue-collar jobs. "I remember thinking I never want another job where I watch the clock."

In 1978, Neu enrolled as a graduate student in linguistics at the University of Southern California. She did her doctoral dissertation in "socio-linguistics—the use of language in a social context, looking at language as part of who you are. The focus of all that was to look how people talk in negotiations. What makes successful or unsuccessful outcomes in negotiations? I had outcome measures which included how much money people would make on a deal, but also other measures like how happy you were with the person you were talking to; would you want to see that person again?"

In studying negotiations, she discovered that some "very commonsensical rules" apply: "Things like interruptions are unhelpful, while listening—including the asking of questions for clarification—is helpful," she said. Questions for clarification "are perceived as someone is actually paying attention and listening. Another thing that was important, but surprised me a little bit, was that it was important to actually respond to a question. I was surprised how often people would ask a question and the other person either wouldn't hear them or wouldn't respond. That was a very big surprise to me in the data."

After receiving her doctorate from USC, she taught English as a second language at UC Irvine, then joined the faculty at Penn State, where in 1986 she helped to found the Center for Negotiation and Conflict Resolution.

In 1991 she joined the Carter Center, which is housed at Emory University. Her experiences in conflict resolution and serving in the Peace Corps in Africa were considered real pluses by those who interviewed her for the job as associate director of the conflict resolution program.

"President Carter's main interest (since leaving the Presidency) was in Africa and still is in Africa—Ethiopia, Liberia, Sudan have been really primary focuses for him," Neu said.

She'll never forget the day she started her job. "I came on a day of a big conference that my program was sponsoring, and it included the entire International Negotiation Network, which was based at the Carter Center and was chaired by President Carter and included Desmond Tutu, Oscar Arias, Javier Perez de Cuellar, Andrew Young, Cyrus Vance, and a lot of other eminent people. I sat at dinner with Desmond Tutu; he was my dinner partner. So, I had no regrets about leaving Penn State."

Although she interacted with Carter on numerous occasions—and has hanging in her office a framed letter from him and his wife Rosalynn complimenting her work—"you work closely with him and you don't, in the sense that you are not actually face-to-face with him very often. He prefers to have communication done via memo. . . . We communicated with him 90 percent of the time via memo, and he would respond 'yes' or 'no.' The memos had check-offs, so it would be, for example, 'I recommend you call President Clinton.' And there would be boxes for 'I agree, yes' or 'no' and he would check. That was the way he communicated. President Carter spent about a week a month at the Carter Center. He was very busy while he was there. He had a very tight schedule. It was not like you could sit down and chat."

Everyone on the staff was familiar with Carter's autobiographical book *Why Not the Best?* in which he told about working for Admiral Hyman Rickover, who was considered a very hard boss. Carter, like Rickover, "is a very demanding man, and he demands the same of himself," Neu said. "So, when you do a particularly good job it is unusual for him to comment on it. He just expects it. He expects it of himself and he expects it of you. Every now and then you would get a 'good' on a memo, or 'I agree.'"

The first major project in which Neu became involved was "in late '94 when we went to Bosnia to negotiate a cease fire in that war and to try to get everyone back to the negotiating table. . . . It was one thing negotiating a cease fire, but then we had to see that it was implemented. So, it meant we were on the phone every single day, sometimes calling State Department people, explaining why the Serbs had violated the agreement yet again, or being told by the United Nations in Sarajevo that the Serbs were violating the agreement, so could we please call our Serb friends and get them to comply."

President Carter had been invited to Bosnia by Radovan Karadzic, leader of the Bosnian Serbs, to talk about a ceasefire. Carter then informed Bosnian President Alija Izetbegovic "that we had been invited to do this and would not accept, unless he agreed," Neu recalled. "Then, because we didn't trust Karadzic to keep his word, we gave him five things he had to do within 48 hours to indicate his sincerity in actually doing something. I don't remember all five conditions; we worked them out in the back of the van, but one of them was that there were 17 U.N. humanitarian convoy trucks that were being prevented by the Serbs from getting to Sarajevo. One of those conditions was that those trucks had to be moved. Another condition was that there had to be a cease fire in Sarajevo. Another was that they had to release all Muslim prisoners of war under the age of nineteen. . . . "

The conditions were met by the Bosnian Serbs, with whom the United States was not on direct speaking terms in December of 1994, although the U.S. did interact with them as part of a five-nation Contact Group. "President Carter has a belief that as long as people are causing destruction and killing people, you have to talk with them. Even if they don't keep their word, you have to talk with them. So, we went in and President Carter negotiated a ceasefire agreement between Karadzic and Izetbegovic. It was not perfect. There was one word that was different in the two versions of the agreement . . . . One (favored by the Bosnian Serbs) implied that they would be starting from scratch; the other (favored by the Bosnian Muslims) implied they would start with the Contact Group plan . . . ."

The Carter-brokered ceasefire was subsequently subsumed under a United Nations ceasefire, which later broke down. But eventually an agreement was forged in 1995 at the Dayton Conference.

In April of 1999, the Carter Center received invitations from President Omar Al-Bashir of the Sudan and President Yoweri Museveni of Uganda to help the neighboring countries reestablish diplomatic relations. Each country had been supporting rebel groups in the other, although there was not parallelism, Neu said.

"The rebel group in southern Sudan (backed then by Uganda) is a legitimate opposition movement with an ideology, and popular support of the people although it doesn't always have good tactics and had done some horrific things," Neu said.

"On the other side you had a Ugandan group, based in Sudan, which was a fundamentalist Christian group, whom Rights Watch did a whole book about," she said. "UNICEF estimates that they have abducted up to 15,000 children. They terrorize their own people and burn their own villages, and it not clear that they have any popular support. It was a difficult negotiation because it was not a *quid pro quo.*"

Neu was dispatched by Carter as head of a team to lay the groundwork for an agreement by which the two countries resumed diplomatic relations and pledged to stop supporting each other's rebel groups.

"This is still something that is ongoing and I am still following it every day in the news because it hasn't been resolved," Neu said. "We did get an agreement signed," but it still has to be implemented.

Neu said Carter "knew that I put myself in physical jeopardy" in Uganda and the Sudan. "The night that he concluded the agreement, I got a call saying he wanted to have a drink with me, which was very unusual—not to have a drink, but the notion that he would think about it. I asked if I could bring the team and he agreed, and I brought the whole team. There were maybe eight of us, and he toasted them, congratulating them, which was really something."

The IPJ director said resolving the Uganda-Sudan conflict is a piece in a much larger effort by the Carter Center to bring an end to the civil war in Sudan. She described that conflict as one of the bloodiest wars in history, with up to two million people killed. The Uganda-Sudan agreement helped the Carter Center to establish its credibility with the Sudanese, she said. Perhaps next, it will be permitted to broker peace in the larger Sudanese civil war.

Although there are numerous peace centers around the world, including another one named for Kroc at Notre Dame University— the Joan B. Kroc Institute for International Peace Studies—Neu said it is an unfortunate fact that there is more than enough conflict in the world to keep all of them busy.

Judaism under the Shade of a Torrey Pine: Adat Yeshurun Builds a New Home in La Jolla

San Diego Jewish Press Heritage,
August 3, 2001

Congregation Adat Yeshurun will relocate from relatively tiny, leased quarters to a beautiful new home, ten times as large, in the hills of La Jolla on Sunday, August 19.

Joyous congregants will depart on foot from the residence of Rabbi Jeff Wohlgelernter at 10 a.m. and carry Torahs up La Jolla Scenic Drive North to the 15,000-square-foot complex.

Wohlgelernter, who walks at a determined clip, normally can cover the distance in 4 1/2 minutes, but the actual procession is expected to take considerably longer than that. And why not? It has been 14 years since Wohlgelernter and a handful of families began the Orthodox congregation. Over the course of the walk, members of Adat Yeshurun, which now numbers 230 families, will have the opportunity to savor how far their congregation has come.

The rabbi provided *Heritage* and a congregant, Dr. Barry Kassar, a preview tour of Adat Yeshurun's new building last week. Most of the structure already was in place.

However, carpeting, a new coat of paint, and some of the windows remained to be installed by the Kvaas Construction Company before such furnishings as the walnut Aron Kodesh and reader's table—both made by hand by the rabbi's late father, David—could be moved into their places in the sanctuary.

From the street, one is impressed by the sleek curve of Adat Yeshurun's roof line and by a large Torrey Pine tree, to the right of the sanctuary building, which dominates a courtyard connecting the shul to its school building and offices.

The Torrey Pine is a protected species. In carefully building around the mammoth tree, the synagogue not only showed great respect for the environment but provided itself with a place for meetings, outdoor weddings, and *kiddushes.*

Without the Aron Kodesh (Holy Ark) to draw a visitor's eye, the sanctuary's all-wood ceiling commanded immediate attention. Made from Douglas fir, the ceiling is reminiscent of the storied ceiling in the Hotel del Coronado's fabled Crown room.

The main space in front of the Aron Kodesh will be the men's section, capable of seating 220 persons, theater style, but expected to be configured normally with tables for 150 persons who will both pray and study. To the left, and above the men's section is the women's gallery which will have seats for 180. A slatted *mehitza* will be angled in such a way that it will provide everyone in the women's section a clear line of sight to the *bima*, Wohlgelernter said.

When not in use, the *bima* can be rolled under the elevated women's section, thereby enabling the sanctuary to be converted into a room for wedding receptions and other *simchas.*

To the right of the men's section, and just a few steps higher, is an area for holding a *kiddush*, or other small ceremony. There is a similar area behind the men's section, which can be used for a variety of purposes. Rolling bookshelves will partition these areas from the men's section—giving the synagogue the look and feel of the study house that it is intended to be.

For High Holidays, the bookshelves may be rolled away, creating a far larger space for worship. The auxiliary area behind the men's section would be divided into supplemental men's and women's sections, and the *kiddush* area also would become a men's section.

Connected to the *kiddush* area is a kosher kitchen, and a few steps away, outside the sanctuary building, is a "vessel mikvah" for the ritual immersion of dishes, glasses, pots, pans, and other eating utensils.

To the right of the *kiddush* area will be large glass doors leading to the Torrey Pine-dominated courtyard, and to the congregation's offices and classrooms.

After conducting us through the courtyard area, Rabbi Wohlgelernter took us back in front of the synagogue, and then down a private pathway to the left of the sanctuary building. This is the entry to the regular mikvah, for congregants observing the laws of family purity. Although there will be special hours for men, most of the mikvah's usage is expected to be by female members of the congregation.

The mikvah not only includes a pool fed by rainwater (mixed with city water) for immersion, but also preparation rooms where the women may first take a regular bath or shower to clean their skin of any impurities before entering the ritual bath. There also is an area for the mikvah attendant to station herself throughout the day.

"It is a very exciting realization of a dream to have our own facility," Kassar said. "It is a carefully designed facility that meets everyone's needs and stays within the guidelines of the rabbi's desire to have a halachically kosher place. . . . It is so exciting to be part of a new shul, not a new congregation, but a new shul."

Wohlgelernter said he too was excited about the move. "This will allow us to do the things that we want and need to do but in a much more terrific way," he said. "You need to feel like you are settled somewhere, that you are not temporary, and not just a little makeshift thing. When you really have a home and a place to spread out, you can do all the programs and the things you want to do."

The design by architect Mark Steele is simple, functional, and beautiful.

Wohlgelernter instructed: "You take a Torah scroll and put a beautiful mantle on it. Why not just a *shmata* (old rag)? The answer is because everything about the Torah has to be beautiful, and the building it is in, that has to be beautiful too."

'Sneak Preview' of the New Beth Israel

San Diego Jewish Press Heritage,
August 31, 2001

Rabbi Ben Kamin, addressing a crowd of members and prospective members at Congregation Beth Israel's still-being-built 70,000-square-foot facility near University Town Centre drew on the thoughts of King Solomon to describe his feelings upon looking at a beautiful new House of God.

"Solomon beheld his structure [the first Temple in Jerusalem], the buildings that he helped design, and he actually spoke out to God," the Reform rabbi related on Sunday, August 26. "He said, 'The building is beautiful God—glorious—but Your name is bigger than this place. How do we possibly incorporate Godliness into this house?' and he felt the answer, and it came from God to Solomon's heart; that in this place, when we invoke God's name, then the building's glory and the majesty of God will be paired."

Standing on the steps leading to the complex which architecturally invokes Jerusalem's Old City, Kamin added to the assembled crowd: "That is what we intend to do here with you for decades and decades to come: to invoke the name of God, which includes every human being, regardless of economic status, of how you became a Jew or why you became a Jew, or how you even hear God.

77

"If you are connected to someone who is Jewish, and you are not a Jew, you are included in this House of God, because the name of God incorporates everything and everyone," the rabbi added.

With that, the rabbi's clerical associates, Cantor Arlene Bernstein and Rabbi Sheila Goloboy, joined by the congregation's president, Jerry Goldberg, led the group in singing *H'nai Matov*. The four leaders linked arms together in the first congregational ceremony at the property since the groundbreaking in January 2000.

The seven-building, $18.5 million complex includes a 500-seat sanctuary with adjoining social hall, a separate building with a 150-seat domed chapel, invoking the feeling of the congregation's current quarters at 3rd and Laurel Streets in downtown San Diego; administrative offices, and a large educational complex.

It was built on three acres that were purchased in 1993 from Donald Bren of the Irvine Company, which developed the La Jolla Gateway project next door. Originally the developer had planned to use the parcel for a third office building in the complex, even building a parking structure large enough to accommodate that use. Beth Israel has made arrangements to use the parking structure for services in the evenings and on weekends, and leases parking spaces for staff and weekday visitors to use.

The event on Sunday, billed as a "sneak preview," was intended to acquaint Jewish families within a short driving radius, to investigate becoming members of the congregation that now counts 1,350 family "units" as members.

Still under construction—with dedication ceremonies not planned until October 28—the tour route around the complex was lined with yellow "Do Not Cross" construction tape and congregants were given numerous warnings to watch their steps. "If you want to look at the majesty of these buildings, stop, look up, and then continue your walking," the temple's executive director, Stuart Simmons, pleaded before the tour got underway. "Every step of the way, there are tripping hazards . . . ."

Sure enough, two people lost their balance and fell to the ground, suffering what appeared to be minor cuts and bumps. The congregation summoned paramedics to the scene just to make certain the man and woman were okay, and after being examined, the couple drove themselves home.

Board members and congregants wore ribbons and buttons to encourage prospective members to ask them questions. For many, it was their first close look at the project.

"I think it is great," board member Harry Guterman told *Heritage*. "I guess history is being made here. It will be a wonderful temple, and it will bring in a lot of Jewish people from the area."

Guterman said he was pleased that the social hall will be much larger than the one at the existing facility—and will more easily accommodate social functions like wedding and bar mitzvah receptions.

Ann Mound said with more than twice the square footage than the congregation has at 3rd and Laurel, it has more space for meeting rooms and therefore will be able to program more events simultaneously.

Kara Kobey said she was particularly excited about the greatly expanded educational facilities. Beth Israel operates not only an after-school religious program for public school students, but also has a full-time day school, the only one in San Diego County which is affiliated with a specific synagogue.

"I am very happy," Kobey said. "I have one child in the day school, my son in second grade, and my daughter in sixth-grade religious school, and I can't wait for the sanctuary to be finished."

Carter, at USD Peace Center, Hits Bush Tribunals

San Diego Jewish Press Heritage,
December 14, 2001

Former President Jimmy Carter, helping to dedicate a peace center that might be considered a granddaughter of the Camp David talks between Egyptian President Anwar Sadat and Israeli Prime Minister Menahem Begin, on Thursday, December 6, urged President George W. Bush to reconsider the administration's plans to bring accused terrorists before closed military tribunals.

Carter acknowledged that it is unusual for former American presidents to criticize sitting incumbents, but said he had heard from Democratic members of Congress who were concerned, but fearful politically, to speak out against what they consider to be an unwarranted erosion of defendants' civil rights.

Even though his stand might be unpopular, Carter said, he believed it is important to safeguard the right of persons accused of crimes to have a public trial and the possibility of appeal to a higher court—even if the crime they are accused of is terrorism.

Besides, Carter quipped, unlike the unnamed Democrats in Washington: "I don't intend to seek public office in the future and I have Secret Service protection."

The former U.S. president participated in the first panel discussion sponsored by the new Joan B. Kroc Institute for Peace and Justice at the University of San Diego, a Catholic university. The Institute's Jewish director, Joyce Neu, used to work for Carter at the Carter Center at Emory University.

Joining Carter on the panel were former Costa Rican president Rodrigo Carazo Odio, who now heads the Peace Action Council of the Unrepresented Nations and Peoples Organization, and Ahmedou Ould-Abdallah, a former foreign minister of Mauritania and special United Nations representative to Burundi, who now serves as executive secretary of the Global Coalition for Africa.

Both Corazo Odio and Ould-Abdallah had participated in Carter Center activities in the past, so the initial forum at the new Kroc center brought together people who all knew and had worked with each other.

Neu, who had helped Carter negotiate ceasefires both in the Bosnian conflict and in a running guerrilla war between Uganda and the Sudan, appeared to relish the moment when she, as executive director of the Institute, took her place at the dais between two former presidents.

In his remarks, Carter spoke of hosting Begin and Sadat at Camp David, noting that Sadat had spent most of his military career trying to wipe out Israel. Begin, according to Carter, had been widely regarded as a former terrorist.

Notwithstanding those fierce reputations, Begin and Sadat were able to conclude a peace pact—with Carter's help. The former president remembered shuttling between the two adversaries, always trying to craft a solution that afforded each of the negotiating teams the impression that it was extracting more compromises than the other.

That was an important lesson to learn, said Carter.

With the insights that he developed into the art of negotiation at Camp David, he said, he was able to start the Carter Center which utilizes his prestige as a former U.S. President to help arrange cease-fires, or to conduct international negotiations.

As Neu learned the art of peacemaking at Carter's side, then developed the program for the Kroc Institute, the USD center can be viewed as a granddaughter of that historic Camp David negotiation.

The easy camaraderie among panelists and members of the audience indicated that the demand for peacemaking expertise around the world is so great, that there is little sense of rivalry among the various peacemaking institutions.

Unfortunately, audience members agreed, there are plenty of conflicts in the world to go around.

Orthodox Girls School Finds a Happy Home on Reform Campus

San Diego Jewish Press Heritage,
May 10, 2002

Although not precedent-setting, it is unusual: An Orthodox girl's school has taken up residence at a Reform congregation.

The 26 students of the Torah High School's Girl's Division, along with their principal, Rabbi Shimon Zehnwirth, relocated earlier this year from quarters at the Soille San Diego Hebrew Day School to the grounds of Congregation Beth Israel. Now reaching through 11th grade, the school next year will have its first 12th grade class, so sufficient room was at a premium.

Stuart Simmons, executive director of Congregation Beth Israel, said a number of issues had to be settled before the arrangement could be made.

First, Beth Israel had to check with its own Beth Israel Day School (which goes through fifth grade) and with its supplementary (after-school) religious program to make certain that sufficient space even would be available for the girls.

With the supplementary school students using the classrooms only two weekday afternoons, it was clear the Torah High School students could use the same classrooms five mornings and three afternoons. During the time that the supplementary school classes are in session, the girls move to other facilities, such as a science room used by the day school, or to the library.

The space problem solved, there were the more mundane issues of how much rent the school should pay, matters of insurance liability and the like.

Finally, there was the issue of how well the Orthodox rabbis of the Torah High School—an affiliate of the Chofetz Chaim Yeshiva in Jerusalem—would get along with the clergy of the Reform congregation.

A meeting among Rabbi Michoel Peikes, dean of the Torah High School, Zehnwirth and Beth Israel's clergy—Rabbi Ben Kamin, Rabbi Sheila Goloboy, and Cantor Arlene Bernstein— "went very well," Simmons said.

While there are numerous theological issues formally dividing the Orthodox and Reform movements, Zehnwirth said on a personal level the rabbis are able to coexist amicably.

"All Jews of all walks of life should get together, no matter where they are coming from or what their background is—that is without question," the principal said.

"They were very welcoming," Rabbi Peikes added. "Part of our education is dealing with Jews of different backgrounds. The children are very happy."

The girls, all post-bat mitzvah, conduct *Shacharit* services in their classrooms every morning, and on occasion Cantor Bernstein has come to join them. "To be Jews together *davening* is a very beautiful thing," Zehnwirth said. It is not a matter of Bernstein leading services because she is a cantor, "it is just a matter of Jews coming together."

Like the boys' division of Torah High School, which has met since last year on the grounds of the Conservative Congregation Beth El, the girls division "gets along just fine" with members and clergy of other movements, Zehnwirth said.

"I think what is very special here are the warm relationships we have with the administration," Zehnwirth said. "Every single person has a smile for you, without exception. They love the girls and the girls love them; it is a special environment."

Simmons said when the idea of the Torah High School relocating to Beth Israel was first raised, "I had a hope that somehow the subliminal message would be that when there are so many places in the world where Jews are conflicted with each other, where they discount or disrespect each other, that here were a Reform institution and an Orthodox institution cooperating and working together."

"I think both the Torah High School and Beth Israel overcame our mutual hesitancy to do this, due in fact to Rabbi Peikes' openness and enthusiasm in recognizing this would be a wonderful environment for the girls, coupled with our desire to break down another barrier in the Jewish community," Simmons added.

"I love the fact that we are doing this!"

What Swallowed Jonah? Sea World Educators Identify the Prime Suspects

San Diego Jewish Press Heritage,
September 13, 2002

In the popular imagination, it was a whale that swallowed Jonah. But when you read the English translation of Jonah this coming Yom Kippur this afternoon, you'll find that in most Bibles and *chumashim*, it was a "great fish."

So, we have a biblical what dunnit, as it were.

Over at Sea World, Keith Robinson and Donna Parham agreed to speculate about the mystery.

The biblical text tells us that the prophet Jonah tried to flee from God on a ship that left Jaffa (in modern day Israel). Furthermore, the text said his ship was headed toward Tarshish when it was beset by a storm. There are various hypotheses where that was. Some sources say Turkey; others say Spain.

In either event, the ship would have been sailing on the Mediterranean Sea. So, Clue Number One: the suspect was a denizen of the Mediterranean.

In the Stone Tanach, Jonah 2:1 is rendered: "*Hashem* designated a large fish to swallow Jonah and Jonah remained in the fish's innards three days and three nights."

In the King James version of the Bible, that verse is numbered Jonah 1:17 and is rendered: "Now the Lord had prepared a great fish to swallow up Jonah. And Jonah was in the belly of the fish three days and three nights."

One version says God "designated" the fish, the other says He "had prepared" it. Could that make a difference? If God "had prepared" the fish, perhaps He had created it anew, especially for the purpose of swallowing Jonah. If such were the case, the fish may have simply existed for that particular moment in time. There may, therefore, be no modern-day equivalent.

Based on that premise, Robinson and Parham offered the first in a series of "suspects." The Jonah Fish, created by God specifically to swallow Jonah and hold him inside for three days, was a fish that was never seen before and was never seen again.

The alternative translation in the Stone Tanach allowed for other possibilities. If God "designated" the fish, He might have looked into the waters of the Mediterranean, spotted a likely-looking fish and commanded it to wait with its mouth open at the storm-tossed spot where Jonah would be thrown overboard from a bucking ship.

Whatever that great fish was, Robins and Parham agreed, in order to swallow Jonah whole it would have needed a very big mouth and very large esophagus.

And have lived in the Mediterranean.

Robinson said most whales don't have big enough throats to swallow a man whole. For example, the orcas that perform in Sea-World's shows couldn't do it.

So, Shamu is "off the hook," as it were.

One whale that does have a big enough esophagus is the sperm whale—an albino version of which bedeviled Captain Ahab in Herman Melville's 19ᵗʰ Century masterpiece, *Moby Dick*.

Robinson said that large sperm whales have esophagi that measure as large as 50 centimeters, or roughly a foot-and-a-half wide. They can be found in the Mediterranean.

He said sperm whales don't have to chew their food, they can move it into their stomachs by peristaltic or muscle action—so Jonah could have been swallowed whole.

The sperm whale, therefore, is the second "suspect."

However, men often measure more than a foot and a half across their shoulders, so in order for his swallower to have been a sperm whale, Jonah would have to have been of fairly light build.

Whales are mammals with digestive systems similar to those of humans, noted Robinson. Think of "all the digestive juices, hydrochloric acids, the heat, just suffocating heat, the lack of air . . . ."

A whale's stomach would be no place for a human to spend three days, Robinson said. Not to live to tell about it.

An active member of the fundamentalist Maranatha Chapel in Rancho Bernardo, Robinson noted that Christian theology suggests that Jonah actually died in the belly of the great fish and then was resurrected by God. As Christians understand Jonah's ordeal, it prefigured the death and resurrection of Jesus.

Parham said the belly of a fish is a far more hospitable possibility for a human dwelling than that of a whale. The whale's metabolism "is a lot faster so they digest their food a lot faster" than fish do, Parham said. "Fish are cold-blooded, so things move at a different rate."

Parham and Robinson in turn considered as suspects two species of fish.

Until the international society in charge of naming fish responded to protests from the Anti-Defamation League and officially withdrew the moniker, one species of giant grouper had been known popularly as the jewfish. There were various theories why the fish got that name, most of them anti-Semitic in origin. But one theory suggested that the giant grouper was called the jewfish because it was the one that swallowed Jonah.

Robinson said that the grouper can grow to 800 pounds, and, "I know that there have been divers who have had their legs sucked into the mouths of groupers. The way they feed, all they do is open their mouths and the water just flows in, so divers' legs have been sucked in."

Mark down the giant grouper as the third suspect. However, neither Robinson nor Parham considers it to be a very strong suspect. In detective lingo, they don't "like" the grouper for gulping Jonah.

Sure, giant groupers have sucked down divers' legs, but there is no evidence they've ever ingested a whole person. To swallow a person whole, there is a far better candidate, one known throughout the Mediterranean, Robinson and Parham said. Thanks to Steven Spielberg, director of *Jaws,* this species is known throughout the world, even in regions remote from the sea. Suspect number four is the great white shark.

"Elephant seals are one of the favorite meals of the great white shark," Parham said. "And some elephant seals are bigger than Shamu."

Robinson told of seeing a photograph of "a great white shark opening its mouth and it had within its gullet a whole blue shark. You could see the head of a six-foot blue shark, so it could easily swallow a man."

Parham added that "in the cold water, with the metabolism of a shark, a man's body could last three days without deterioration."

How Jonah might have found air to breathe inside the stomach is another question—an unanswered one. Even though some other fish species have been known to surface from the sea and gulp down air, like the lungfish for example, there is no known explanation for how such air could be transferred to the fish's stomach.

After Jonah was swallowed, he prayed to God. Three days later, the great fish "vomited" Jonah onto dry land, according to the King James version of the Bible. It "spewed out" Jonah, according to the Stone version of the Tanach.

Robinson thumbed through the book *Great White Shark* by Richard Ellis and John McCosker to a page where it noted that in the 16th Century, the French naturalist Guillaume Rondelet had sought to identify a marine mammal capable of swallowing a man and then bringing the prey back up later on.

The authors said the great white shark was a great substitute choice.

Every scientist knows that a theory is simply a best-informed guess, until perhaps new facts come along. But based on the foregoing, Parham and Robinson have their hypothesis.

What dunnit? The great white shark dunnit. "Jaws" swallowed Jonah!

Elephants in the Garden

San Diego Jewish Press Heritage,
January 17, 2003

In honor of the approaching Tu B'Shevat holiday, *Heritage* assistant editor Gail Umeham and I, with our respective spouses Okoronkwo and Nancy, decided to take our grandchildren Amy, 4 1/2, and Shor, 20 months, to visit City Farmers Nursery to learn about trees and other plant life.

Bill Tall, owner of the nursery, grew up at Congregation Beth El back in the Conservative congregation's Clairemont days. Today, he is a member of Temple Beth Sholom in Chula Vista.

He cherishes days like Tu B'Shevat when his passion for growing and his religion come together. His daughter, Rebecca, today a business student at San Diego State University, and his son, Samuel, a Crawford High School student, became b'nai mitzvah with ceremonies right at the nursery, amid the trees, shrubs, farm animals, and fish. A similar experience may await daughter Sarah, now a student at Horace Mann Junior High School.

Tall also enjoys teaching children about plants, possibly realizing that the adults who accompany the children to the nursery will hang onto his every word, because they don't know much about horticulture either. Tall is a natural teacher.

Do you know why some trees shed their leaves in winter? Tall explained to us that in cold climates the leaves fall on the land above the tree's root system, thereby insulating the roots from freezing. Furthermore, the fallen leaves provide nutrients for the roots, enabling them to force food back up into the plant system.

I'm not sure how much of that either little Amy Lupsha or Shor Masori absorbed. However, while Tall educated the grandparents, he also kept the tykes interested.

At one point, he broke off a piece of sugar cane, stripped it, and instructed Shor to put it in his mouth so he could see how sweet it tasted. Shor chewed and sucked it for the rest of the tour, and only relinquished the cane afterwards when we stopped at Nate's Deli, which the Tall family also operates on the property at 4382 Home Avenue. The deli is named for Bill's late father.

For Shor, sugar cane was good, but the deli's chocolate chip cookie, accompanied by a glass of milk, proved even tastier!

During the tour, Amy seemed fascinated by an elephant-foot palm, so named because the bottom of the palm looks like an elephant's foot. "If you ever felt an elephant's foot, this is what it would feel like," Tall told Amy. I couldn't make up my mind if that were true or just a Tall tale.

As Amy inspected the tree more closely, the nursery man told us elephant-foot palms had been planted as "street trees" in Los Angeles, but "they grew so wide that they grew over the curb and into the street and became a nuisance."

It was apparent to me that Amy has a fondness for animals, whether of the "elephant" palm variety or of the barnyard variety such as the sheep, goats, horse, ducks, turkey, geese, chickens, and roosters that the Tall family keeps in an outdoor menagerie. When Shor started to put his fingers through the fence to pet the animals, Amy was quick to protect him from such folly.

Tall told fascinating stories about some of the strategies that Mother Nature employs to ensure that trees are able to reproduce. Fruit, for example, is a device to protect the seed that is maturing inside. When the fruit falls off the tree in the summer, either on its own or with the help of birds, the fleshy material around the seed rots away. However, the seed still is protected from the ensuing cold climate by a seed coat, or pit.

During the winter, the coat will begin to weaken. Next, in the spring, it will break down sufficiently to permit the seed to come out and germinate.

Another strategy employs insects, Tall said. Caterpillars will defoliate a passion-flower shrub completely, and when there is no food left, they will go into their cocoons. Mother Nature requires the plants to suffer such marauders because later in the cycle, when the passion flowers come out, butterflies will emerge from the cocoons and begin their work of pollinating the flowers. Of course, pollinating the flowers is essential to the production of seeds.

"The sole reason a plant is on the Earth is to reproduce," Tall instructed. I figure if his parents don't tell him first, Shor and I will have a variant on the birds-and-the-caterpillars conversation some years from now.

Soille's Headmaster Passes on His Passion to a New Generation

San Diego Jewish Press-Heritage,
June 6, 2003

Rabbi Simcha Weiser, who has been headmaster of the Soille San Diego Hebrew Day School for 22 of its 40 years, counts among his greatest delights learning about graduates who have gone on to become officers of their synagogues or board members of Jewish day schools in the cities where they live.

In that, no doubt, he is a link in a chain on which the late Rabbi Yaacov Kulefsky and the retired Rabbi Shlomo Goldstein preceded him. Goldstein was one of the teachers whom Weiser credits with motivating him to become a better student at the Hebrew Academy of Washington, D.C. And Kulefsky? He was the head of Ner Israel Rabbinical College in Baltimore and the rabbi whom Goldstein credits with being his mentor.

Kulefsky to Goldstein to Weiser— from one generation of Jewish teachers to another.

In keeping with that theme, not only Weiser will be in the spotlight at Soille San Diego Hebrew Day School's 40th anniversary scholarship banquet on Sunday evening, June 15, but so will alumni Yael Schwarz, Dr. Abraham Broudy and Dr. Karl Jacobs, who will recall memories of their years at Hebrew Day.

The evening's festivities will culminate with the dedication of a sefer Torah, symbolically linking generation after generation of teachers to the giving of the Torah on Shavuot.

Weiser told *Heritage* that as a young teenager he was far more interested in the Washington Redskins than in Rashi. "I was a very mediocre student, to be honest with you," he said. "I was not the most model citizen in school. I did fine academically, but was going through the motions like most of my classmates."

Then along came Rabbi Goldstein. "If you didn't do well on a test, he'd come over to a child and say, 'Hey, you didn't do well. Why didn't you do well? What is the problem? How can I help you study better? How can I help you take better notes? How can I help you understand the material better? Because I expect you to get much better grades than this. I expect you to succeed because what I am teaching you is important!"

Goldstein was one of the youngest members of the faculty, and American-born. Many of the other teachers at Washington's Hebrew Academy were Holocaust survivors, recently moved from Europe, who seemed to feel American kids never could understand what real Judaism was about, Weiser recalled.

Weiser remembered that at first he resisted Rabbi Goldstein's efforts to have him take his studies seriously. "My deal was 'Hey, Rabbi Goldstein, I have an idea for you. You leave me alone and I will leave you alone.' And his attitude was: 'That is just not acceptable. You are going to do well. You are going to learn, you are going to accomplish. What I am teaching you is important and it is important for you!'"

After a few years, Goldstein left teaching to become a successful lawyer. Now that he's retired, he's teaching again, and remembers

95

Weiser by his boyhood name of "Steven." (Weiser took the name "Simcha" when he received his ordination or *smicha* as a rabbi).

Why does Goldstein think he had such an impact as a teacher? "Part of the reason, perhaps, was that I was not much older than Steven and the other students," he speculated in a telephone interview. "I was 26 and they were around 14. The other teachers were beyond middle age. Today when I teach, I find that the younger teachers have a better relationship with the students than I do."

Goldstein, who grew up in Los Angeles, remembered on one vacation visit home, he tentatively decided to leave his yeshiva in Baltimore and try to find one in Los Angeles. "Rabbi Kulefsky was my *rebbe*; he called me up and had a long conversation with me, that I should really return," Goldstein recalled. That such an important person, the *rosh yeshiva*, took a personal interest in him was inspirational, he said.

The year after Goldstein was Weiser's teacher, another remarkable teacher came along. He was Rabbi Avraham Baharan, member of a long-time Jerusalem family, whom Weiser remembers as a "charismatic" person.

"He forged a much more personal relationship," Weiser recalled. Baharan had a remarkable memory, which he demonstrated by playing three chess games with his students simultaneously— without ever looking at the chessboard.

Students would tell them where they moved their pieces, and he would visualize their boards and tell them what move to make for him. "Although we occasionally beat him, he held his own," Weiser marveled.

After a Shabbat meal, "he would speak to us and we would study something together and he really walked the extra mile and engaged us as individuals."

Onward to Yeshiva High School of Greater Washington, and there was another mentor, Rabbi Zechariah Mines, a person "whose home was open to us, who spent casual time with us, who took the time to get to know us as individuals," Weiser said.

Weiser's mentors shared one important characteristic: each took a personal interest in his students' progress.

During Weiser's long years of study for ordination at the Chofetz Chaim Yeshiva in New York, he followed two tracks: one that could lead him to be a pulpit rabbi and another that did lead him, upon graduation in 1979, to the field of Jewish education.

"I was pretty convinced in my last years of yeshiva that my interest really was education," Weiser said. "I felt as if there was a huge need. I felt that there were so many kids going through the classes of Jewish day schools uninspired, untouched, and I really wanted to see that changed.

"To be honest, I also figured a day school has a bigger place in the life of the Jewish community than does the synagogue. I have tremendous respect for the synagogue and tremendous respect for pulpit rabbis, I really do. But given the choice, if you ask me 'where is the bigger opportunity to have an impact on the community?' I felt that this was a better place."

Besides affecting the lives of students, "schools like ours engage families," Weiser said. "Families have to make parenting decisions. They have to decide first of all if they want a Jewish education and how intense a Jewish education it should be. You are educating the whole family."

* * *

After incorporating in 1964, the San Diego Hebrew Day School moved so often that it might have been called the "school on wheels." Its first home was the old Jewish Community Center on 54th Street. Next, it moved to Temple Beth Israel at Third and Laurel Street. Then to the home of a former restaurant (Aspen Mine Company), and after that to Tifereth Israel Synagogue. Next, it went to Beth Jacob Congregation, and when that proved too small, the school's nursery and kindergarten were relocated to a home on Adams Avenue. Then the nursery (preschool) was moved to another home. Seven homes in less than seven years.

In 1971, Hebrew Day School purchased a historic public school building on 8th Street in National City. It seemed like a good idea at the time, especially since students were being drawn both from San Diego and Tijuana.

But none of the students lived in National City, and after his arrival here in 1981, Weiser soon determined that if the school were to grow and flourish it would have to move again.

"Being in National City was a tremendous, tremendous detriment," Weiser said. "Rabbi Marvin Hier of the Simon Wiesenthal Center in Los Angeles clarified this to me. He has a Lower East Side (of New York City) manner about him, and he said: 'Look, Rabbi, you've got three strikes: You're in the old neighborhood, it's an Orthodox school,' and, I forget the third, maybe that we had no strong financial support group. 'You've got to change that; no matter what it takes, get out of there!'"

"So the second year I was here, we were in trailers, portable buildings... in the College Area. We had our parents out on the Sunday before school, planting shrubbery and making sure that it looked like a school. That was a throwback to the old days of the Hebrew Day School moving every year. I really didn't want to see that, but that showed the intensity of conviction that we had to get out of National City, because staying in National City meant consigning the school to the past."

When San Diego public schools decided to lease out unneeded land, Hebrew Day went to the grounds of the former John Muir school, across the street from the old Congregation Beth Tefilah. Later, it moved to the former grounds of Cleveland Elementary School and, finally in the 1993-94 school year, to its present site, a property it purchased at the corner of Afton Road and Aero Drive in the Kearny Mesa area. It took the name Soille San Diego Hebrew Day School in memory of Rabbi Henry and Esther Soille, who helped the school during their lives and who left a financial legacy to it upon the rabbi's death.

"Location, location, location" was not all of Weiser's worries. Hebrew Day School was once the only Jewish day school in San Diego, but others were then competing for students. In 1980, the year before his arrival, the San Diego Jewish Academy got under way, and in 1981 Beth Israel Day School got started. Furthermore, Chabad announced that it would soon be beginning its own day school.

To make matters more complicated, board members of the United Jewish Federation were dubious at best that Hebrew Day School was viable enough to qualify for funding. Only 40 students were enrolled when Weiser arrived.

"I looked around and thought, 'Does this community really need a Hebrew Day School?' Weiser related. "And that was not an easy question to answer."

In deciding that the day school, in fact, was necessary, he promulgated a vision that "it really wasn't a question of the school being the biggest, but a question of the school doing its job of raising awareness in the community of the importance of Torah study and seeing to it that anyone who walked through the doors felt a sense of comfort, warmth and feeling at home."

To have an "anchor" for the school's Judaic program, the new headmaster recruited Rabbi Chaim Hollander, who had graduated from the Chofetz Chaim Yeshiva some years before Weiser and who then was teaching in New Orleans.

"The first challenge was getting kids into the school," recalled Hollander, who today serves as pulpit rabbi at Young Israel Synagogue in the San Carlos neighborhood in addition to his teaching duties at the day school.

"People felt that the building in National City was unclean, not secure, unsafe," Hollander recalled. "Rabbi Weiser promised people that it would be brought up to standards, and that we would move in a year."

Weiser made telephone call after telephone call to parents, urging them to re-enroll their children in the school. He told them about Hollander, about his philosophy of involvement with their students, and by the time the new term opened a month later, there were 115 students enrolled. Weiser also placed many a phone call to Jewish philanthropists, successfully seeking funding to keep the school viable.

"There was no real (Judaic) curriculum in place," Hollander remembered. With eight years of experience teaching Judaic studies in different schools, Hollander said he was able to "wing it" pending the development of a more professional curriculum for the following years.

Together, the two compatriots, who had known each other only casually before, forged a Judaic program which set as goals that "children should be able to read Hebrew fluently, be comfortable with the prayers, be able to read prayers, be able to pick up a Chumash and be able to translate it well enough to understand, to be able to read the Rashi commentary, understand what his point is, and then finally to have experience or a feel for the Talmud," Hollander said.

In the middle school years, boys would study Talmud while girls would take "Yahadut" in a program developed by Weiser's wife, Betty. This Yahudut program "goes into the basis of Judaism in great depth, with lots of philosophical material," Hollander said.

Weiser's father had balanced his life as an Orthodox Jew with a career as an accountant for the U.S. Defense Department. Similarly, "balance" became a hallmark of Weiser's view of the school's academic programming. Judaic studies were important, but so too were the secular studies. They had to be so excellent that graduates of the middle school could qualify for any private high school (or public school) they might desire *en route* to a top-rated college education. Weiser said parents should never be forced to choose between "Harvard or Judaism."

When Weiser arrived, Elaine Lepow was teaching third grade as well as English in seventh through ninth grades. She remembered an occasion when she was teaching ninth-grade English and was asked to come downstairs to have her picture taken with the third-grade students. Rabbi Weiser volunteered to take over the ninth-grade English class temporarily. She had been teaching about noun clauses and gave him the book, assuming that would not be an area with which he was familiar.

After the photograph was taken, she ran back upstairs and found him "explaining noun clauses in depth and diagramming them with the kids. It was my first understanding of the thoroughness of preparation of this person to be not only headmaster of the school and rabbi for our school community, but extremely well prepared to go into economics because his math background was strong, and even into noun clauses in English."

Lepow, who today serves as the school's principal, said although when Weiser arrived he was younger than everyone else on staff except one custodian, he had the charisma to forge a team. "He is extremely intelligent and by nature very sensitive," almost, in her view, "a Renaissance man who can meet issues whether they are financial, rabbinic, personnel, of deep emotional impact, or just academic interest."

Of immediate significance to Lepow was that under Weiser, "there was never any censoring of what I was teaching. I had the freedom to teach everything I felt was important, whether in third grade or junior high. In addition to that, I found someone I could discuss Shakespeare with intelligently and get into some of the main threads that I was weaving between our philosophy as Jews and that of the universality of the play."

Under Weiser and Lepow, "we hired Karen Wellner, who became involved in the San Diego County Science Fair, and we have been winning awards ever since," the principal noted.

"We also spun out from that to make sure that our kids were given opportunities to compete in math contests, poetry competitions, secular things ..."

As an administrator, Lepow learned a philosophy from Weiser reflecting what he had learned from his own teachers: "Within our own faculty, we are constantly meeting, evaluating, going over and assessing all the time, how do you meet the needs of every single child in the school, not just every single child in your classroom?"

Faye Snyder, today director of the preschool, had served as the day school's lead preschool teacher for a year prior to Weiser's arrival. She said she believes a good school needs to have fewer than 400 children, "because the principal of the school has to know every child. To know every child, you have to know every adult that is connected to the child, and any other child who might be connected to that child, but is not in that school.

"Currently, Soille San Diego Hebrew Day School has an enrollment of 265 students (48 in preschool), and I know every child and every person connected to every child," Snyder said. "So does Rabbi Weiser. There aren't too many headmasters who can do that. He is busy, yet he makes it his business to know everybody."

* * *

Simultaneous devotion to Torah and secular studies was rewarded in 1992, when San Diego Hebrew Day School was named one of the nation's "Blue Ribbon" schools by the U.S. Department of Education. That led to Weiser, Lepow, former school president Eilene Cummins and Dr. Michael Mantell, who then was the school's president, flying to Washington D.C. for a variety of ceremonies, including a meeting on the South Lawn of the White House with President Bill Clinton and a kosher luncheon in the Capitol with U.S. Rep. Duncan Hunter (R-El Cajon). Other indelible memories for Weiser: the warmth with which Lynn Schenk— then a congresswoman, today chief of staff to California Gov. Gray Davis— spoke about her own Jewish upbringing, and the chance to attend a reception with other educators in the Library of Congress, in a newly restored room that even his father, a life-long government employee, had never been inside.

On any given school morning, Rabbi Weiser typically is standing at the front door of Soille San Diego Hebrew Day School, greeting students as they come in. "I ask them how they are doing and I tell them the price of admission to Hebrew Day School is a 'smile on your face,'" the headmaster said.

"You'd be surprised how many kids walk around with an expression that says 'the world is not my friend.' I want them to realize this is a place that is safe for them, that cares for them."

Greeting the children, Weiser said, "you can get a lot of insight. You can see if there is tension in the family, if no one is taking the time to give a kid a hug."

After 22 years as headmaster, with a second generation of his students attending the school, Weiser describes himself as a "grandfatherly figure, a friendly figure, not the authoritarian figure" that the principal of his own boyhood school days represented.

When a student's family is beset with difficulties— a death or the trauma of divorce— "I will call up the parents, offer to meet with them and their children...and in the adolescent years, if there is a rift in the family and the parents are having a hard time parenting a child, we become involved. We make it a partnership with parents."

Hollander commented that even after more than two decades at the helm of Hebrew Day School, Weiser is always alive with new ideas about how to make the school better, how to re-invigorate its program, how to keep education ever fresh.

"I have tremendous goals for the school," concurred Weiser. "There is room in the community for many schools, but I want Hebrew Day School to be an engine of progress. I want to see the school do more in terms of parent education in the next few years. I am also thinking about a program of once-a-week family learning in the Day School, having them come to school for an hour or an hour and a half and have the kids and parents together."

Weiser estimates that, over the years, the number of students who graduated from Hebrew Day School or spent enough time there for the experience to be formative is somewhere between 800 and 1,000. Since leaving the school, many of these graduates "have spent time in Israel, or at a yeshiva, or doing specifically Jewish things— activities that absolutely can be traced back to the school," he said.

For example, at UCSD, two students who have been leaders of the pro-Israel campus movement are Wayne Klitofsky and upcoming banquet speaker Yael Schwarz. Both are Hebrew Day School graduates. While not taking total credit, Weiser said "the fact that the school gave them that kind of confidence, and sense of security to do so, is something that makes me very proud."

San Diego Names Bayside Circle after Louis Rose, its First Jewish Settler

jewishsightseeing.com
January 21, 2005

The Point of the matter is San Diego has named some land specifically for Jewish pioneer Louis Rose. It is called Louis Rose Point.

San Diego Mayor Dick Murphy, City Councilman Michael Zucchet, Park and Recreation Director Ellie Oppenheim, and Steve Solomon, president of the United Jewish Federation of San Diego, had participated in a ceremony at the proposed site last September 22 to mark the San Diego aspects of the 350th anniversary of Jewish settlement in North America.

But formal approval for the naming of the site on a boat channel leading to San Diego Bay awaited action by the Park and Recreation Board. That came yesterday (January 20), the same day President George W. Bush was inaugurated for his second term.

The small circle of land at the foot of Womble Street occupies a small portion of what was formerly Naval Training Center—but as a result of the Base Realignment and Closure (BRAC) process, is now called Liberty Station. The location alongside the boat channel was specifically chosen in honor of Rose's dream to move the City from Old Town San Diego to the edge of San Diego Bay in order to develop the area as a commercial port. To that end, Rose in 1869 laid out the 30-block-long townsite of Roseville—an area that is to-day part of the Point Loma neighborhood of San Diego.

The San Diego Park and Recreation Board—after hearing from a succession of speakers, including this writer—voted unanimously to formally bestow the name "Louis Rose Point" on that circle of land, which will be an enclave in a larger, as yet-unnamed city park. The sprawling former Naval Training Center property overlaps Roseville, and from Louis Rose Point, one can see a panorama of the genteel community that grew up on the pioneer's town site.

Park and Recreation Board member Norman Greene led a succession of speakers in favor of the project, noting that his colleagues had voted in 2002 to name something in that area for Rose, and that two years before that the City Council and then-Mayor Susan Golding also had indicated their approval of the project—but somehow nothing got done. Saying that cities do not have good institutional memories—except in the cases of formally adopted resolutions and ordinances— he urged the board to complete the naming process. Once that was completed, he said, a campaign could get underway to raise private funds to build a suitable memorial to Rose.

Other speakers included former California Assemblyman Howard Wayne; Dr. Paul Thomas, president of Trinity Lutheran Church; Rabbi Scott Meltzer of Ohr Shalom Synagogue, and long-time San Diego resident and columnist Gert Thaler.

As Louis Rose's biographer, I was given the three-minute time allocated for individual speakers to tell why he was important to the city. I explained that when San Diego was founded in 1769 by the Spanish, they chose Presidio Hill because it was high and could be defended, was near a source of fresh water, and had Indian villages nearby where the Franciscan padres could preach Christianity. It made sense for the Spaniards, but for Rose, who grew up in Neuhaus-an-der-Oste near Germany's busy Elbe River, and immigrated to New Orleans on the Mississippi River, the fact that it was several miles removed from the bay made no commercial sense at all.

Next, Rabbi Meltzer, speaking for his Conservative synagogue and the San Diego Rabbinical Association—"and to what extent I can, for the entire Jewish community"—said it is a matter of pride that the city chose to recognize "one who had a grand vision of what this city could be at a time when this city's future looked bleak, at least for some."

Wayne, a Democrat who served three terms in the state Assembly, told the board, "I know that we have a rich and distinguished history here in San Diego, but it is often for many people not well known. One thing that we can accomplish with this motion is to help bring history to light to people who would visit this Point . . . ."

Thomas said his church has been enriched by the merger of two congregations, one traditionally white, the other traditionally black, and added about Louis Rose Point "This is an ecumenical type of project we are looking at. Particularly on this inauguration day, it seems appropriate for all of us to look back and remember those who have come before us—to honor their memories, their sacrifices, to honor their spirits and their commitments to make San Diego a better city."

"Further," Thomas said, "it seems appropriate to point out that the Old World sent us their wanderers and dreamers. Louis Rose was one of the immigrants who came here with little but had a vision for the future. Only in America could an immigrant and a member of a minority religion rise to the heights of a Louis Rose. He was quite an example. We should remember him. Our children should know of him for the example he set."

Thaler concluded the period for public comment by telling the board members of "having lived here for many years—84 of them. I hope that if there is a dedication of this memorial to Louis Rose in '08 or '07 that I would be here with all of you to enjoy that.

"I grew up on the Bay of San Diego, my father's business was established in 1890 and I know the bay very well and I know the vision that people had and shared with Louis Rose," said Thaler, a columnist for the *San Diego Jewish Times*. "I attended the dedication of the park, and as I stood there, I thought this vision should come true, because truly San Diego is still the most beautiful city in the world."

When public comment ended, board members were quick to signal their approval of the idea. Moving approval, board member Daniel Mazzella told of growing up in New York City and attending a school called PS 12—for Public School 12. "How exciting is that?" he asked about the name. "How much more exciting and interesting for our culture that we can start to add some of those pieces that are missing. I think that this is a promise kept . . . I think this is an important cultural augmentation to the story of San Diego."

Board Member Kevin Faulconer, who had seconded the motion, said he and other residents "hear the term 'Roseville' a lot in Point Loma, as some of you folks might now, but not too many folks may know what that means."

Board Member Olivia Puente-Reynolds said she hoped that ultimately a statue of Rose would be built, along with a marker explaining his significance to the community's development. She said she liked his famous quote to doubters about San Diego's rich prospects: "Just Wait Awhile and You Will See!"

Greene, Mazzella, Faulconer, and Puente-Reynolds were joined in voting for the project by Daniel Coffey, Darlene Gould Davies, and M. Virginia "Ginny" Barnes, the latter of whom chaired the meeting in the absence of the regular chairman, Jim Austin. Three other board members—Aurora Cudal, Robert Ottilie and Robert L. Robinson—were absent.

San Diego Jewish Academy: A Quarter Century of Teaching

San Diego Jewish Times,
February 9, 2005

Metaphors and analogies to seeds and plants sprouted throughout the day, on January 25, as the San Diego Jewish Academy celebrated its 25th anniversary and dedicated a garden in memory of popular kindergarten teacher Levana Estline. Fittingly, the occasion coincided with the Jewish holiday of Tu B'Shevat, known popularly as the "Birthday of the Trees."

On hand to help plant the garden were people who were important to the school at its various stages of growth. Among the celebrants were San Diego Jewish Academy's first three presidents, respectively, Charles Wax, Dr. Allen Jay, and John Adler; two teachers who have taught at SDJA its entire quarter century, Karen Rund and Edna Yedid; and a former student who was a member of SDJA's first class, Scott Meltzer, today the rabbi at Congregation Ohr Shalom.

Marsha Berkson, who chaired the 25th anniversary celebration, recalled that Wax, the first president, once related that at its founding in 1979, the Jewish Academy had no money, no students, and no facility. Today, there are 700 students on a 40-acre campus. Originally based in San Carlos, it branched out to La Jolla, where first an elementary school and, in 1984, a junior high were established. From La Jolla, the campus moved north to the current facility in Carmel Valley, where its high school took root. To those involved in each stage, said Berkson, "we thank you for cultivating the seeds."

Berkson called to the stage a group of elementary school students—"The Class of 2017," she kvelled—who performed the school song, "Acharai" (Follow Me), written by teacher Sara Geller. Apropos to the day, the lyrics instructed that San Diego Jewish Academy is a place:

Where all the seeds we plant today
Become the leaders of their day
And as they reach up to the sky
Proud voices shout out "Acharai"
We are the lights that lead the way . . .

Another teacher, Shana Lew, retold the Talmud story often recalled on Tu B'Shevat, about a certain Honi who laughed at an old man who was planting a tree. Did that man think that he ever would see the fruits of that tree? No, the man patiently explained, but as his ancestors had planted for him, so too would he plant for future generation. Honi grew tired and slept in a shady place for 70 years. He awakened to see a beautiful tree, and asked an old man standing nearby if he were the same man whom he had seen plant it. The old man replied that, to the contrary, he was the grandson of the planter.

"Mordechai Rap" from the forthcoming musical, *Esther*, was previewed for the donors and parent activists. The rap's rhyme scheme could be interpreted as a salute to the "gardeners" who had planted and tended Jewish education:

You got to stand up for what you believe in

Cause that's the only way you're gonna be achievin . . .

You know you gotta stand up, you gotta stand up . . .

The musical, based on the Book of Esther, will be performed by a cast of 110 SDJA students March 23-26 at UCSD's Mandeville Auditorium.

The ceremony for adults was followed outside by a ceremony for the 700 students and their teachers, with many of the horticultural metaphors repeated.

There were poignant moments as well: Larry Acheatal, SDJA's executive director, told students that Estline, who died in 2003 at age 63, had served as a kindergarten teacher at the school for 18 years, and that present for the occasion were members of her family—husband Tsvi, and children Ofer, Einat, and Yael. Teachers and students participated in a short program memorializing Estline before the gates to the 5,000 square foot garden were opened. The family assisted in ribbon cutting and gate-opening ceremonies for the garden.

Inside the gates were various stations, Levana's Garden being a place not only to cultivate plants—but also minds. In one area, close to the gate, there is a "butterfly garden," so named because it would be seeded with plant species that naturally attract butterflies. Down a pathway is a "California garden, that will be planted with indigenous California plants," said Acheatel, and in another area "there are plants and trees that are native to Israel . . . ."

There also is a "knotted garden" utilizing plants that weave together in the "shape of a Magen David," Acheatel said. Beyond that there will be a "secret garden," to be screened by high hedges, where students may have quiet classes. A series of raised flower beds—one for every grade from preschool through fifth grade—will be dedicated to growing vegetables Gan Levana also includes a green house, on top of which "there will be a weather station and our students in middle school will be using that to report weather here in the Carmel Valley area," Acheatel said.

Some of the fruits and vegetables grown by the young gardeners will be donated to programs for the hungry; tzedakah being another form of San Diego Jewish Academy produce.

Many Farseeing Visions behind Ratner Children's Eye Center

San Diego Jewish Times,
February 23, 2005

D*or l' dor,* from generation to generation, Jewish tradition teaches. Anne Ratner of San Diego remembers that her father-in-law, Isaac, always helped anyone who approached him on the street with a hard-luck story. He was concerned lest he fail to respond to the one person who might really need his assistance the most, "so he didn't turn anyone down," she recalled.

Now in her 90's, Ratner said she also remembers how her late husband, the clothing manufacturer Abraham Ratner "always was interested in helping children"—thus, Anne's decision to underwrite Tifereth Israel Synagogue's Abraham Ratner Torah School.

Both Anne and Abraham had eye problems and while being treated at UCSD's Shiley Eye Clinic, Anne also became interested in Dr. Stuart Brown's dream of creating a center that would deal exclusively with children's eye problems. She quoted Brown, chairman of UCSD's Ophthalmology Department, as telling her that for some children "if you don't get to them before they are five, they can have a problem that can never be repaired."

So, she provided the financing to build the Abraham Ratner Children's Eye Center, but her interest did not end when the center named in her husband's memory opened nine years ago. She also donated the funds for the Anne F. Ratner Endowed Chair of Pediatric Ophthalmology, which has been occupied from the outset by Dr. David Granet. Additionally, she has helped finance an eye mobile that is a critical part of UCSD's outreach to children in the under-served communities of San Diego County.

"They go in and give exams and glasses to kids who can't afford it," she said, "and some kids come home and see their mothers for the first time. This helps to make their lives what they should be."

And yet, neither Ratner nor other members of her extended family, believe they have done enough. Modestly declining to tell the extent of their donations, they are involved in a campaign to double the size of the children's eye clinic, which UCSD has decided to rename as the Anne and Abraham Ratner Children's Eye Center.

The Ratner Children's Eye Center's program for children is wide in scope. Among those playing an important role is Barbara Brody, a PhD whose responsibilities include overseeing the Ophthalmology Department's community outreach program. Digital photographs are taken of thousands of children's eyes at preschools and Head Start programs at approximately 170 locations throughout San Diego County. A computer reads these images, flagging those that indicate possible eye problems. In such cases, parents are invited to bring their children to the eye mobile for a follow-up examination.

Recently, at the Brooklyn Child Development Center at 3303 A Street, San Diego, Sharie Ford, in response to one of those invitations, accompanied her four-year-old son. As Patrick was given a series of eye tests, his mother expressed appreciation to Brody and to Marcia Hazan, the granddaughter of Anne Ratner, not only for Patrick's examination but also for the fact that the eye mobile comes right to the school grounds. For working parents, she pointed out, "this is very convenient." If the examination had to be conducted somewhere else, "I would have to pick him up, take him somewhere else, and then bring him back."

It is a trailblazing program. Hazan, at the eye mobile for a tour, commented that her daughter, Shana, wishes there could be a similar outreach effort in Chicago where she teaches fourth grade. In that city, she reported, many students "have problems and can't see and there is nobody to really address those issues."

Bill Orvis, a UCSD graduate in history who manages the eye mobile, administered a series of vision tests to Patrick, a bright and energetic child. Patrick particularly enjoyed one requiring him to put on the type of 3-D glasses that moviegoers used to wear and to look at a picture of a fly. Orvis asked young Patrick to try to grab the fly in his hand, and Patrick swiped at the image above the paper on which it was printed—a good result because it meant that Patrick was seeing in three dimensions. If he had reached all the way down to the paper, it might have meant he could only see flat images.

Meanwhile, inside a compact examining room in the back of the eye mobile, Dr. Lara Hustana, an optometrist who also did her undergraduate work at UCSD, tested Fabian Caballero, 4, for visual acuity, eye posture, and diverse eye diseases. In one examination, in which grandmother Maria Elena Enriquez was asked to click a button to project simple images on a wall, Fabian was asked in Spanish to identify what he was seeing. In essence, the exercise was a diversion—a way to hold the engaging young Fabian's interest while Dr. Hustana searched his eyes with her machines.

As in the cases of Patrick and Fabian, examinations often indicate no serious problems. Many students simply need eyeglasses, which UCSD makes and delivers to them at their pre-schools.

However, if an eye examination indicates more serious problems, then an appointment will be made at the Anne & Abraham Ratner Children's Eye Center. From the way it is furnished, to the clothing worn by the doctors, the Ratner Center is designed to make children feel comfortable in what otherwise might be intimidating surroundings.

The reception area boasts a large fish tank—with a puffer fish inside never failing to draw the interest of children—that was donated to the center by Anne Ratner's daughter, Pauline Foster and her late husband, Stan Foster—both of them well known leaders of the United Jewish Federation of San Diego County.

The lobby is bright and sunlit, and there is a television that continuously runs animated movies. Jo Adamcik, office manager at this happy place, notes that "we have games on the other side of the partition for the older kids; we have a movable art piece out on the patio; books all over the place, tons of little toys and things—we want to make it fun and relaxed and exciting for the children."

The examination rooms, painted in separate colors of the rainbow—red, yellow, green, and blue—also have cartoons playing to keep the children amused while they are waiting for the doctor. After eye examinations are completed, Adamcik confesses, "the parents often are ready to leave but the kids aren't."

The 5,000 children who visit the facility yearly may be treated by Granet—who shuns white coats as too forbidding, and likes to wear ties and even socks decorated with children's favorite cartoon characters—or by Dr. Shira Robbins, who, like Granet is a member of the Jewish community and knows how a bespectacled teddy bear can help a child relax during an examination.

Explaining why a special center was needed just for children's eye problems, Granet said that as a child grows, and especially in the first 18 months of a child's life, dramatic changes are occurring in his or her visual system. "If you don't have a system that works properly at the right time, that child will never see—it is not something you can fix later in life."

But how do you find out that a child has problems? The children are too young to talk about it, "they don't have the verbs, the nouns; they don't have language," and even if they can talk, "they don't know that there is anything wrong because this is the only world that they have ever known," Granet pointed out. "So, you have to have special tests, special skills and special approaches to first interact with that child."

Granet said he just had spent 25 minutes on the floor with an 18-month old child "trying to get him to play with me" so he could do an examination. In the case of a child's vision, unfortunately, "if you don't use it, you lose it," Granet said. "So, for example, if a child needs significant glasses in one eye and we find them at age 9, I can put the prescription on him, but he will not see because the connection between the eye and the brain was never made. That is a completely treatable blindness if it is caught early, but irreversible if it is caught late. That is why catching kids early is so important."

One of the programs of the Ratner Children's Eye Center attempts to measure the impact on a child's life of having vision problems successfully treated. Granet said that a fellowship named after Stan Foster goes to a PhD who "looks at the consequences of all these visual things on the children that we have been working on—to demonstrate the effect and value of catching these kids early."

The center also trains foreign doctors, with one from the Philippines and another from Brazil currently in residence.

Dr. Stuart Brown, who had the initial "vision" of the children's eye center, says San Diego Schools Superintendent Alan Bersin—who is married to Anne Ratner's granddaughter, Superior Court Judge Lisa Foster—helped the eye center reach out to pre-school children served by the San Diego Unified School District. "It is still inexplicable to me that the previous superintendent had said no,"

Brown said. Bersin comprehended how much difference it could make to a child if a vision problem were corrected early, "and became a champion" for the program.

"We realize that children's brains start working early, and that the earlier they start learning, they better they perform," Brown said. "The earlier you read to your child, the earlier that they are challenged, the better they perform in life. But how do they do it, if it is uncomfortable for them to see, or if they can't see well—if a good part of their brain isn't getting what it needs?"

Anne Ratner's father-in-law, Isaac Ratner, worried about missing the person who might really need his assistance the most. As it doubles its size, and continues to spread its net, the Ratner Children's Eye Center is doing everything it can to find the children who are similarly in need.

Rock Formations and Belief Systems Co-mingle in San Diego's Mission Trails Regional Park

jewishsightseeing.com
March 4, 2005

The Mission Trails Regional Park is one of the largest urban parks in America—covering about 7,500 mostly primitive acres at the locale where San Diego embraces the inland suburban city of Santee.

By following Father Junipero Serra Trail named for San Diego's first non-baseball playing padre, or by availing oneself of the dirt paths meandering near the San Diego River, pedestrians can glimpse unspoiled Southern California as the Kumeyaay Indians knew it in the years prior to San Diego's settlement by the Spaniards in 1769.

Visualization of the Kumeyaay's lifestyle is aided not only at a visitors' center, which looks like a modernistic raptor perched on a natural hillside, but also by various trailside story boards and exhibits.

Living a short way from the park, I am one of its frequent visitors—and often as I muse during my hikes, the stories in Hebrew Scriptures and sacred Kumeyaay beliefs co-mingle. This sense that Mission Trails is a place of spiritual democracy is reinforced on my walks whenever I look at rock configurations and imagine them to be the depictions of legends, sometimes theirs, sometimes ours, sometimes those of other cultures.

At one spot along the road, there is a whale-like boulder, ready to swallow Jonah. Not too far down the road, there is a large boulder on a hillside against which two snake-like objects appear to be leaning toward each other in a friendly conversation —perhaps one is chortling over what he told Eve.

Farther along, an outcropping looks very much to me like a man holding a pair of tablets crooked in his right arm—Moses coming down the mountain. I told you this place is spiritually democratic, so farther still there is a tight cluster of large globular boulders, some of them patterned with what appears to be the maps of continents. Astronomers might call this configuration "Before the Big Bang."

Some of my friends who are deeply conversant with Kumeyaay culture do not appreciate my comparing these ancient rock formations to scenes from the Bible. We should appreciate the ancient Kumeyaay culture for what it was—without overlaying upon it something foreign, they tell me. I can appreciate, even applaud, their desire to appreciate Kumeyaay culture in its original form and in situ, but I also have a feeling that the ancient Kumeyaay would not have been such purists about it.

121

Their own creation legend, while different from what we read in the first portion of Genesis, has some points of comparison. Reading from the Stone version of the Tanach, we Jews learn in Genesis that initially there was darkness upon the surface of the waters, and that God decided to create light.

On the third day, our biblical account continues, God separated the Earth from the sea. Then, on the fourth day, "God made the two great luminaries, the greater luminary to dominate the day and the lesser luminary to dominate the night; and the stars."

Jack Scheffler Innis recounts in *San Diego Legends* (Sunbelt Publications, El Cajon, Calif: 2004) the Kumeyaay Creation story, which he, in turn, found in *The Religious Practices of the Diegueno Indians,* a 1910 book by T.T. Waterman. ("Diegueno" was the name that the Spaniards called the Indians in the vicinity of Mission San Diego, whereas "Kumeyaay" is the name the Indians called themselves.)

"In the beginning, there was no land, only salt water," their creation tale begins. "In the water lived two brothers who kept their eyes closed, so that the salt would not blind them . . . . On one occasion, the older brother swam to the surface and looked around. He saw nothing except the vastness of the water. . . . [He] then decided to create ants. Little red ants sprang from the depths and were so numerous that they filled up portions of the water with their bodies and made land."

Next the older brother made birds, "but since there was no light to show the way, the birds became lost and could not find anywhere to roost. So, the older brother kneaded together the colors of clay: red, yellow and black to form a flat round disk. This he tossed up into the sky. It stuck to the sky and began to emit a dim light. Today we call this object, Halay, the Moon. The Moon's light was too dim to be very useful, so he took another piece of clay and tossed it skyward across from the Moon. It was very bright and lit up everything. We call that Inyau, the Sun."

So, in both Genesis and in the Kumeyaay story, we start with a shapeless deep, and supernatural beings separate the waters from land (by different means). Later, they create the Sun and the Moon as lights for the day and the night. If you really want to knock yourself out, I suppose you could compare the story of the bird not being able to roost in the waters to the story of the raven that flew from Noah's Ark after the flood.

In Genesis 1, we are taught that God "created man in His image, in the image of God. He created him; male and female He created them." In Genesis 2, we are told the Adam and Eve story, wherein God "cast a deep sleep upon the man and he slept; and He took one of his sides and He filled in flesh in its place. Then Hashem God fashioned the side that He had taken from the man into a woman, and He brought her to the man . . . ."

In the Kumeyaay story, the mythic "older brother . . . decided to create people. Working with light-colored clay, he split one piece in two. First, he made man, then he took a rib from the man and made woman. The children of this man and woman were called Ipai, people."

In Genesis 2, we learn that "Hashem God commanded the man, saying 'of every tree of the garden you may freely eat, but of the Tree of Knowledge of Good and Bad, you must not eat thereof; for on the day you eat of it, you will surely die.'" A serpent however persuaded the woman that "God knows that on the day you eat of it your eyes will be opened and you will be like God knowing good and bad . . . and she took of its fruit and ate; and she gave also to her husband with her and he ate . . . ."

A serpent also figures in the Kumeyaay story about how people obtained knowledge." After the older brother had created people, a big snake arose from the ocean in the West. . . . When he reached the civilization, he devoured all learning and slithered to a place called Wicuwul, possibly the Coronado Islands (small, rocky islands owned by Mexico, clearly visible from San Diego Bay). Thus,

123

all the arts, including singing, dancing, basket making, and speaking resided inside his body far away. . . .

"A medicine man heard about the problem and decided to try to reach the serpent. But before setting foot in the water, he changed himself into a bubble." The legend continues that the medicine man was swallowed by a second serpent, but (Jonah-like) remained alive in its body, until he was able to cut a hole through the serpent's head and escape.

Eventually the medicine man reached the knowledge-eating snake and persuaded it to follow him back to the village, where the snake coiled its body inside a ceremonial hut. Frightened by the snake's large size, the people set it on fire. "The serpent burst, and knowledge within him scattered throughout the lands. Each tribe got something different. That is why one tribe may be good at dancing, another good at basket making, and still a third tribe at singing."

The scattering of knowledge is somewhat similar to the Genesis story of the Tower of Babel, in which common language was changed to many languages, and the peoples were scattered to different places around the world.

I cannot say whether the Kumeyaay creation story predated the arrival of the Spanish missionaries, or whether the various biblical stories somehow were woven into the Kumeyaay's spiritual basket.

Be that as it may, on my walks through Mission Trails Park, I never fail to gaze at the rock formations to see within them the kinds of pictures other people find while cloud-gazing. At one place up on the hill, I have espied a formation resembling the kind of stone lion you see guarding the entrances to public buildings and some homes in China.

This gives me further confidence that Mission Trails Regional Park is a place big enough in spirit to accommodate not only Native American beliefs but also those of the newcomer Europeans and Asians.

Zion Avenue in San Diego: An American Street with Just a Bit of Jewish Flavoring

jewishsightseeing.com
May 1, 2006

A large American flag waves above a much smaller Zion Avenue street sign, symbolic perhaps of how Jewish influences can be found within the greater, heterogeneous American landscape. Along Zion Avenue's 1.2 mile, west-east course, one will encounter a major hospital, four churches, four small shopping centers, an elementary school, a public library, and numerous single-story residences, many of them built in the 1950s.

As you head east, about midway up the avenue, you pass from the Grantville community of San Diego into the Allied Gardens community. Both communities were named by land developers who wanted to appeal to war veterans hungry to purchase their own homes.

Grantville, named for Union General Ulysses S. Grant, was developed in the 1880s with the idea of attracting Civil War veterans to one of San Diego's historic areas—Grantville being in the vicinity of Mission San Diego, which stood as a solitary outpost through the last quarter of the 18th Century and the first two-thirds of the 19th Century.

Grant, who became the 18th president of the United States in 1869, was an icon to Civil War veterans. His son, Ulysses S. Grant Jr., also was a well-known civic figure in San Diego, to which he relocated in 1890s. One of the city's best-known hotels downtown is the U.S. Grant Hotel, developed by the son.

If you start at its western end, Zion Avenue begins at the intersection with Riverdale Street—the name being a reference to the nearby San Diego River, which follows an occasionally meandering course from the Cuyamaca Mountains in the eastern portion of San Diego County to the Pacific Ocean. When the Spaniards settled San Diego in 1769, they built their first mission above the river, but moved it farther upstream five years later. Today Mission San Diego with its signature bell tower is one of San Diego's best-known landmarks. Numerous streets and places in San Diego have mission-influenced names, among them the San Diego Padres professional baseball team, Friars Road, Padre Dam, and Mission Trails Regional Park.

Less than one-tenth of a mile from the street's western terminus is Zion's commercial intersection with Mission Gorge Road, a major artery that connects with San Diego's Interstate Highway 8. There are businesses on all four corners of this intersection, with a Kentucky Fried Chicken now occupying a former gasoline station lot on the northeast corner, and dozens of other businesses arrayed among three shopping centers covering the other corners.

One of the businesses in the shopping center on the northwest corner is Mr. Chick, whose owner, Amir Benami, was raised in Holon, Israel. He decided to take a traditional "see-the-world" trip after his military service in Israel. Because he had relatives in San Diego, he decided to vacation here, and, he says cheerfully, "I'm still on vacation the last 15 years!"

His uncle. Rami Vana, owner of the Chicken Nest restaurants in San Diego, taught him the family business. The Mr. Chick on Zion Avenue is Benami's second restaurant. He continues to operate another Mr. Chick in San Diego's Kearny Mesa neighborhood, where there are a variety of electronics companies. In fact, says Benami, quite a few of his customers live near the Grantville location but commute to Kearny Mesa, so he had a built-in customer base.

Benami says he also attracts many of the health-conscious medical professionals of the Kaiser-Permanente Hospital and Medical Center which is just a short distance east on Zion Avenue. He says that whereas the minimum requirement for cooking chicken healthfully is at temperatures above 165 degrees, "we cook them at 500 degrees."

I asked the Israeli about the coincidence of his business being along "Zion Avenue," and he said the location is not far from the home he shares with his American-born wife, and 3-year-old son. When the location became available, after housing a Thai restaurant, he decided to grab it.

Across Zion Avenue at the southwest corner of the intersection is a shopping center anchored by Petco, a store that caters to the needs of dogs and cats and other pets. Among a number of eating establishments, including a Greek restaurant, a brewery, and a Rubio's—credited as the chain that pioneered San Diego's famous fish tacos—is an Einstein Brothers bagels store, where assistant manager Linda Fossen smilingly agrees that you don't have to be Jewish to love bagels.

In my youth, bagel choices were limited to "plain" and "egg," but Fossen told me that more than 20 varieties of bagels are served by Einstein Brothers, which has more than 400 outlets across the country and 17 in San Diego County. The most popular with her customers, she said, is the "Everything" variety, meaning it has "all the different seeds, sesame, poppy, garlic, onion, and salt." Are you more a traditionalist? Fossen says another popular item is an old Jewish favorite: bagels with cream cheese and lox, garnished with tomatoes, onions, and capers.

The intersection with Mission Gorge is quite busy, with Zion Avenue having dedicated left turn lanes in each direction to help speed the traffic. The shopping center across Mission Gorge, on the southeast side of the intersection, is anchored by Vons market, which keeps numerous varieties of kosher products on its shelves— as does Albertsons market, a competitor, located one-mile farther east on Zion Avenue in a shopping center at the Waring Road intersection.

Before leaving the businesses surrounding the Zion Avenue-Mission Gorge intersection, you might take notice that some of their advertising is quite eye-catching. Next to Mr. Chick, for example, is Manhattan Pizza which features a large stand-up sign of the Statue of Liberty. But that's no torch in her hand. Obviously in a spirit of cooperation, La Mirage Hair Salon boasts a large American flag in its window. And, the European and American Car Center across Mission Gorge has a Volkswagen that is a good reminder to drive carefully through the busy intersection. It is perched on the company's roof!

Looming behind the Vons shopping center at the southeastern corner is the Kaiser-Permanente Hospital and Medical Center. I have jokingly called my son, David, and grandson Shor "Zionists" because they were born in this hospital, 26 years apart.

The hospital maintains an "apothecary garden" with plants that are healthful for you, and a "sinister garden" with plants that are toxic. All of them grow in the San Diego County area . . . . If you knew nothing but their common names, where would you assign the following four species—Angels Trumpet, Jerusalem Cherry, Bird of Paradise, and Deadly Nightshade?

Notwithstanding its name, the Deadly Nightshade (*Atropa belladonna*) is valued both as an anti-spasmodic and as a pupil dilator. On the other hand, Angels Trumpet, Jerusalem Cherry (a ground cover) and the leaves and berries of a Bird of Paradise are all toxic.

On the other hand, as beautiful as its name sounds, the Jerusalem cherry plant contains solanine, which can ulcerate one's gastrointestinal system, and cause seizures, depression, respiratory problems, and shock.

Sylvia Wallace, Kaiser-Permanente's manager of media relations, said the garden was planted about 20 years ago as a community service project. She said it features plants that grow in the San Diego County.

Across from the Kaiser-Permanente Hospital is the Grace Assembly Church, one of four Christian-oriented institutions you will find as you drive east on Zion Avenue at lawful speeds of 30 miles per hour except in the school zone, where you must slow down to 25 miles per hour. The street is on San Diego Transit's Bus Route 13, which carries eastbound passengers to San Diego State University and La Mesa, and westbound passengers to the San Diego Trolley station at Euclid Avenue in southeastern San Diego.

The Grace Assembly Church is still within the Grantville neighborhood, while the other three Christian institutions—Zion Avenue Baptist Church; Ascension Lutheran Church; and Genesis, A New Beginning, are in the Allied Gardens area.

Many people knowing that Grantville was named for General Grant think that Allied Gardens was named for the Allied powers, who fought the Axis powers in World War II. However, that is just a suburban legend. In actuality, Allied Gardens was named for the company that built it, Allied Contractors. According to Leland Frazer, author of *San Diego County Place Names A to Z,* partners Louis L. Kelton and Walter Bollenbacher developed the area in the 1950s after purchasing 1,000 acres of the nearby Waring Estate, owned by the family whose name is given to Waring Road. Allied Contractors offered 13 different styles of single-family homes. Throughout the area, one mainly sees California bungalows, as these tract ranch houses are called.

Proceeding east on Zion Avenue, one passes a playground on the south side of the street. This is part of Stephen Foster Elementary School which fronts on 51st Street. The school was named for America's most popular composer of songs in the 19th Century. Even today, most Americans can hum—even if they mangle the lyrics—such songs as "Oh, Susannah"; "Old Folks at Home" (Also known as "Suwannee River"); "Jeanie With the Light Brown Hair", and "Beautiful Dreamer."

There's plenty more Americana in the Edwin A. Benjamin branch of the San Diego Public Library, which is named for a local Jewish philanthropist who donated $500,000 to assure others could share his love for books. Linda Moskovics, the branch librarian, estimates that there are 60,000 items in the 6,900-square-foot facility. A member of the Jewish community, Moskovics says the Judaica collection isn't as good as that in the neighboring San Carlos branch library from which she was promoted two years ago. But she says there are good resources on Jewish holidays, and anything else that someone might need can be quickly obtained from other libraries via an inter-branch loan. She is building up the Benjamin branch's collections of juvenile literature and DVDs.

A very short distance east of the library is the intersection of Zion Avenue with Waring Road. Here, a traffic triangle was dedicated in 2005 as one of the civic beautification projects of City Councilman Jim Madaffer, who represents the area.

Flowers are planted within the triangle. There is a large, old-style, standing clock, and a sign welcoming visitors to Allied Gardens is carved in granite.

Across the intersection with Waring Road is yet another shopping center, this one anchored by Albertson's and by Blockbuster Video.

Once one passes that shopping center on the southeastern corner of the intersection, one enters a residential neighborhood which extends another one-tenth of a mile before Zion terminates at Eldridge Street. Testifying to the American feel of the 1950's era neighborhood is the fact that on the portion of Eldridge Street facing Zion, there is a house with an American flag fittingly displayed for all driving up the street to see.

Stopping at San Diego's Airport for a Little Hometown Sightseeing

jewishsightseeing.com
May 8, 2006

Many of us drop off people at airports, or rush to and from the gates, but how many of us have an opportunity to sightsee at our hometown airport?

I decided to do just that today (Monday, May 8) at San Diego's Lindbergh Field after my daughter, Sandi Masori, and I took her husband, Shahar, and child, Shor, to Delta Flight 1024 to Atlanta, from which they would catch a connecting flight to Tel Aviv.

I had mixed feelings about artist John J. Whalen's large mural of Charles A. Lindbergh on Harbor Drive as well as the double-figure sculpture by Paul T. Granlund showing Lindbergh as a boy, with arms outstretched, and as the man who flew the first solo, New York-to-Paris flight across the Atlantic Ocean May 20-21, 1927. The sculpture was dedicated in 1987, sixty years after the famous flight.

Given the important role Lindbergh played in aviation, I can understand the pride San Diego takes in him, especially since his plane, *Spirit of St. Louis,* was built locally by Ryan Air Lines Inc. San

Diegans like to joke that the famous monoplane would have been called *Spirit of San Diego,* except for the fact that benefactors in Missouri paid for it.

The reason I cringe seeing Lindbergh so lionized was because of his role later in life as a sympathizer for the Nazi regime in Germany. Others may be willing to overlook this unsavory part of Lindbergh's biography, but I cannot bring myself to do so.

I like the sculptures of the boy and the man because it encourages little boys like Shor, 5, to dream big. I just wish some other aviator had been so honored.

There is a large sculpture in the parking lot of Terminal Two depicting what to me looks like two geese having tumbled together into a heap.

The legend carved around *In Search of Wilderness* by Les Perhacs states that "lessons learned through the observation of nature benefit all." With Shor and Shahar flying half-way around the world, the sculpture made me shiver. I wasn't at all sure man should learn such a fowl lesson.

Inside the entry rotunda of Terminal Two, one becomes immediately cognizant of *Sunlight Juxtaposed,* a large abstracted stained-glass mural created by glass designer Joan Irving.

I had thought that I might have to say farewell to Shahar and Shor at this point as only passengers normally are permitted to go through security screening. But the kindly ticket agent, noticing that grandpa was entertaining Shor while daddy schlepped the carry-on luggage and handled tickets, asked me if I would like a pass to accompany them to their gate. Indeed, I would. I cheerfully took off my shoes and belt and put them with my camera into the tray for x-raying. I never complain about airport security. As far as I'm concerned, the more vigilant it is, the safer we all are.

Beyond the metal detector, there was an installation by Terry Thornsley called *Sea Rhythms,* into which many passengers who had preceded us had tossed pennies for good luck. Not finding a penny, I gave Shor a dime, so he could be ten times as lucky as anyone else.

Their flight had been assigned to Gate 40 at the very end of the long terminal corridor. Along the way, there were posters from the San Diego Hall of Champions with photographs and brief career descriptions of well-known athletes who had either resided in San Diego County or had played for a San Diego team.

These included baseball players Tony Gwynn, Ted Williams, Trevor Hoffman, and Dave Winfield; basketball player Bill Walton; boxer Archie Moore; football players Dan Fouts, Marcus Allen, Marshall Faulk, Junior Seau, Terrell Davis, and Kellen Winslow; golfers Phil Mickelson, Billy Casper, and Mickey Wright, skateboarder Tony Hawk, swimmer Florence Chadwick, tennis star Maureen Connolly, track star Gail Devers, and tri-athlete Paula Newby-Fraser.

None of these athletes is Jewish, but the man who started San Diego's Hall of Champions, Robert Breitbard, is a member of an old and distinguished San Diego Jewish family. Who knows, I thought, perhaps someday the posters of former San Diego Chargers coach Sid Gillman and player Ron Mix will be placed in that corridor, or perhaps, if he has a successful career, Igor Olshansky, a defensive lineman currently playing for the San Diego Chargers will have compiled such an impressive record that his poster too will be placed with those of the luminaries.

Also, on the long corridor wall was an advertisement for UCSD's Rady School of Business, named for Jewish philanthropist Ernest Rady.

I was not surprised when Delta announced that there would be a half-hour delay in the boarding of Flight 1024 because of weather problems in Atlanta. We were, after all, *en route* to Gate 40.

There's something about Jews, the number 40, and long trips—as in raining 40 days and 40 nights in the days of Noah and his Ark (grandpa's and Shor's favorite biblical story), and Moses and the Hebrews wandering for 40 years in the desert.

Not to worry! Near the large indoor installation, *Water and Sun* by Christopher Lee, in which a suspended orb represents the Sun and a small bubbling fountain serves as water, we took a seat at Cramer's Bakery & Deli. There, Shor and I shared a combination as perfect for us as water and sun may be for others: a toasted onion bagel with cream cheese! In my opinion, there could be no more perfect start for his trip to Israel!

Restoration of Casa de Bandini Wins Support from Religious, Ethnic Groups

jewishsightseeing.com
May 17, 2006

When the California Cultural and Historic Endowment reserved slightly more than $1.8 million last month for the restoration of the Casa de Bandini/Cosmopolitan Hotel, it did so knowing that this building located in Old Town San Diego State Historic Park represented a unique opportunity to tell "a multitude of stories from overlapping cultures."

The 10-member board, chaired by State Librarian Susan Hildreth, did not have to look very far for proof that a large variety of historic, ethnic, and religious groups, including Jews, felt a warm sense of connection to the building originally erected as a one-story hacienda for Don Juan Bandini about 1827, and converted by Alfred Seeley after 1869 into a two-story hotel and stage stop.

An information packet assembled for the CCHE board's April 27-28 hearing in Sacramento contained letters of support for the project from 26 businesses, organizations, and individuals. Bill Mennell, technical director at Old Town San Diego State Historic Park, led the successful presentation. As a matter of disclosure, I should report that I served on Old Town San Diego State Historic Park's advisory committee, chaired by former State Sen. James R. Mills (D-San Diego), whose members liaised with many of the people and organizations who sent these letters.

Allocated from a fund created by the California Clean Water, Clean Air, Safe Neighborhood Parks, and Coastal Protection Act of 2002, better known as Proposition 40, the $1.8 million grant will be used to strip from the building more than a century of non-historic additions and to bring the structure back to its historic configuration as a hotel and stage coach depot.

The $1.8 million public grant will be matched by Delaware North Corp., which recently won from the State Parks a long-term lease to operate the two-story building as a restaurant and hotel while facilitating its use for the interpretation of history.

And what a history the building has had, according to a paper prepared for the CCHE board by Victor Walsh, the state historian at Old Town. Bandini, a Peruvian who became related to San Diego's oldest families by marriage, was an opponent of Mexican rule in San Diego, joining in uprisings in 1831 against Governor Manuel Victoria and in 1836 against Governor Juan Bautista Alvarado.

When the village of San Diego was occupied by a small American force commanded by Commodore Robert Stockton, the Bandinis made their home available for his headquarters. Bandini's daughters Arcadia, Ysidora, and Josefa, are credited with sewing from their petticoats the first American flag to fly over Old Town. You might call them, the Betsy Ross sisters of the west.

Like other landholders, Bandini protested the expropriation of Mexican grant lands by the Americans, eventually transferring his property to Arcadia's husband, Abel Stearns, another well-known

California pioneer. Stearns by 1856 leased the Casa de Bandini to Jacob Elias, a merchant who was successful enough to purchase, four years later, the 36,000-acre Rancho San Rafael, site of the present-day City of Glendale. To run the store selling "ready-made clothing, fancy goods, hats, boots and trunks," according to historian Walsh, Elias hired Heyman Mannasse.

Of interest to the Jewish community, Mannasse was the brother of Joseph S. Mannasse, who along with his partner Marcus Schiller, followed in the footsteps of San Diego's first Jewish settler, Louis Rose, and became actively involved in the city's civic life. J.S. Mannasse was on the city Board of Trustees that proposed setting aside land for a large city park—later to become Balboa Park—and Schiller was on the successor three-member board that designated the land for permanent public use. Schiller also was the first president of Temple Beth Israel, a Reform congregation which opened its doors for High Holidays in 1889.

One of the letters in the packet was from Norman Greene, who co-founded with me the Louis Rose Society for the Preservation of Jewish History. Greene noted that the street that extends perpendicularly from the Cosmopolitan Hotel once was known as Avenida de Judios, or Jews' Avenue, because so many merchants of the period were, in fact, Jews.

California State Sen. Denise Moreno Ducheny (D-San Diego) praised plans for focusing in the building on the "untold stories of 19th Century Old Town San Diego's ethnic groups and social classes." Karla L. Shiminski, site administrator for the "Old Town Program" of San Diego City Schools struck a similar note, saying, "The histories of those people—the leather-jacketed soldiers from the presidio, the Indians from the nearby mission, wealthy Spanish-speaking ranchers like Bandini, vaqueros and servants, Mormon soldiers, American tradesmen and settlers, and Jewish merchants— needs to be told because it is both meaningful and relevant to the children of today and future unborn generations."

Bruce G. Gallagher, board president of the San Diego Archaeological Center, said: "The work regimens, social activities, and songs of servants, stage hands, and other workers—many of whom were California Indians and Mexicanos—is the 'untold story' of Old Town San Diego State Historic Park. It is a story that State Parks intends to tell through historic reenactments, storytelling, games, and musical performances."

U.S. Rep. Bob Filner (D-San Diego) suggested in another letter that the "building's design—a Mexican adobe on the first floor and an American wood-frame addition on the second—symbolizes Old Town San Diego's history during the 19th Century." Lloyd Schwartz, chairman of the City of San Diego's Historical Resources Board, on which I'm also privileged to serve, noted that "the building has considerable historic fabric and integrity that include the original adobe walls on the first floor, the tongue-and-groove wainscoting and window seats in the dining areas on the first floor, the stairway banister in the entrance area, and many of the doors, window sashes, and cornices on the second-floor balcony."

Msgr. Mark A Campbell, pastor of the Catholic Church of The Immaculate Conception across the street from the state park, pointed out that in its first configuration, the "U-shaped single-story was an adobe brick casa grande with twelve to fourteen rooms and rear walled courtyard by the 1840s, of thick adobe walls, clay tile sloped roof, deep set windows with shutters, tiled floors (originally earthen), and muslin-covered ceilings—symbol of the family's wealth and status."

Furthermore, the clergyman noted, "The home was the pueblo's social and political center: a place where Bandini and other town leaders met to discuss politics, trade, and the missions, which Bandini wanted to see secularized. It was also the scene of elaborate Catholic weddings and community festivities, like the reenactment of *La Pastorela* . . . ." His reference was to a Mexican folk play in which the devil tries to win the souls of shepherds on their way to Bethlehem to see the baby Jesus. . . .

139

Jeanne L. Ferrell, president of the Boosters of Old Town, wrote to the Endowment board, "When you walk into the Casa de Bandini, one can almost hear the Californio music and hear the laughter of those who came to dance the evenings away. It was the social and political hub of the little community."

Tom Vilicich, president of the San Pasqual Battlefield Volunteer Association which reenacts one of the few battles in San Diego County during the Mexican-American War—a battle won by the Californios—observed that "many of the Californios who fought in the battle at San Pasqual had casas in Old Town. The San Pascual Indian Pueblo had ties to Mission San Diego. And the U.S. Dragoons (who lost to the Californios at San Pasqual) were rescued by Commodore Stockton's men who had taken over Old Town . . . ."

Dale Gubler, director of the Mormon Battalion Historic Site located close to Old Town San Diego State Historic Park, wrote another of the letters. The Mormon Battalion, marched overland from Kansas to California in one of the longest recorded marches in history, arriving in San Diego after warfare was concluded. Thereupon, members of the battalion "built the first kiln-fired brick building in California (the Old San Diego Courthouse)" along with other projects. Gubler noted that the Casa de Bandini "was here in 1847 when the Battalion was here. The historic value of the building is inestimable."

Marsha Snelling, vice chairperson of Descendants of Old Town, wrote: "Although our personal preference would be to see the adobe restored to its earliest use as a family home of the Californio Bandini family, which we think is the era under-represented in the interpretive program of the park, we still can and do wholeheartedly support the restoration of the adobe as the Cosmopolitan Hotel. It is a bona fide historical landmark from 1869 and as such, represents a real phase of San Diego's Old Town's history."

Similarly, Mimi Lozano, president of the Society of Hispanic Historical and Ancestral Research, wrote: "So many historical renovations in California seem to concentrate on much later periods, neglecting or minimizing the wonderful contributions of Hispanic citizens, such as Don Juan Bandini. It appears that the Casa de Bandini historic building is a perfect structure to give public awareness concerning the Mexican and U.S. transition periods in the 19th Century."

Bruce Coons, executive director of the Save Our Heritage Organization (SOHO), said restoration of the structure to its former incarnation as the Cosmopolitan Hotel—while stripping away evidence of later periods as "an olive packing plant, lodging house, tourist motel and restaurant"— would permit the public "for the first time in San Diego to visit a fully operational 19th-Century hotel and stage stop. The building is an invaluable historic link to San Diego's frontier heritage under Mexican and early U.S. rule."

Geoffrey Mogilner, chief of Racine & Laramie, an old-time tobacco store in the State Park, described the Cosmopolitan Hotel as "the most significant stage stop in the county."

When Albert Seeley made the Casa de Bandini into a hotel and stage shop, he "owned the only stage company to make the rough route to Los Angeles pay," commented Mike Dillon, president of the Encinitas Historical Society—located in a coastal area through which stage coach service could have passed.

Many stage companies before Seeley's attempted to make a profit, Dillon said. "An assumption is the ticket cost of $16 was not as profitable as the Cosmopolitan Hotel would be. The addition improved the bottom line. Mr. Seeley was in the transportation business for well into the '80s. This project is a part of the history of a struggling young city."

Others who sent letters supporting the project included Lynne Newell Christensen, the historian of the County of San Diego Department of Parks and Recreation; Jim Vann, president of the Gaslamp Quarter (San Diego) Historical Foundation; Joseph Ditler, executive director of the Coronado Historical Association; Ronald V. May, board chair of the Fort Guijarros (San Diego) Museum Foundation; John Rotsart, executive director of the San Diego Model Railroad Museum; Walter Nelson, president of the Lively Arts History Association, and Rudecinda Lo Buglio, chair of Los Californianos Publications.

Business representatives inside and near the State Park who likewise urged the grant included Consuelo Puente of El Fandango Restaurant; Dennis and Heidi Toler of Toler's Leather Depot; Leroy Brown, owner of San Diego House of Coffees and Tea, and Lorin Stewart, director of San Diego Operations for Old Town Trolley Tours of Historic Tours of America.

"Old Town San Diego is an important part of history, not only of San Diego, but of California, the United States and Mexico, as well," Stewart wrote. "As the 'Birthplace of California,' Old Town has a story that should be actively and accurately told for all to enjoy and to learn from. The State Park's original mission is pure in that vision, and the historic restoration of the Casa de Bandini/Cosmopolitan Hotel is a significant and important project towards realizing that mission."

A Star of David Button Is Intriguing Find at Presidio Golf Course

jewishsightseeing.com
May 27, 2006

When operators of the Presidio Golf Course started building a driving range last year, an old bottle on top of what appeared to have been a filled-in well was uncovered. A passerby sensitive to the importance of archaeology notified Myra Hermann, a senior environmental planner with the City of San Diego's Development Services Department.

Construction was stopped and arrangements were made promptly to have an archaeological survey done by the firm of Mooney, Jones & Stokes of the site located between the old Spanish Presidio and what today is known as Old Town San Diego State Historic Park.

Stacey C. Jordan-Connor, Mooney, Jones & Stokes director of cultural resources, said a metal button with a simple Star of David design was among the artifacts recovered from a 35-foot long, 4-foot wide trench that was cut down to the level of disturbance during a four-day dig.

Although today part of an 18-hole pitch and putt golf course, the land that was excavated by the archaeologists formerly featured a corral and stable owned by Prussian-born partners Joseph S. Mannasse and Marcus Schiller, two 19th Century Jewish entrepreneurs who also were important historical figures in San Diego.

Mannasse immigrated via San Francisco to San Diego in 1853 in the company of his brother, Heyman, and cousin, Moses. Schiller arrived in San Francisco about the same time that the Mannasses were leaving that city. Schiller migrated to San Diego in 1856, becoming partners with Mannasse in a general store located across what today is Juan Street from the subject property.

During the 1860s, Schiller became a grand master of the San Diego Masonic Lodge, and like his partner, served on the Board of Trustees of the City of San Diego. Mannasse, in fact, was on the Board that cleared the way for a large tract of land to be set aside for a city park; Schiller, replacing his partner on the board the following year, formally voted to create the park. Many years later that large city park would become known as Balboa Park. Schiller also was active in the affairs of San Diego's small Jewish community, becoming the first president of Temple Beth Israel, which opened its doors for High Holiday services in 1889.

As a matter of coincidence, the Temple Beth Israel building where Schiller presided now is located just a few blocks up Juan Street in Heritage Park. The building's original location was at 2nd and Beech Street, closer to downtown San Diego, but it was relocated and restored nearly a century later thanks to the efforts of philanthropist Jim Milch, the Save Our Heritage Organization, and the County of San Diego, operator of the Heritage Park.

Together Mannasse's and Schiller's laid out a real estate development known as the Mannasse & Schiller Addition, located between Old Town San Diego and Roseville, a town site created on San Diego Bay by San Diego's original Jewish settler, Louis Rose. Mannasse's and Schiller's real estate speculations also prompted them to purchase ranch land covering the coastal area of San Diego County now occupied by the City of Encinitas.

There is no way of knowing whether the Star of David button found during the 2005 archaeological dig belonged to either of the partners, as there were other Jewish merchants and family members who lived in San Diego during the 19ᵗʰ Century who might have visited Mannasse and Schiller's corral and stable.

Other interesting buttons also were found at the site, including some from military uniforms. Four of these buttons bear a relief image of the mythical Phoenix bird and an encircling motto in French, "Je renais de mes cendres" ("I am reborn from my ashes").

In a recent interview at the golf course, Dr. Jordan-Connor said team members recognized from published materials the Phoenix buttons as having been made in England for the troops of self-proclaimed King Henri Christophe of Haiti, who reigned over the former French colony from 1811-1820. These buttons may have reached San Diego in the complex web of international trade—and, one might speculate, so too could the little Star of David button have reached the Mannasse and Schiller corral site serendipitously.

The Presidio Golf Course is adjoined by the tiny Casa de Carrillo, which was built in 1821 and is considered the oldest standing structure in San Diego. The property is associated with one of San Diego's best-known love stories. Josefa Carrillo, forbidden to marry Yankee sea captain Henry Delano Fitch by the jealous Mexican Gov. Jose Maria Echeandia, ran one night in 1829 from her adobe home to the nearby Pear Garden, where her friend Pio Pico—a future Mexican governor of California—waited with two horses. Together, they rode to San Diego Bay, where Josefa met Henry and the couple boarded a ship and sailed off together for marriage in Chile.

The land had a succession of owners between the time it was owned by Mannasse and Schiller and 1931, when it was purchased by George Marston, an influential lover of history who also constructed the Serra Museum atop nearby Presidio Hill.

Wanting to keep the land between the Presidio and Old Town an open space, Marston hired William P. Bell to lay out a par-3, 18-hole golf course. Bell already was renowned as the designer of golf courses in Balboa Park and at the La Jolla Country Club, as well as at the Bel Air Country Club in Los Angeles and on the Wrigley family-owned Catalina Island. Later in his career, he would lay out the golf course at Tilden Park in Berkeley, and designed a course at Torrey Pines, which was completed by his son, William F. Bell.

Jordan-Connor said that most of the material found in the trench can be dated to the mid-19th Century when Old Town was the center of commercial activity in San Diego. However, there are less likely possibilities that some artifacts may be from other periods. To build the golf course, Marston had the land scraped and re-shaped. So there is at least a chance that Marston himself or people associated with the golf course project might have lost those interesting buttons. Similarly, it cannot be known definitively whether or not some of the artifacts landed at the site in the interim period between the Mannasse and Schiller period and the golf course construction, or even from the period prior to Mannasse and Schiller's ownership when the land was traversed by a path leading from the old settlement to Presidio Hill.

In addition to 23 buttons recovered during the dig, thousands of other items were turned up by archaeologists who sifted dirt through one-quarter inch mesh. There was an intriguing arrow point made from porcelain, perhaps an adaptation of Native American (Kumeyaay) culture using European materials.

Additionally, there were shards of pottery, clay pipes, marbles, bottles, jars, tumblers, stemware, nails, tacks, screws, washers, a gun flint, a writing slate, a bone knife handle, bottle fragments, bones from butchered cows, and an interesting variety of shells—to name only some of the catalogued finds. The City of San Diego, in cooperation with the San Diego Archaeological Center, maintains such collections of artifacts.

Here's Something on which Two Jews Can Agree: Torrey Pines State Reserve Is Uniquely Beautiful

jewishsightseeing.com
July 6, 2006

In our self-deprecatory humor, we Jews like to joke, "two Jews, three opinions," in recognition of what might be our Talmudic penchant for debating, refining, distinguishing, differentiating, clarifying, expanding, or expounding upon a point. But if you should ever happen to spend some time in the visitors center of Torrey Pines State Reserve, you can find proof-positive documentation that two Jews can occasionally agree—even two Jews who were elected to the state Assembly from neighboring districts in San Diego County.

On display along with photographs of botanists Charles C. Parry and John Torrey, and in addition to stuffed examples of mammals and birds which may be encountered in the 2,000-acre state reserve, is an October 9, 1999, resolution by State Assembly Members Susan Davis and Howard Wayne congratulating a number of local organizations in connection with the celebration that year of the 100th anniversary of the reserve being named a city park.

In the following year, Davis went on to be elected as a member of Congress. Wayne continued in the Legislature, eventually reaching the three-term limit for service in that body and returning to a position in San Diego as an assistant state attorney general. The two colleagues, both Jewish Democrats, noted in their joint resolution that the park, was "possibly the oldest region in the nation set aside as a wilderness preserve" and that its namesake Torrey Pine is a species found only on these bluffs on the northern coastal edge of La Jolla and, curiously, on Santa Rosa Island off the California coast near Santa Barbara.

Parry, who visited San Diego in 1850, the same year that California became a state, recognized that the trees growing at a place that Spanish explorers had named Punto de Los Arboles (Point of the Trees), were a unique species of pine. He named the species in honor of Torrey, his former professor, sending to him some seeds. Torrey never traveled to California, so never got to see the tree named in his honor. Today, the Parry Grove Trail is one of the popular walks overlooking the Pacific Ocean at Torrey Pines State Beach. Another is the Guy Fleming Trail, named for a naturalist who worked hard to preserve the park. The longest trail is the Beach Trail leading over the bluffs, past gullies and caves, to the beach below. From the Beach Trail one may take detours to such colorful-sounding venues as Red Butte, Razor Point, Broken Hill Overlook, and Yucca Point.

Along with cousins Harry and Sherry Jacobson-Beyer of Louisville, Kentucky, I hiked along the beach trail on Wednesday, July 5, finding it to be an easier hike than I had imagined. Besides the namesake Torrey Pines, there were numerous plant species to see, including several varieties of cactus, juxtaposed against dramatic panoramas of the Pacific Ocean and deep gullies which suddenly presented themselves as the fenced trail wended its way westward. We had hoped to walk all the way down to the beach, but were advised that rain damage had forced the closure of the portion of the trail that descended all the way down to the sand. So, we hiked to an overlook, then turned around, and retraced our steps, finding in the ascent as much fascinating scenery as we had encountered in the descent.

There are signs along the trail system alerting hikers to the fact that rattlesnakes may be encountered. At the visitor center, I had heard a docent telling one woman who inquired that she need not fear the rattlers: "They are much more afraid of you, and because you are too big to eat, they have no interest in attacking you." He advised her that if she saw a rattlesnake, she should simply give it time to slither off the path. I am certain that the docent was correct; I've long believed that snakes have been getting unjustifiably bad press ever since that little incident that the Bible describes as having occurred in the Garden of Eden.

We saw a few birds and lizards but nothing particularly exotic from the animal kingdom on our hike, but the rock formations more than made up for this, and come to think of it, the rocks looked quite a lot like an animal. "A camel," I said.

"No, a sphinx," said Sherry. "Okay, well, maybe a lion." See what I mean about two Jews and three opinions? Harry kept uncharacteristically silent during the brief debate.

One of the impressive sights along the walk was the root system of a Torrey Pine, which had penetrated through the side of the sandstone where it had grown and now was dangling over the deep gully below. I imagine that sometime in the future, as more of the bluff is eaten away by wind and rain erosion, the tree will lose its footing and tumble down toward the beach far below.

After returning to the visitor center, where our car was parked, we drove down the hill to the beach parking lot. The $6-per-vehicle

149

admission to Torrey Pines State Reserve permits you to shuttle between the two parking lots. We headed to the water that had been
tantalizing us from the bluffs above. How good it was to soothe our
feet after trudging up a trail!

Because there is an admission charge to the Torrey Pines State
Reserve, the beach typically is less crowded than nearby beaches. It
took us naturalists no time at all to find a spot to observe frolicking
humans.

"Any Hotel that Would Have Groucho as a Guest" Prompts Other La Valencia Stories

jewishsightseeing.com
July 11, 2006

Both La Valencia Hotel and the nearby Grande Colonial Hotel of La Jolla like to make a point of mentioning on their websites that Groucho Marx, along with other Hollywood celebrities, stayed in their hotels—particularly in the years when the La Jolla Playhouse, under the tutelage of actor Gregory Peck, offered film stars the chance to hone their stage skills during its summer season.

The plays were put on at La Jolla High School from 1947 through 1964. Today, of course, the La Jolla Playhouse offers year-round fare at its home on the UCSD campus.

It's hard not to wonder about Marx, whose multitudes of quips include two which ought to make the manager of any prestige-conscious hotel blanche: "Please accept my resignation. I don't want to belong to any club that will accept me as a member" and perhaps, more to the point, "Room service? Send up a larger room."

Although it wasn't considered one of their best films, the Marx Brothers starred in 1938's *Room Service,* a movie that had the added advantage of including Lucille Ball in the cast. Its premise was that a Broadway troupe had to convince the hotel where they were staying on credit that their play soon would be produced—even though the producers and everyone else associated with the play were dead broke.

With nightly rates at the 117-room hotel starting at $300 and some "ocean villas" renting at a daunting $3,500 a night, the clientele portrayed by the Marx Brothers in that film hardly are the kind the management of the 80-year-old hotel is hoping to attract.

Groucho was born in 1890 as "Julius" Marx, a name which may have made him grouchy, or blue—certainly, it didn't make him Orange Julius. A Jew to the end, though hardly an Orthodox one, his ashes are inurned in San Fernando Valley at Eden Memorial Park in a building within a short distance of the graves of my own parents, Martin B. Harrison and Alice Harrison Walters. There, any semblance of a connection stops.

In that Nancy and I are residents of San Diego County, we don't sleep at either hotel, but La Valencia has been the site of some notable occasions in our family history. For example, when my son David decided it was time to ask Hui-Wen Chang to marry him, he took her to the fancy 12-table Sky Room atop La Valencia. He then invented some excuse for suggesting that they go out on the balcony, which affords a glorious view of palm-tree studded La Jolla Cove and the Pacific Ocean. He got to his knees in the night air and asked her to become his bride. At that height, I'd hate to think of what might have happened if the romantic moment had caused either of them to swoon. And, thank goodness, she said yes!

Just this last Sunday, Nancy and I attended another La Valencia event, a luncheon in the Mediterranean Room and connecting Tropical Patio thrown by Herman Slutzky in honor of the 85th birthday of his wife, Hilda Pierce.

Hilda is an artist and author of an exciting memoir on her escape from Austria after the Anschluss and the life she led subse-

152

quently in England and the United States. Among the celebrants were Slutzky's daughter, Marsha Sutton, education writer for the *Voice of San Diego,* and Marsha's husband, Rocky Smolin, and their two sons, Max and Noah. Taking advantage of the chocolate fountain that is part of the elaborate buffet offered on the patio, Noah rocked our ark by carefully hand-lettering with a fondue-stick a message for Pierce on the rim of his plate: "Happy Birthday, Grandma." I teased Hilda that unlike her paintings, Noah had the advantage of being able to eat his!

Another well-known spot in the hotel is the Whaling Bar, which is decorated with scrimshaw, pewter, and wood accessories. According to hotel publicists, Gregory Peck used to have get-togethers with the casts of the La Jolla Playhouse productions there.

Today the hotel still has its share of glamorous guests. Over the past six years, *San Diego Union-Tribune* columnist Diane Bell has logged in a few of them, including Priscilla Presley, who was in La Jolla to attend a friend's wedding in 2001, and newly elected Gov. Arnold Schwarzenegger, who had a fundraiser there in 2003 attracting such big givers as Qualcomm co-founder Irwin and Joan Jacobs, Padres owner John & Becky Moores, and hotel developer Doug & Betsy Manchester.

More recently, Bell carried items about surfer/model Veronica Kay having been introduced to her husband Scott Baker, the publisher of *213 Magazine* (that's the Los Angeles area code), at La Valencia, and Rancho Santa Fe financier Ralph Whitworth having engaged the Motown group The Four Tops to perform at his wedding to Fernanda Lopes at the hotel.

If all this gives you the idea that La Valencia runs a little on the expensive side, perhaps Groucho spoke for La Valencia's guests after all, when he said: "Money frees you from doing things you dislike. Since I dislike doing nearly everything, money is handy." Or, perhaps, he was speaking for the hotel on another occasion when he grumped: "Go, and never darken my towels again!"

San Diego Mesa College Librarian Jack Forman a Connoisseur of Jewish Books

San Diego Jewish World,
July 1, 2008

O n the book shelves of librarian Jack Forman's office at San Diego Mesa College are many Jewish stories. Forman serves on the American Library Association's panel that awards the Sophie Brody Medal for the best Jewish book of the year. Named for a late San Diego philanthropist, the award is funded by her husband Arthur Brody and the Broad Art Foundation. Forman and eight other librarians throughout the United States are members of the committee. Their chair is Barbara Bibel, an Oakland librarian.

Forman's office sits near the library reference section of San Diego Mesa College's ultramodern Learning Resource Center, which not only houses 110,000 hard cover books and 25,000 electronic books, but also is home to elaborate networks of computers and audio-visual equipment designed to teach junior college students the e-skills that are required for life in the 21st Century.

The Learning Resource Center was designed by architect Mark I. Steele, who also designed Congregation Adat Yeshurun in La Jolla and is working on the proposed Hillel Center at UCSD. Aspects of the Learning Resource Center's design appear to pay homage to the iconic architecture in La Jolla of the Salk Institute for Biological Studies, which was a collaboration by architect Louis I. Kahn and Jonas Salk, discoverer of the polio vaccine.

Besides evaluating the works of other writers, Forman is himself an author, having written the biography, *Presenting Paul Zindel,* about the author of numerous books for teenagers including *Pig Man* and *My Darling, My Hamburger.* Zindel also became well known to adults as the playwright of *The Effect of Gamma Rays on Man-in-the-Moon Marigolds.*

Forman said many of the teenagers and adults in Zindel's books were eccentric and that the author tried to teach teenagers that it is important to have self-esteem.

I asked Forman the criteria that he and other judges apply to determine the best Jewish book of the year. He responded that the winning entry must have Jewish "substance," literary merit and "be accessible to the largest number of persons."

Examining those criteria one-by-one, I learned that whereas there are numerous books that deal with Jews—such as Walter Isaacson's *Einstein: His Life and Universe,* which Forman described as a "wonderful biography"—the book focused on Einstein's science rather than his Jewishness. Thus, it was not included in the list of books under consideration.

While literary merit may be a matter of perception, Forman said the book must be "something that reads well, and easily, and flows. It is well-organized, and it has a voice that you can connect to, not just a bunch of sentences. There must be some spirit or personality behind it."

155

By accessible, Forman explained that a scholarly article on Judaism might be exceedingly well written, yet nevertheless not appeal to enough people to have much impact.

New winners won't be announced until January, but one gets a sense of the committee's standards in considering that *Ministry of Special Cases* by Nathan Englander was the most recent medalist. "Honor books" were Diane Ackerman's *The Zookeeper's Wife;* Joyce Antler's *You Never Call, You Never Write: A History of the Jewish Mother;* and Shalom Auslander's *Foreskin's Lament.*

Forman said he receives for judging approximately 100 books each year, some of which are solicited and some of which are sent by publishers in the hope of attracting attention. He winnows the great stack of books by setting aside those which don't hold his interest when he skims through them. Those rejected clearly are not up to the standards of the others. Balloting by the judges may further winnow the stack down to about 25 books, and these Forman said he will read cover to cover.

He is able to read some of his books in his office, notwithstanding his busy schedule as department chair of the library and audiovisual department, and also teaching classes in library science, being responsible for ordering books in various categories, including religion, supervising the reference desk, and serving as an advisor to the Jewish Student Union, among other tasks.

Additionally, Forman reads at the home that he shares with his wife, Gail Feinstein Forman, an occasional contributor to *San Diego Jewish World* and author of numerous books and stories for teaching English as a second language.

I told him that I imagined that at their home he had a comfortable easy chair with a good reading light behind him, shining directly onto the pages of the book he's reading. Actually, no, he responded, he usually reads on a couch, with a light at his side, that is "not really great lighting." He's been thinking of ordering a fine reading chair.

In San Diego Mesa College's Learning Resource Center, there are a variety of reading configurations for the faculty and the students. The library has its own coffee shop, "where people can browse through a book," he said. "We also have a small reading area off to the side, where we have new copies of magazines. On the second and third floors of the buildings, there are several study areas that are supposed to be quiet areas. There is a mixture of chairs at long tables and individual carrels where students can have more privacy, and 19 group study rooms where they can meet as groups."

Furthermore, he noted, "there are some easy chairs on the first floor and on the second floor, and students like them a lot. Unfortunately, often they fall asleep in them. We get comments on the cards, on the one hand thanking us for the chairs, and on the other, telling students to stop sleeping in them."

The comment card program is taken quite seriously at San Diego Mesa College. The suggestions and the responses are posted conspicuously in the Learning Resource Center and together they make for some interesting reading.

New Americans Museum Celebrates Some of This Country's Richest Blessings

San Diego Jewish World,
July 8, 2008

When my friend Dan Schaffer and I set out to visit the recently-opened New Americans Museum in the Liberty Station area of San Diego, we thought we were going to visit just one museum. As it turned out, we visited three museums all occupying the same large building. What was remarkable was that the three experiences—plus a side trip to a new restaurant—all were interrelated. They all reflected how rich America has become because it is a land of immigrants.

The 4,000-square-foot New Americans Museum is the brainchild of Deborah Szekely, perhaps best known internationally as the founder of the Golden Door spas and the Rancho La Puerta health resort of Tecate, Mexico. The daughter of Jewish immigrant parents, Harry Shainman (also spelled Szainman) of Warsaw and the former Rebecca Sudman of Austria, Szekely was raised in the Far

Rockaway Beach area of Brooklyn, near Coney Island, with the sound of her mother's German and father's Yiddish in her ears. Szekely also learned English as a child.

Her parents' marriage was of the Only-in-America type, her father having immigrated steerage class to America to avoid being conscripted as a poor youngster into what was then the Russian Army. Her mother, the child of wealthy fur traders, steamed in elegance to America's shores. Not one to put on airs, Rebecca worked as a nurse in New York, eventually meeting Harry. When the Depression came, Rebecca, able to draw on her parents' resources, prevailed on her husband to relocate the family to Tahiti.

Many years later, after returning to the United States and making her success in the spa movement, Szekely became president of the Inter-American Foundation, traveling extensively throughout the Western Hemisphere. During a telephone interview, she told me that it was the stories that she encountered in this U.S. diplomatic assignment—rather than her own immigrant background—that motivated her to create the non-profit New Americans Museum.

"Every place I went, whether the Caribbean or Latin America, I was chatting with the women," she recalled. "They would point out their young kids, bright, and say, 'That is the one that we are going to send to America.' People don't realize that the children were these families' investments in the future—like venture capitalists. The best of the best of the family is sent to America, and everyone in the family chips in . . . whether from Latin America, South Africa, or Cambodia. And the kids repay their families' investments with their successes."

For example, said Szekely, Mexican immigrants to the United States send billions of dollars per year in remittances to their families. "They hold two jobs, one to repay the investments of their families to bring them here," she said. As strong as the sense of gratitude is in the first generation of immigrants, it typically diminishes in the second generation, Szekely said. "The kids don't send as much money back as the parents, who feel the obligation."

There are benefits and drawbacks to such patterns of immigration, the museum founder said. "They come here full of high hopes and get treated as second-class citizens. Not speaking English doesn't mean that you are not bright. How many of us [Americans] can speak Spanish? But people see things out of context. None of the kids came here because they were looking for a free ride."

Referring to portraits now on exhibit of teenage immigrant children photographed for the Smithsonian Institution by Barbara Beirne—in which the subjects wrote their own captions—Szekely said: "Look at these kids: We are truly getting the best of the best, and this has to be recognized!"

In the exhibition, youngsters from throughout the world tell of their families' reasons for coming to America. In many cases, it was to avoid warfare or political persecution in their countries of origin. In others, as alluded to by Szekely, they came because of the economic opportunity that America represented. Some of the youngsters also told of the adjustments their new lives required.

Szekely said it is unfortunate that immigrant children sometimes don't realize how bright, and far-seeing, their parents have been. "Sometimes, the parents are looked down upon because they are poor. The children think if they are poor, they are not bright."

The mistake the children make is to confuse material advantages with intellect. The parents may, in fact, be very bright, even if, "They came from a place where they did their washing in a river, whereas now they have a washing machine, which they think is wonderful, or if the father is a gardener, who thinks it is wonderful to have his own truck and tools," Szekely said. "Some kids think their parents don't have the capacity, or the potential, and they do."

The problem, she suggested, is that, "Stereotypes have been sold to the kids." The New Americans Museum, even while in formation, fought against stereotypes. It sponsored essay contests in which immigrant children were encouraged to interview their parents about their lives in the old country and the circumstances of their immigration. "The kids have been astonished when they ask what their parents what it was like, and there has been a whole new bonding."

Photographer Beirne said her project was inspired in 1999 by meeting teenage refugees from Kosovo and deciding to seek teens from other countries. "I searched for places to meet these newcomers in the hope of being able to photograph them in their new surroundings. My first stop was Grand Street Settlement in New York City, a non-profit organization that has provided services to immigrants since 1916 . . . ." She offered the teenagers autonomy in selecting where to be photographed, what they would wear, and "the messages that would accompany the photographs." She then traveled throughout the United States from 2000 to 2006 meeting immigrants, refugees, and American-born children of immigrant parents.

As Dan and I read the teenagers' comments, we could not help but remember the immigrant generations of our respective families. In my case, my paternal great grandparents arrived approximately in the 1880s from Rzezow in what is now Poland (then Austria-Hungary), and my maternal grandparents arrived early in the 1900s from Lithuania. Dan's parents were of a similar Eastern European background; his mother, the former Norma Diamond, was from Poland, and his father, Maurice, hailed from Lithuania. They met in Cleveland, where they were married in 1921.

Both of us were particularly interested in the comments of teenagers from Israel and of Palestinian background that reflected the hurt on both sides of the conflict. Tahani Salah, 16, wrote under her photo: "My blood is P.L.O. My blood flows through the Ramallah roads. My skin one shade lighter than peach. The road home is just too weak. Why can't I speak the same Arabic? I'm a Muslim

161

Palestinian; that has never seemed real to me. Can't you see I have never been home. When will it ever be safe to go home?"

In contrast, Marina Krichevsky, 16, wrote: "We immigrated from Israel two years ago. Israel was a pretty scary place. There are terrorist attacks all the time and I do mean all the time. Some kids never leave their neighborhood. Other kids feel they might as well move around because they could be killed in their own backyard. If we still lived in Israel I would be in the military."

A second exhibit was locally produced: "Contemporary Story: Perspectives by Immigrant and Refugee Artists," in which refugee teens studying photography made studies of the lives and works of other immigrants involved in both the performing and creative arts. In most cases, the subjects were from different countries than the photographers.

A four-photo study was of classical piano teacher Yevgenia Nisman from Odessa, Ukraine, as seen by Ahmed (Last Name not given), 18, from Somalia. There were two different views of Nisman playing her piano; another, closer up, of her sitting at the piano, and finally, a study of her hands on the keys. Nisman is a member of our Jewish community.

The museum describes its mission as being "a catalyst to celebrate America's past and promise" and providing "inspiring and compelling educational and cultural programs and activities of our diverse immigrant experience."

The executive director of the museum is Gayle Hom, a third-generation Chinese American whose father, Tom Hom, once served on the San Diego City Council and later represented San Diego in the California State Assembly. Her late mother, Dorothy, was deeply involved in the creation of the Asian Pacific Thematic District in downtown San Diego.

Hom is married to a Jewish man, Sheldon Zemen. Their wedding incorporated Chinese and Jewish customs. Hom became a

Jew-by-choice and both their children have become bar and bat mitzvah at Congregation Beth Am. Her story resonated with me because my own son David and his wife, Hui-Wen, similarly had a wedding that encompassed both their rich heritages.

An interesting side note about the museum is that its location at 2825 Dewey Road in "Liberty Station," as the former Naval Training Center is now named, sits in the Roseville section of the Point Loma neighborhood of San Diego. Roseville was the town site laid out in 1869 by Louis Rose, the first Jewish settler in San Diego. As Rose was an immigrant from Neuhaus-an-der-Oste, Germany, it turns out that the museum honoring immigrants is itself located in an area laid out by an immigrant.

After visiting the New Americans Museum, Dan and I walked a few paces into the gallery operated by the San Diego Watercolor Society, which offers a new exhibit the first Friday of every month. The current one, in celebration of the opening of its neighboring New Americans Museum, is patriotically themed "Red, white and blue and all the other colors too," according to the society's former president, Risë Parberry, who, like other board members, volunteers as a docent.

"1850 . . . *New Roots* is an eye-catching painting depicting two Chinese in traditional dress against a background of the American flag. The painting is the work of Tom Hom, father of Gayle Hom."

Another work that drew my attention was *Entrance to the Garden of Eden,* an abstract by Rachel Hasson utilizing acrylic paint on a Japanese plastic material known as yupo. Hasson had been born in Lvov, Poland, and avoided the Holocaust by immigrating to Palestine in 1939. She later studied medicine in the United States, becoming a professor of pathology and pediatrics at Albert Einstein College of Medicine in New York. She took up painting in her retirement. Besides her work on display in San Diego, she currently has a one-woman show in the community of Laguna Woods, where she now resides.

Located on another end of the building is the Visions Art Quilt Gallery, where a touring exhibit cleverly called "Material Men" (a pun on Madonna's signature song "Material Girl") shows the works of male quilters. One of the volunteers at the gallery was Boatema Boateng (the 'o's in names are pronounced like 'w's), an expatriate from Ghana who is an assistant professor of communications at UCSD. Dan, who once had served as a teacher in Nigeria before settling down to a long career as a high school teacher in San Diego County, conversed with her about pedagogical styles and educational techniques in the United States and in West Africa.

Eventually, Dan and I left the museum building to continue our tour of Liberty Station, an area that may well become another great cultural center of San Diego similar to Balboa Park. We wandered through a long, arched walkway, soon finding Tender Greens, a new restaurant emphasizing local organic foods, which co-owner Rian Brandenburg (a former chef at the Lodge at Torrey Pines) told us is intended to bring cuisine that is both healthy and imaginative to casual diners. The young woman who seated us for a very tasty lunch was Dasha Bondurovska, a recent immigrant from Ukraine. Another member of the staff is Rachel Roos, a new arrival from Brazil.

Wherever we went that day, Dan and I encountered "New Americans" who are enriching our country's cultural and economic lives. How apropos that we should now have a museum to celebrate our nation's good fortune.

Tibor Rubin, Jewish Recipient of Medal of Honor, Heads for San Diego Exhibit

San Diego Jewish World,
August 26, 2008

During the Korean War, there was a 24-hour period that neither Corporal Tibor Rubin nor a grateful United States of America, which awarded him the Medal of Honor, will ever forget.

Rubin is one of 17 Jewish winners of the Medal of Honor who are profiled in a Jewish War Veterans-sponsored exhibit that will run through September 30 at the Veterans Museum and Memorial Center 2115 Park Boulevard, in Balboa Park. He will make a personal appearance at the exhibit from noon to 4 p.m. on Sunday, September 28, according to Nicole Nore, the museum's events director.

According to the official citation, while American forces were retreating to the Pusan perimeter, machine gunner Rubin took a position on a hill with the assignment of keeping open the vital Taegu-Pusan Road link used by his withdrawing unit.

"During the ensuing battle, overwhelming numbers of North Korean troops assaulted the hill solely defended by Corporal Rubin," the citation for the Medal of Honor said. In Rubin's "personal 24-hour battle," he single-handedly slowed the enemy advance, "allowing the 8th Cavalry regiment to complete its withdrawal completely."

As it turned out, that was just a preliminary engagement for Rubin. "On October 30, 1950, Chinese forces attacked the unit at Unsan, Korea, during a massive nighttime assault," the citation said. "That night and throughout the next day, he manned a 30-caliber machine gun at the south end of the unit's line after three previous gunners became casualties . . . . He continued to man his machine gun until his ammunition was exhausted. His determined stance slowed the advance of the enemy, permitting the remnants of his unit to reach safety."

Rubin was wounded during the battle and was captured by the Chinese. As he was a native of Hungary (and a Holocaust survivor), the Chinese offered to return him to that country. He refused, however.

Then, according to the citation, "Corporal Rubin disregarded his own personal safety and immediately began sneaking out of camp at night in search of food for his comrades. Breaking into enemy food storehouses and gardens, he faced almost certain death." Additionally, he "provided not only food to the starving soldiers but also desperately needed medical care and moral support for the sick and wounded in the POW camp. His efforts were directly attributed to the saving of the lives of as many as 40 of his fellow prisoners."

The citation concluded: "Corporal Rubin's gallant actions in close contact with the enemy and unyielding courage and bravery while a prisoner of war were in the highest traditions of military service and reflected great credit on himself and the United States Army."

Service personnel like Rubin who receive the Medal of Honor warrant a salute from any member of the military, no matter how great that person's rank. Even a general, or the chairman of the Joint Chiefs of Staff, would feel privileged to salute Rubin in honor of his bravery.

From the Civil War through the War in Vietnam, Jews have been earning the Medal of Honor, according to the exhibit.

A sample of recipients from each war or military operation covered by the exhibit include:

Civil War—Born in Guttentag, Silesia, Prussia, Sergeant-Major Abraham Cohn helped rally Union forces during the Battle of the Wilderness. According to the citation, "he coolly carried orders to advance under severe fire."

Native American Wars—Simon Suhler also was known as Charles Gardner. Born in 1844 in Bavaria, Germany, he fought against Native Americans in Arizona in 1868 while serving with the U.S. Army in Cavalry B of Company B of the 8th U.S. Cavalry. The museum legend did not provide specifics of his heroism.

Haiti—On November 17, 1915, Samuel Margulies, also known as Samuel Gross, a Marine attached to the U.S.S. *Connecticut,* participated in the attack on Fort Riviere, Haiti, "in an effort to cut off all avenues of retreat for the Caco bandits. Approaching a breach in the wall, which was the only entrance to the fort, Gross was the second man to pass through the breach and faced constant fire from the Caco bandits." The citation continued: "For a ten-minute period, he engaged the enemy in desperate hand-to-hand combat until the bastion was captured and the Caco resistance neutralized."

World War I—First Sergeant Sydney Gumpertz of San Rafael, California, an infantry man with the Army's 33rd Division, encountered enemy machine gun fire which held up his unit's advance near Blois de Forge, France, on September 29, 1918. He "started with two other soldiers toward the machine gun nest. His two companions soon became casualties from bursting shells but First Sergeant Gumpertz continued on alone in face of direct fire from a machine gun, jumped into the nest and silenced the gun, capturing nine of the crew."

World War II—U.S. Army Capt. Ben Salomon was serving as a surgeon in Tanapag Village in Saipan in the Marianas Islands, where the Japanese had a 32,000-strong garrison. The first and second battalions of his regiment were attacked on July 7, 1944 by a force of between 3,000 and 5,000 Japanese soldiers. According to the citation: "Although both units fought furiously, the enemy soon penetrated their combined perimeter and inflicted overwhelming casualties. In the first minutes of the attack, roughly 30 wounded soldiers made their way into Captain Salomon's aid station. As the perimeter began to be overrun, it became increasingly difficult for Captain Salomon to work on the wounded. He then saw a Japanese soldier bayoneting one of the wounded soldiers lying near the tent. Firing from a squatting position, Captain Salomon quickly killed the enemy soldier, then as he turned his attention back to medical care, two more Japanese soldiers appeared in the front entrance. As these enemy soldiers were killed, four more crawled under the tent. Rushing them, Captain Salomon killed three of the four and butted the fourth in the stomach and then a wounded comrade shot and killed the enemy. Realizing the gravity of the situation, Captain Salomon ordered the wounded to make their way as best as they could back to the regimental aid station while he tried to hold off the enemy as best as he could. Captain Salomon grabbed the rifle from a wounded soldier (and) rushed outside and captured a machine gun after the four Japanese manning it had been killed. When his body was later found, 98 enemy soldiers were piled in front of his position." The Medal of Honor was awarded to Captain Salomon posthumously.

Korea—Tibor Rubin's story is retold at the beginning of this article.

Vietnam—Air Force Sergeant John Levitow was a loadmaster aboard an AC-47, which, according to the citation, was "struck by a mortar round" with the resulting explosion ripping "a hole 2 feet in diameter through the wing, and fragments made over 35,000 holes in the fuselage. All the occupants of the compartment were wounded. The explosion tore and activated a flare from the grasp of a crew member who had been launching flares to provide illumination for Army ground troops engaged in combat. Sergeant Levitow, although stunned by the concussion of the blast and suffering from over 40 fragment wounds to his back and legs, staggered to his feet and turned to assist the man nearest him who had been knocked down and was bleeding heavily. As he was moving his wounded comrade forward and away from the open compartment door, he saw the smoking flare ahead of him in the aisle. Realizing the danger involved and completely disregarding his own wounds, Sergeant Levitow started towards the flare. The aircraft was partially out of control and the flare was rolling around from side to side. Sergeant Levitow struggled forward despite the loss of blood from his many wounds and the partial loss of feeling in his right leg. Unable to grasp the rolling flare with his hands, he threw himself bodily on the burning flare, hugging the deadly device to his body. He dragged himself to the rear of the aircraft and threw the flare through the open cargo door. At that instant the flare separated and ignited in the air, but clear of the aircraft. Sergeant Levitow by his selfless and heroic actions saved the aircraft and its entire crew from certain death and destruction . . . ."

A Conversation with Andrew Viterbi, National Medal of Science Laureate

San Diego Jewish World,
September 16, 2008

D r. Andrew Viterbi learned too early about the National Medal of Science that will be bestowed upon him in a White House ceremony September 29. Conversely, he learned too late about the presidential medal he received some years ago from his native Italy.

"I have been honored in more ways than I deserve, but I don't believe in knowing that I am being considered," Viterbi told *San Diego Jewish World* in an interview at the Viterbi Group offices on La Jolla Village Drive. Viterbi was the discoverer of what is known to fellow scientists as the "Viterbi Algorithm," a formula that is imprinted on the chips in cell phones throughout the world. He also is a pioneer in Code Division Multiple Access (CDMA), a process that Qualcomm patented to improve cell phone technology.

About two years ago, Viterbi heard his office phone ringing, and because the secretary was out, grabbed it himself. The party on the other end was a representative of the University of Southern California, home of the Viterbi School of Engineering, to which the Viterbi family made a gift of $52 million. The caller asked if the university could have a list of Dr. Viterbi's publications.

That call tipped Viterbi off that something was in the works and he dutifully sent the publication list to USC, after first having to search for it. More than a year later, Viterbi received a letter from the Office of White House Science Advisor John Marburger saying that he was being considered for "presidential recognition."

The letter went on that it couldn't be divulged what the recognition might be, but that in order for the matter to proceed, the FBI needed a copy of his signature—apparently for a handwriting analysis that is part of a background check. Viterbi dutifully sent a copy of his signature to the federal officials.

Then came a telephone call from Marburger, but Viterbi was out. When Viterbi returned the call, Marburger was out. Finally, an assistant to Marburger told Viterbi what was becoming obvious, that President George W. Bush would bestow upon him the Presidential Medal of Science.

He will be among eight honorees. Viterbi said that he and perhaps three others are Jews—problematic in that the White House award ceremony has been scheduled for the morning of Erev Rosh Hashanah. The White House promised that everything would be concluded by noon, thereby enabling Viterbi to fly back to San Diego to be with his family for the High Holidays.

The White House ceremony will be in the East Room on a Monday morning, but there will be a blacktie dinner the evening before, Viterbi was advised. The President usually doesn't attend this dinner, but such luminaries as the Science Advisor, the Secretary of Commerce and, of course, the other medalists will be in attendance.

In addition to Viterbi, the National Medal of Science Laureates for 2007 are: Fay Ajzenberg-Selove, University of Pennsylvania, Philadelphia; Mostafa A. El-Sayed, Georgia Institute of Technology, Atlanta; Leonard Kleinrock, University of California, Los Angeles; Robert J. Lefkowitz, Duke University, Durham, North Carolina; Bert W. O'Malley, Baylor College of Medicine, Houston; Charles P. Slichter, University of Illinois, Urbana-Champaign, and David J. Wineland, National Institute of Standards and Technology, Boulder, Colorado.

Viterbi, whose parents fled with their family from Italy to avoid the Holocaust when he was four years old, had been awarded his native country's second highest award—that of a Grand Officer— several years ago.

"What was funny about it, just by coincidence, I was in Italy at the time with an interesting group, the University of Pennsylvania Judaic Studies Center, doing a tour of all the Italian ghettos, most of which I had toured on my own, but having a professor, a specialist in the area, is nice," Viterbi recalled. "So, we were there, and it was the Second of June, which is the national holiday, because it marked the time in the post-War that the Italian Republic was declared, and that is the day that the president gives out the honors.

"But I didn't know anything about it, and I didn't find out until I got back to the States and I got congratulatory messages from friends and family and I said, 'for what?' and finally someone sent me the newspaper that I was on the honors list from the President."

Eventually, Viterbi was invited by Italy's Consulate in Los Angeles to be an honored guest at an annual conference for Italian scientists so that he could formally receive the award.

That was the second award from Italy; Viterbi previously had received the Christopher Columbus Award for Science bestowed by the City of Genoa. He also has been recognized by governments and academic institutions in Israel, Finland, Germany, and Japan.

While the U.S. National Medal of Science citation makes reference to Viterbi's overall career, it places particular emphasis on the Viterbi Algorithm, which he developed while he was a faculty member at UCLA.

I asked Viterbi if he would explain in "layman's terms" just what the Viterbi Algorithm is.

He responded that the algorithm permits cellular communications "to operate in a channel that is noisier and which is more prone to multi-path interference." The latter problem, he explained, particularly affects urban cell phone users. Pointing out the window of his conference room in La Jolla, Viterbi said "if you used your cell phone in here, it [the signal] might bounce off the building next door, or somewhere else, and so when it arrives at your [receiving] station, it will arrive in multiple forms. . . . All these deflections tend to interfere with each other, causing fade." By using the algorithm, cell phone manufacturers can predict and eliminate some of the variances that would otherwise interfere with communications.

Viterbi said his algorithm built upon the theory of the 19th Century Russian mathematician Andrey Markov "who came up with a model for statistical sequences." Unlike a roulette wheel, Viterbi said, "what happens next depends on what happened last, along with some other random phenomena."

Not only does the Viterbi Algorithm enable more certain cellular communications, but to Viterbi's surprise, it also "has applications in all sorts of things—recording . . . voice recognition . . . even DNA sequencing."

Given that he discovered the algorithm while a professor at UCLA, why did he give his $52 million gift to arch-rival USC? I, as a former UCLA Bruin, couldn't help but wonder.

"I have a very good relationship with both schools," Viterbi laughed. But the gift from Andrew and Erna Viterbi to USC also was a matter of sentiment.

He explained that when his family relocated from Italy to Boston, his father had to be recertified as an ophthalmologist, and did not start up his American practice until he was already 60 years old. The family was able to send Andrew (né Andrea) to Boston Latin School (which is one year older than Harvard University) and to the Massachusetts Institute of Technology, but to do so, the family had to watch over its pennies very carefully.

After receiving a master's degree from MIT, Viterbi came out west to work at CalTech's Jet Propulsion Laboratory in Pasadena during an era when the U.S. government—then in a space race against the Soviets—made funding for science and technology a priority. Viterbi worked on projects so advanced, he felt certain they were at a doctoral level, and so he decided to pursue his studies with an eye towards becoming a professor.

The problem was that Viterbi needed to work to support his parents—his father was now 75—and within a few years Viterbi was married, and he and Erna had two children. So, Viterbi couldn't enroll full time in a doctoral program. USC allowed him to work on his doctorate part-time, a concession that other institutions were not willing to make. Viterbi obviously was quite grateful, and after he became wealthy as the co-founder with Irwin Jacobs of Qualcomm, he decided that USC would be one of the institutions to which he would give back.

Albert Einstein on occasion wondered whether the world was better or worse off for his having discovered the formula leading to the development of nuclear fission. I asked Viterbi if he ever had similar thoughts about whether the world was better or worse off as a result of the fast and sure communications enabled by the Viterbi Algorithm and CDMA.

He responded with characteristic modesty. First, he said, he certainly isn't in the same league as Einstein, who was one of the greatest scientists of the 20th Century. Second, he said, cell phone technology would have developed with or without his algorithm.

With those caveats, he suggested that fast communications—whether by the Internet or via cell phone—in fact have improved the world, despite some drawbacks such as people walking along the street and driving their cars while talking on the cell phone and paying minimal attention to each other.

"One interesting statistic is that worldwide in the year 2000, there were 600 million users of wired telephones," Viterbi recounted. "That year the number of cell phones reached the number of the fixed, and then fixed went down and then cell kept rising at an exponential rate, so now there are about 3 billion, so that means that virtually every country has service. In countries like China, or India, every village has at least one phone. There is the 'phone lady.' When they talk about 'micro-loans,' it is usually to a woman who buys a cellular phone, and then rents it out to the whole village. It takes the place of the phone booth."

Furthermore, he said, in developing nations, the infrastructure costs for cellular are far less than for fixed systems. If such inventions as cellular and the Internet had been available in previous periods of our history, he said, they might have averted some man-made disasters.

"Everybody who can read or write can access it; that to me is the most important thing," he said. If you think about the greatest catastrophe that confronted us [Jews] as a people—the Holocaust—the total lack of information, the lack of wanting to believe or to listen to what was happening, today that couldn't happen. You would have had 100 million bloggers and it couldn't be ignored."

Viterbi retired from Qualcomm in 2000. Today, an energetic 73, he was interviewed last week in the offices of the Viterbi Group, to which he devotes approximately one-third his work time. He said that a number of the companies in which his group has invested are based in Israel, but that the attraction is not only that they are Israeli but that they are run by "some very clever people."

175

Among those he mentioned were Provigent, Sandlinks, and Cellint. Provigent provides software solutions for cell phone transmission from tower to tower. There are numerous companies that have produced hardware for this purpose, but Provigent "has put it all on one chip." In that there are many different companies with cell towers, having a single chip that can communicate with them all enables interconnectivity, according to Viterbi.

Sandlinks is involved in radio frequency identification (RFID) tags, which not only identify their product but also relay information to other tags and readers, Viterbi added.

And, Cellint tracks the number of cellular calls being made from various stretches of the road systems to develop real-time traffic density portraits, he said.

Giving lectures mostly at USC but also at various venues around the world also takes about a third of Viterbi's time. Of particular interest to the Jewish community is the remaining third of his working time, which he spends on family philanthropies.

With education being his and Erna's priority, major beneficiaries of the family largesse include such Israeli institutions as the Technion; the soon-to-be-built Sha'ar Hanegev High School, in the partnership region of the United Jewish Federation of San Diego; and the Israel Venture Network which offers advanced training for principals in smaller and poorer school districts. In San Diego, the Viterbis support such local Jewish institutions as the Agency for Jewish Education and San Diego Jewish Academy. They contribute to secular schools as well, from preschool all the way through post-doctoral studies. Most of their contributions are given either through an advised fund with the Jewish Community Foundation, or through a JCF Family Foundation.

Health is another arena to which the Viterbis like to give, with their donations covering "everything from help for the elderly" through Jewish Family Service and Seacrest Village Retirement

Communities to "cutting-edge biological research such as at the Scripps Research Institute or the Burnham Institute. Also, we just made a commitment to [Rady] Children's Hospital," he said.

Viterbi is an important contributor to the United Jewish Federation of San Diego County. In fact, the community building at 4950 Murphy Canyon Road that houses the United Jewish Federation, Agency for Jewish Education and the Jewish Community Foundation—The Joseph and Lenka Finci Building—is named after the parents of Viterbi's wife, Erna.

But How Do the Fish Like Tashlich?

San Diego Jewish World,
October 1, 2008

Tashlich being my absolute favorite service on the day of Rosh Hashanah, I have imagined that it probably is also well-regarded by the fish and the ducks at Lake Murray who become the beneficiaries of the bread to which we Jews symbolically transfer our sins. But, this year, I figured I'd confirm my impressions with someone at the Scripps Institution of Oceanography.

I asked Jules Jaffe, PhD and member of the local Jewish community, if he could try to imagine what a fish might think of Tashlich. Would it be as happy as I imagined? Or would the fish find some reason to object to all that bread representing our sins being dumped into its watery home by so many people all at once?

Jaffe said that much of the bread thrown upon the waters likely would be gobbled up by ducks, seagulls, or other swimming birds, long before the fish could get to them—but such bread which did sink down to the bottom likely would attract smaller organisms and bacteria.

These in turn would attract the fish which, in consuming the organisms, might also eat the bread.

In all likelihood, "there are lots of animals that would be more happy with the bread than the fish," said the scientist, explaining that fish prefer such foods as plankton, which are higher in protein content.

Whether eaten by small organisms, fish, or marine birds, "the bread will be recycled in one form or another," Jaffe said.

I wondered what, if fish could think, they might feel about being invited to gobble up the symbolic sins of others.

"My views on animal consciousness are not conventional," Jaffe responded. "It's an interesting question whether animals have remorse or guilt. I would say it is an open question."

Jaffe noted that he is a biophysicist, not an ichthyologist, so has no data, "but my colleagues tell me fish are the dumbest animals around."

Jaffe's own field of study is in developing remote sensing techniques using sound and light to determine what kind of life forms are populating the top 300 feet of ocean. "What's there? How many are there? What are they doing?" are the questions that propel research into new sonar for detecting species as small as zooplankton.

UCSD Colleagues Recall Former Israel President Ephraim Katzir's Hideaway Life in La Jolla

San Diego Jewish World,
June 3, 2009

After Ephraim Katzir completed his term as the fourth president of Israel in 1978, he wanted to get away from politics, international affairs, and the stresses of public life and back to his beloved science.

So, keeping as low a profile as possible, he moved with his wife Nina and daughter Irit for six months to La Jolla, California, where he used a fellow scientist's office on the UCSD campus to rest, recuperate, study, and write.

So successful was Katzir in keeping quiet his half-year-long stay at UCSD that following his death last Saturday at age 93 in Rehovot, current-day UCSD public relations officials were unaware that their campus had been the venue for a short chapter in the former Israeli President's long life. However, after spreading their information-gathering net wide, they eventually were able to confirm the low-profile ex-president's stay on campus.

William Allison, a researcher who investigated mitochondrial diseases and professor emeritus of biochemistry, subsequently told *San Diego Jewish World* that while Katzir never became a formal member of the UCSD faculty, he was extended the courtesy of being able to move into the office of Professor Nathan Kaplan to do his writing. Kaplan at the time was visiting mainland China—one of the first American scientists permitted to do so following the thaw in China's relations with the United States, Allison said.

Given that his UCSD sojourn was 30 years ago, there is some question over exactly whose office Katzir used, or if perhaps he had used two different ones over the six-month period. Prof. Ed Dennis remembered Katzir using Room 4080 of what was then called the Basic Science Building, and which is now called the Biomedical Sciences Building.

That room was Biology Professor Morris Friedkin's "scientific office while he was Provost of Revelle," and was "adjacent to Nate Kaplan's office," messaged Dennis.

It's possible that Kaplan returned from China while Katzir was still at UCSD, necessitating a change of offices, Dennis suggested. He said he has a recollection of seeing Kaplan and Katzir together at a social function that year.

Regardless of all that, Katzir "was very low key, interested in discussing his science as a biochemist studying protein structure and function," Dennis said. "I had several interesting chats and conversations with him during his stay."

"I don't recall there being any security presence or concerns expressed, which is surprising given our current times," added Dennis of UCSD's Chemistry/Biochemistry Department.

Known to scientists around the world as Ephraim Katchalsky before he Hebraicized his surname, Katzir had met Kaplan—a former chairman of the Biophysics Department at Brandeis University—at various scientific conferences around the world. Similarly, he had a long-standing friendship with Murray Goodman, then chairman of UCSD's chemistry department—a relationship that predated Katzir's acceptance of Israel's presidency in 1973.

Allison had been a student of Kaplan's at Brandeis University and, like him, migrated across country to the UCSD campus, where he was assigned the office next door to Kaplan. That was how he became Katzir's temporary next-door neighbor, he recalled.

"I remember that he was a great biochemist, and that I was in awe talking to him about science," Allison said in a telephone interview. "He never talked about the presidency—the only insight I got was that he was very happy that he was no longer president."

Katzir had served as Israel's president during some tumultuous years. The Yom Kippur War occurred while he was in office, as did Egyptian President Anwar Sadat's subsequent surprise offer to fly to Jerusalem, thus beginning the process that led to the Camp David peace accord between Israel and Egypt.

Katzir was among the Israeli dignitaries who lined up to greet Sadat at the Ben Gurion Airport, a place of considerable pain for him because the same airport was where his brother, renowned chemical physicist Aharon Katzir, was one of 24 persons indiscriminately murdered in 1972 by three members of the Japanese Red Army on behalf of the Popular Front for the Liberation of Palestine. Ben Gurion Airport then was known as the Lod Airport after the city in which it is located.

Aharon Katzir, like Ephraim, had been on the faculty of the Weizmann Institute in Rehovot. During the Independence War, the two worked together to develop explosives for the Haganah—a process that people used to joke about later because it was so stinky. In order to keep the project secret—and not to offend the noses of other Haganah members—the two brothers had to mix up their chemicals in a cave, according to a story told by the *Jerusalem Post* in Katzir's obituary.

Eligible for a second five-year term as Israel's President, Katzir turned it down, saying his wife Nina had been ailing.

In La Jolla, however, Mrs. Katzir's health apparently had rallied. Zelda Goodman, wife of then-Department Chair Murray Goodman, said the Katzirs rented a house in La Jolla Shores, and that she and Nina often went shopping together. In contrast to her husband, who was quiet and preferred the company of books and academic colleagues, Nina, an educator who was interested in children's books, was quite social, Zelda Goodman recalled.

As one who would become a driving force in the development of the San Diego Jewish Book Fair at the Lawrence Family JCC, Goodman and Nina Katzir were kindred spirits.

The Goodmans entertained the Katzirs in their La Jolla home, with dinners often being a time when the men who were scientists would get into earnest discussions about their work. Sometimes, quipped Zelda, the "more mature ones" remembered to occasionally discuss other topics that their spouses could enjoy as well.

Ephraim Katzir had a worldwide reputation for his work with polyamino acids, which were useful in developing a drug for the treatment of multiple sclerosis. Goodman on the other hand was considered an expert in peptides.

Allison said that while Katzir had his own scientific emphasis, he clearly enjoyed hearing about all related areas of biochemistry and biophysics.

After considerable coaxing, Murray Goodman was able to persuade Katzir to give one lecture to scientific colleagues who came from the UCSD campus, from the Salk Institute, Scripps Clinic, and from various private scientifically-oriented companies near the campus. Allison recalled that a lecture hall for approximately 400 persons was packed with colleagues.

The ex-Israeli president also would sit among graduate students in seminars conducted by her husband Goodman said.

In contrast, Katzir was quite reluctant to give talks about Israel, even to the Jewish community, knowing that if he gave one speech, he would be besieged with other invitations—just what he had wanted to get away from, according to Zelda Goodman.

She said that back when Katzir was President of Israel, she and her husband visited him at the Presidential residence in Jerusalem, which was a thrill. The last time she saw him was about five years ago, shortly before her husband Murray died, when they visited him at the Weizmann Institute, where he had a residence on campus.

She recalled that Katzir at that time expressed a great deal of concern about Iran's intentions in the Middle East, but in a quiet, thoughtful way, rather than in a bombastic way. He didn't urge any particular course of action, she said.

It was in Rehovot that Katzir was buried on Sunday evening. Although he was eligible to be buried at Mount Herzl in Jerusalem with Israel's other heads of state and prime ministers, he chose to be buried close to the Weizmann Institute, with which he had been associated for six decades.

Mingei International Museum

San Diego Jewish World,
June 4, 2010

O utside the Mingei International Museum in Balboa Park stand two large, fanciful sculptures by Niki de Saint Phalle, an internationally celebrated sculptor who lived in La Jolla in the final years of her life. One created in 1998 from glass, stones, mirrors, and polyester, called *Poet and Muse,* depicts a male poet with a female muse on his shoulders, his arms transforming into her legs.

The other, playfully called a *Nikigator,* is an elongated, exaggerated alligator made from similar materials and sitting on playground foam, a delightful magnet for preschoolers who can scamper through the *Nikigator's* innards.

Poet and Muse is a tribute to the creative process that drives the folk artists and craftspeople whose works are on exhibit at the Mingei, whereas the "Niki-gator" matches the museum's theme, which is celebration of artisans who turn everyday objects into works of art through their care and talent. Playground equipment could simply be functional, but not in Saint Phalle's world. This piece, intended to be touched, caressed, and climbed upon by tykes, is a stimulus for the young imagination.

Saint Phalle's works are exhibited throughout the world, and especially in San Diego County. *Coming Together* is a large circular piece outside the downtown San Diego Convention Center; *Queen Califia's Magic Circle* is in Kit Carson Park in Escondido, and *Sun God* is a prominent feature on the UCSD campus. Saint Phalle also has an entire menagerie of imaginative, fanciful animals on permanent exhibit at the Jerusalem Zoo in Israel.

Inside Balboa Park's re-created House of Charm, built in its original incarnation for the 1915 Panama-California Exhibition, the Mingei held a major retrospective of Saint Phalle's work. Following her death in 2002, what had been planned as another exhibit for her at the Mingei's smaller facility in Escondido, was transformed into a tribute to her life and works.

Saint Phalle and the museum's founder, Martha Longenecker, were close friends. Saint Phalle not only was represented in the museum's collection, she became one of its important financial benefactors. One day, according to Martha Ehringer, the museum's public relations director, Saint Phalle told Longenecker she wanted to purchase for the museum any piece it wanted. Thrilled, Longenecker suggested a grand piano. But Saint Phalle decided anyone with sufficient funds could make such a gift, she wanted something much finer, much more memorable. So, she commissioned a long table suitable for board meetings to be made by Mira Nakashima at the Nakashima Woodshop in New Hope, Pennsylvania, and purchased 18 chairs fashioned by Mira's father, the late master woodworker George Nakashima—two chairs to be placed at each end of the table, and seven along each side.

Doug Smalheer, a docent who taught U.S. history for 40 years, a majority of that time at San Diego Mesa College, is enamored of the table and chairs, and tells the story of Nakashima's life and works with all the zest of one describing Washington crossing the Delaware, or Lincoln signing the Emancipation Proclamation.

Nakashima grew up in Seattle, Washington, and earned a master's degree in architecture from the Massachusetts Institute of Technology. He went overseas to France, Japan, and India after graduation, becoming an admirer of Eastern thought and religion. Not long after he returned to the United States, Japan bombed Pearl Harbor, and as a Japanese-American he was resettled in a camp in Idaho, where he practiced carpentry before being permitted to relocate to the arts colony at New Hope, Pennsylvania, where his family still lives.

Smalheer explained that Nakashima believed that a tree was intended to be a tree—and that therefore artisans who must transform it to other uses should, to the greatest extent possible, honor the tree's original purpose. If one follows the edge of the table from one end to the other, it is not in a straight line, but instead maintains the original contour of the tree. It flares at one end, where its roots might have begun, and it bulges slightly at the other, where its branches might have originated.

After being felled, the tree had been sliced lengthwise, but not entirely severed, so that its front and back could be laid side by side while still connected. These halves were reinforced by Nakashima in several places by wood patches described variously as "bow ties" or "butterflies." Although he was not the first to use the technique, they were a trademark of Nakashima's. Smalheer tells a story about a collector who ordered a table like Nakashima's. The artisan emphasized its grain and its natural contours, but the patron was dissatisfied. He wouldn't finalize the purchase until the artisan put in the butterfly patches.

The Nakashima conference table and chairs are found upstairs amid the museum's permanent collection. Ehringer said the museum has collected many more works than it ever can display at one time, even with two museum locations—and this is especially true because exhibits from around the world are continually being rotated in and out of the museum.

Another exhibit from the permanent collection displays 56 Chinese hat boxes in what Ehringer describes as a Xanadu type setting. Uniforms were required of officials serving the Qing Dynasty—the last dynasty to rule China—and these uniforms included hats. Depending on the office, the hats were of different shapes, with all being adorned with badges of office.

Families saved the hats in their boxes through the rise of Sun Yat-Sen and Chiang Kai-Shek. But after the Communists took control of the mainland—and especially during the Cultural Revolution—being proud that family members served the Imperial Household could bring suspicion, even censure, upon the owners of these hats. So, the hats either were destroyed or hidden. But the boxes were kept, because they still had utilitarian purposes—things could be stored in them. And it was these boxes that were collected by exhibition designer Peter Cohen, and eventually donated to the Mingei.

Tables, chairs, hat boxes—these are everyday objects, and yet those at the Mingei Museum are exquisite in their beauty. For a visit to the Mingei to be properly enjoyed, one should schedule enough time to survey the objects and savor their stories.

Model Railroad Museum, Balboa Park

San Diego Jewish World,
June 8, 2010

At the San Diego Model Railroad Museum you can enjoy trains that are 1/48 scale, 1/87 scale, and 1/160 scale among others. As you walk along the large exhibit cases observing to-scale scenes of San Diego and the Southwest, you also can learn about a Jewish railroad woman whose persistence was a model for other feminists who wanted equal opportunities.

Her name was Leah Rosenfeld and although she had more se-niority than the men who applied for the job of Southern Pacific station agent in Saugus, California (today part of city of Santa Clarita in Los Angeles County), she was denied the position. Southern Pacific said that the job would require her to occasion-ally work more than eight hours per day, and to lift articles weigh-ing more than 25 pounds. California's protective laws prohibited companies from giving jobs exceeding such weight and time limits to women.

According to a narrative board researched and written by Shirley Burman, Rosenfeld's male-dominated telegraphers union wasn't interested in coming to her aid. There was not much she could do about the matter until after Congress passed and President Lyndon B. Johnson signed into law the Civil Rights Act of 1964 prohibiting discrimination on the basis of race or sex.

Rosenfeld filed a complaint with the federal Equal Employment Opportunities Commission (EEOC), chaired in 1966 by Franklin D. Roosevelt Jr. The station master position, she wrote, was "denied to me and assigned to a junior employee because I am a woman and he is a man. The question of ability was not raised, the company stating only that position might require working more than 40 hours a week or lifting articles in excess of 25 pounds prohibited to women by California Industrial Act."

She said that while Southern Pacific had used that "excuse" to deny better paying jobs to women, when it came to undesirable jobs, the "prohibition is seldom enforced." She added that the discrimination worked a hardship against her; noting that "I pay the same for groceries as do men."

In 1971, "California's Protective Laws were declared unconstitutional; Leah had won her case," the narration continued. According to Judge Colleen W. McIlwirth, the decision not only helped the women of California, but by creating a precedent, it helped women throughout the United States.

The railroads did not treat women uniformly throughout its history—their hiring and promotion practices were influenced by pragmatism and work force availability. As early as the Civil War, Abbey Strubel was working as a telegrapher, even though alarmists "feared that the physical stamina and nervous systems of women would be wrecked if they operated machinery," according to the narrative.

"Isolated duty stations were preferred by many female operators because they were good places to raise children," it went on to say. "They could keep their eyes on the kids and still do the jobs."

In rural communities along the tracks, trains did not make regular stops. "Mistresses like Ina Adkins of Caliente, California, hung the outgoing mail on the mail crane to be grabbed by a hook on the moving post office car. After the train had passed, she picked up the thrown off incoming mail."

Englishman Fred Harvey in 1876 created a series of restaurants in Santa Fe train stations across the country, and "hired young girls between the ages of 18 and 30 of good character and who radiated an image of wholesomeness. The 'Harvey Girls' were more than waitresses; they were hostesses. The girls dressed in a simple black dress with a white neck collar and black bow with a starched white apron with no jewelry or make up. The Harvey Girls brought a civilizing influence to many communities with their good manners and social poise. Many married local ranchers, miners and railroaders."

An offshoot of the "Harvey Girl" program came in 1926 with the establishment of "Indian Detour Couriers"—sightseeing guides who took passengers from trains on detour excursions to break up their transcontinental trips. The women guides were called "couriers" with preferred hires being "college-educated women who had a knowledge of native people, languages, culture, and the landscape."

In 1935, another opportunity opened for women as "registered nurse stewardesses" on passenger trains. "The duties were to assist women and children and to attend to the needs of the elderly on cross-country journeys. The nurses were known for their intelligence and candid friendliness. Babies and small children required extra attention. Formula had to be made and bottles warmed while games kept small children amused on long journeys." Some railroads created programs in which little girls could be helpers as junior stewardess nurses.

Even before one enters the model railroad museum, one can pick up bits of railroading knowledge. On the bottom floor of the Casa de Balboa, which the museum shares with the archives of the San Diego Historical Society, one finds a semaphore—the old mechanical signaling device for railroads—with an explanation of how they worked.

191

The device standing beside the track had an upper and lower arm, with the top one telling about track conditions over the immediately upcoming mile-long block; and the lower about track conditions on the following mile-long block. The blade for the upcoming or "home block" was painted red; while the one for the "distant block" was yellow with a fishtail. Red, green, and yellow lights in connection with each arm indicated whether the train should stop, proceed with caution, or go.

Immediately inside the museum doors one encounters a scale model Cabrillo Yard on the right side of a walkway and the depiction of the San Diego & Arizona Eastern Railway exhibit on the left. Wending one's way around the San Diego and Arizona Eastern exhibit takes one to the Tehachapi Pass scale model and to the Pacific Desert Lines exhibit.

A sign board informs that "construction on all layouts began in 1982" with some 300 club members volunteering on the average of one night a week to construct the railroad. The volunteers put in over 10,000 hours a year from 1982 to 1987.

"There are approximately 115 scale miles of track in all the exhibits," said the sign. "This equates to about 6,560 actual feet or 1 ¼ miles" of model railroad, exclusive of the many feet of sidings and yard trackage.

Currently the San Diego Model Railroad Club is working on a diorama that will recreate, in miniature, downtown San Diego as it appeared in the 1950s. Club members are working from photographs in the San Diego Historical Society's archives and from Sanborn maps showing the location of each building.

Three Generations of Commanding Officers Probe *Star Trek's* Popularity

San Diego Jewish World,
July 22, 2011

Three commanding officers of the *Star Trek* television series pondered for a Comic-Con audience on Friday, July 22, what has made the science fiction show remain popular over four decades.

William Shatner joined Avery Brooks and Scott Bakula at a press conference at the San Diego Convention Center, headquarters for the annual Comic-Con fan fest. Each actor had played the commanding officer in a *Star Trek* series. Shatner was Captain James T. Kirk in the original series; Brooks was Commander Benjamin Sisco in *Star Trek: Deep Space Nine,* and Bakula was Capt. Jonathan Archer in *Star Trek: Enterprise.*

Their news conference was called to promote the documentary *Captains,* now showing on the premium cable channel Epix, in which Shatner conducts conversations with other *Star Trek* captains to probe their feelings about the series and some of their most memorable moments.

Shatner said that the show's popularity surpassed those "tale well told" shows which could be recounted the following day around the office water cooler, and touched something deeper. "There is the family—the family of players in each of our iterations," he said. The show captures their interactions. "The fact that they care for each other and that we were in this lonely environment and all we had was each other, I think, resonated," Shatner said.

Brooks, whose talents as a jazz musician were utilized in the documentary, agreed with Shatner, while suggesting that the show was "an affirmation of the ancient in modern ways." He said the show not only was imaginative, but was able to provoke imaginative responses from its audience. "It is the people who hold the connection," he said. "If you don't turn it on, it doesn't last for 44 years and counting."

Bakula said he was a fan of *Star Trek* long before he ever was cast as Captain Jonathan Archer—who, in an interesting twist of *Star Trek* chronology was a predecessor of Kirk's, rather than a successor.

"The reason we are all here is this man seated here and his group of players who created this mythology who captured us," said Bakula, indicating Shatner.

When he watched Shatner play Captain Kirk in the 1960s, he recalled, he was living in St. Louis, which he described as "a pretty white town, certainly where I was growing up, in my day. What the show represented was the way everyone treated everybody equally without question," he said. "They dealt with their emotional differences, but not other differences—no color, no anything—none of that existed.

194

"It blew all that stuff away . . . in the middle of the 60s in this country," Bakula continued. "And if you got on board with that, that to me was the ride . . . . If you got on board with that premise, none of that matters and we are going to reach out because the writers imagined it and we can hold that in our own bodies—that this is the future and that's a future that we want to be part of, and here we are. That's why I came to watch it."

Not only was it a realization of the Civil Rights dream of the 1960s, but in addition, Shatner suggested, *Star Trek* offered viewers the premise that mankind still would be alive in the future—that notwithstanding all the earthly conflicts, "we will find a way out."

'Liberation Moment' at Miramar National Cemetery Honors American Ex-POWs

San Diego Jewish World,
September 17, 2011

The first monument at the Miramar National Cemetery, which one day will be the final resting place for nearly a quarter million veterans, was dedicated on Friday, September 16, in honor of American Ex-Prisoners of War. Unveiled was a 15-foot-tall, seven-ton-statue, named "The Liberation Moment," sculpted by Richard Becker of Poway.

On hand to watch the unveiling was Anthony Principi, the former U.S. Secretary of Veteran Affairs in George W. Bush's administration, who said the statue depicts "the happiness of a hero who has finally broken free of the barbed wire boundaries that had kept him in prison." But viewers who gaze at the statue "will also see in the hero's emaciated body and ratted clothing, the hunger and deprivation prisoners of war have endured throughout our history simply for defending freedom for all Americans. In the hero's haunted gaze, we feel both his joy at being liberated and his sadness that some of those with whom he shared this captivity did not survive."

Within the base of the statue is a time capsule to be opened in 2045—100 years after the end of World War II. Among DVDs bearing the testimony of American former prisoners of war and books that some of them wrote, is one volume by Sy Brenner, 89, who sat in the front row for the outdoor ceremony. His book, *The Night I Got Killed*, tells of being a Jewish-American soldier who had to hide his religious identity from his Nazi German captors.

Brenner said he remembered the day of his own liberation from a prisoner of war camp near Stuttgart, Germany, "vividly."

"The guards took off from our prison camp two or three days before the American army came and I was wandering outside of the camp, and some French people told me that the American Army was near the administration building and I went there," Brenner related.

"And I saw the Nazi swastika flag coming down and the American flag going up, and they started playing 'The Star-Spangled Banner,' and I started crying. In fact, I was crying so hard my whole body was shaking. And I was thinking of my parents and wishing they were there to see that Nazi flag come down, and that everyone in the United States should see it come down."

For Thomas Crosby, junior commander of the San Diego Chapter of the American Ex-Prisoners of War, Liberation Day came across the world at a Japanese-run POW camp in the Philippines. His father, a General Electric employee, had been visiting headquarters in the United States when 8-year Crosby, his mother, sister, and grandmother were all captured by the Japanese, and separated for three years—with girls and women in one area of the camp, men in another, and boys in a third. There were 3,500 prisoners in all, 220 in the building where Crosby was kept prisoner.

"February 3rd, 1945, the day of liberation, the 1st Cav (1st Cavalry Division, an armored unit of the U.S. Army) spearheaded 100 miles down to rescue us, and the Japanese held us, 220 of us, hostage, and shot it out with the 1st Cav—65 of them," Crosby recalled. "Thirty-six hours later, after the shootout, we thought we were gone. Colonel Hiyashi wanted to trade us, the 220 of us, for their escort out to their front lines. They couldn't do that right away because the 1st Cav didn't have their reinforcements. When they did, they did what they said they were going to do—they marched them out. When they marched them out, we were free!"

Free, but far from healthy. As an 11-year-old, Crosby weighed only 48 pounds at the time of liberation. Among the adults, weight-losses of 50 to 60 pounds from malnutrition were not uncommon.

Crosby's 18-year-old grandson, Tommy, is of slender build. Three years ago, he modeled over several sessions for sculptor Becker, at one occasion holding the pose for the statue for nearly an hour. Watching the unveiling of the statue with his image portraying the agony and exhilaration of his grandfather, was a "great honor for me," Tommy Crosby said. "Everyone here who is an ex-POW has been through so much; this was an opportunity to be able to give back to them . . . ."

His girlfriend, Kari Hardisty of El Cajon, standing by him, told her reaction: "I was very proud. It's very exciting."

And his grandmother, Nancy Crosby, commented: "Today was really meaningful: I am fighting tears back. The meaning of this statue is so personal, and yet so personal for everyone here."

Grandpa Thomas, Father Thomas Jr., and Tommy Crosby have a proud family tradition. "All of us are adopted!" said the senior Crosby, whose special project was the time capsule.

With the time capsule scheduled to be opened 34 years from now—and grandchildren and great-grandchildren being asked to attend that ceremony—Crosby said he wondered how technology might change by 2045. Will they even be able to play the DVDs? He said he included a DVD player in the capsule, just to make sure that they could.

Steve Muro, undersecretary for Veteran Affairs in the Obama administration, said the Liberation Moment memorial, which has a POW/MIA flag flying near it, brought to mind for him a memorial he once saw in the Himalaya Mountains honoring the war dead of many nations. A legend on that monument read: "Tell them we gave our tomorrows, so you can have your todays."

A Visit to the House of Israel

San Diego Jewish World,
March 31, 2014

Having the pleasure of company from Israel, our correspondent Dorothea Shefer-Vanson and her husband Dr. Yigal Shefer of Mevasseret Zion, I made certain that our itinerary on Sunday, March 30, included some of the attractions of Balboa Park. In particular, I wanted them to see how Israelis and American Jews work together at the two-room House of Israel to make friends for Israel from among the thousands of tourists who visit Balboa Park, which is San Diego's premier cultural center.

On the patio, we found Grossmont College student Guy Yifrah, writing the names of visitors in Hebrew. It's always interesting for people who are unfamiliar with another alphabet—be it Hebrew, Chinese, Arabic, Farsi or what have you—to see what their own name looks like. Certainly Carolina Ramos, visiting from across the California-Mexico border from Mexicali, seemed pleased to see how "Carolina" was spelled, from right to left.

Barely did we go inside the cottage when we were greeted warmly and invited to taste burekas. In the House of Israel version, burekas are similar to spanakopita served at Greek restaurants. They were smilingly served up by Nechama Bunton, 7, a young member of Ohr Shalom Synagogue. Such a warm, beautiful smile! You cannot help answering this sweet girl with a smile of your own.

The children of Ohr Shalom Synagogue—which is located at 3rd and Laurel Streets, only a few blocks from the park (when the Laurel Street Bridge is open)—were among the featured exhibitors at the House of Israel. The mezuzot that they made at their school were on display along with an explanation that whereas the children crafted and painted the casings, the sacred words of Torah inside the mezuzot were not written on kosher parchment, so these *objets d'art* were not kosher for use on anyone's doorpost.

The House of Israel contains numerous video monitors with important information about modern Israel. Yet, what caught my eye was a time line shown to us by Sandy Golden, an American educator who occasionally favors *San Diego Jewish World* with her articles.

Dressed in a blue and white T-shirt adorned with the flag of Israel and that country's name in Hebrew letters, Golden explained that the timeline helps visitors become familiarized with the many epochs and rulers in the Land of Israel's history.

Speaking of timelines, Golden wanted all our *San Diego Jewish World* readers to know that at 2 p.m., Sunday, April 20, the House of Israel will be presenting its annual lawn program during which it will introduce visitors to the folk dances, songs and tastes of Israel.

Featured entertainer will be Yale Strom and his band Hot P'Strom'i. Strom, a violinist, ethno-musicologist, documentary film maker, and artist-in-residence for San Diego State University's Judaic Studies Department, will be joined on the program by young dancers from the Tarbuton, an institution in northern San Diego that promotes the Hebrew language and Israeli culture, as well as by other entertainers. No Jewish event would be complete without food—and Golden anticipates there will be plenty of that.

201

April 20 falls on Easter Sunday as well as in the middle of Passover, and if you already have plans for that time period, don't despair. You can see the regular exhibits of the House of Israel, and maybe even taste the burekas on any Sunday afternoon. The House of Israel is located among the cluster of international cottages located across the interior park road from the Organ Pavilion.

New Americans
Museum Debuts Again

San Diego Jewish World,
January 17, 2015

Nonagenarian Deborah Szekely has succeeded at many enterprises, most notably as a visionary behind the Rancho La Puerta spa and resort in Tecate, Mexico, and the Golden Door spas that even found their way onto cruise ships. In 2010, she experienced what seemed like a failure when the New Americans Museum closed at San Diego's Liberty Station as the civilianized Naval Training Center now is known.

Failure, however, is not in Szekely's personal vocabulary, and on Friday, January 16, she announced at a news conference the re-opening—or as she put it, the "reawakening"—of the New Americans Museum. As she did so, she stood in front of a wall entirely covered by a digitized image created by Los Angeles artist Carolyn Castaño invoking the bright colors of a Colombian rain forest, part of the reopened museum's initial look at the places from which New Americans come.

Other images in the exhibition of Castaño's works portrayed the impacts of warfare upon indigenous people, the works alluding to better-known images. For example, in one striking lightbox piece, with an effect similar to a stained-glass window, there is a portrait of a woman whose son has died in a conflict. If only she could have held him one last time. Castaño pictured her amid the tropical flora holding her dead son's body as the Virgin Mary does in Michelangelo's *Pieta*.

I asked Szekely, who is Jewish, about her own immigration experience, and she said that her father left what is today Poland to avoid being drafted into the Russian army for a lifetime of slave-like conditions. It was a familiar immigration story of the 20th Century, she said. Was her museum here on the West Coast inspired by the Ellis Island Museum in New York City's harbor? No, she responded, as nice a museum as Ellis Island is—that is a "museum of the past" whereas the New Americans Museum is a museum celebrating the present and the future.

What is it exactly that she wants people to take away from a visit to the museum? I asked her as we stood near some indigenous weavings of Colombian life, collected by Szekely between 1984 and 1991, while she served as president of the Inter-American Foundation. Descriptions of the collection were written by Patrick Breslin.

With some passion, she asked me to imagine a child whose immigrant parents are working at low-paying, menial jobs. The child feels mired in poverty, especially as he looks at what other children have, and he feels that he and his parents must be stupid. The child cannot imagine the difference between what his parents have now—tools for their jobs, a home of their own with running water and a refrigerator—and the utter poverty that they escaped when they left their native village. The child does not know that people in that village had no tools of their own, but had to share them; and did not have a steady supply of electricity for their homes, much less a working refrigerator.

People who live under such conditions can't afford on their own to immigrate to the United States; they get here with the help of their fellow villagers, who recognize the immigrants have special qualities that will help them to succeed in the United States, said

Szekely. Children of immigrants who come to the museum will learn and take pride in how far their families have come, in a material sense, and also learn about the beauty, the art, and the music that they brought with them to America, helping to further enrich a well-off country.

Szekely told the news conference that the museum will help to sponsor ceremonies for children recreating the oath-taking that their parents went through when they became citizens, to help the children comprehend the enormity of the process.

Leticia Gomez Franco, the museum's director of programs, said that the museum will host four exhibits a year, each dealing with a place of origin of immigrants, or a theme that illustrates the process of becoming Americanized. Overall, the museum will seek to depict the diversity of America's immigrants and the great value that diversity has for America.

In April, for example, the next exhibition will be one that had been at the National Museum of American Jewish History in Philadelphia examining how baseball—especially the love for it—has aided various immigrant groups in the naturalization process.

A fact sheet said New Americans Museum programming will focus on post World War II immigrant histories, with docent and school tours. Featured artists such as Castaño will give talks; there will be forums, and "Emerging Arts Leaders" internship programs. The museum, at 2825 Dewey Road, will be open Tuesdays through Sundays, from 10 a.m. to 4 p.m. weekdays and 11 a.m. to 3 p.m. weekends.

JFS Dedicates its Jacobs Family Campus

San Diego Jewish World,
January 31, 2016

Jewish Family Service on Sunday, January 31, dedicated a reconfigured and re-imagined campus intended to architecturally incorporate Jewish values and principles within its buildings and on its grounds.

At a ceremony to affix a mezuzah to a property at 8788 Balboa Avenue and to honor lead donors Joan and Irwin Jacobs, the CEO of the social service agency, Michael Hopkins, enthusiastically listed some of the refinements to the building and grounds that were inspired by JFS's building committee and board of directors, and by Safdie Rabines Architects.

Among these were a raised vegetable garden bed to complement the food pantry and kitchen from which JFS distributes and serves food to those in need; a walk-in cooler and freezer for longer and more effective food storage; a corner market, where needy JFS clients can load up on groceries, including kosher meats; solar tubes and panels to decrease dependence on fossil fuels; water-wise landscaping for conservation purposes; and a bioswale system designed to remove silt and other pollutants from rain water that runs off the property into storm drains and the ocean.

Coincidentally, it rained quite heavily during the indoor ceremony, but the deluge subsided when Rabbi Yael Ridberg of Congregation Dor Hadash was called upon to affix a mezuzah to one of the entrances to the JFS complex. The Reconstructionist rabbi noted that within the mezuzah on a piece of parchment are "some of the most powerful words in the Jewish tradition: the Jewish prayer of the *shm'a* which speaks to our obligation not only to be present in this moment but to connect with our past, our heritage, and to bequeath it to our children."

She added that mezuzot are appropriate on the doorposts of "any home, any structure that constitutes a home, whether it is a literal home where we raise a family, or a home where we help families be families, such as JFS."

JFS already had in its Turk Family Center, at 8804 Balboa Avenue, a large complex which served as both administrative headquarters and counseling center for the cradle-to-grave social service agency. About four years ago, the large building next to it at 8788 Balboa Avenue, came up for sale, and at first, board members and agency planners thought it might simply provide an opportunity to house JFS personnel who had been scattered around the county in rented quarters.

But, according to Hopkins, it dawned on key players that the acquisition could be far more than that: it could provide an opportunity to consolidate the administrative functions of JFS in the Turk Family Center, while creating for clients a special building designed to accommodate their needs for privacy, cheerfulness, and for collaboration among the social workers helping them with their problems.

With such goals in mind, he said, the new building emphasizes "natural light, open work spaces, beautiful artwork, the use of glass throughout our meeting spaces, and so many subtle touches that make this campus a positive space." A trellised walkway connects the two buildings which have been painted in complementary fashion.

Initially, it was estimated that the changes to the new building and old building as well as to the grounds might cost $6 million. With Irwin Jacobs, the co-founder of Qualcomm, and his wife Joan making the lead gift, the project was broadened in scope to include many features to respect the "dignity of our clients" and to make the entire complex "client-centered," according to Hopkins.

The complex of two buildings and surrounding grounds was officially named the Joan and Irwin Jacobs Campus in recognition of the lead gift, the amount of which was not specified. At the same time, JFS decided to do some "re-branding." It changed its motto from "One source for a lifetime of help" to "Moving Forward Together" which Hopkins said, recognizes the partnership between clients and the social service agency.

As an example of that partnership, he told the story of Abraham and Irena, an octogenarian couple with slim financial resources whom JFS helps to continue living in their home. He said that Irena visited the corner market and asked where the kosher meat section was. It was a detail which JFS had left unattended, but afterwards the agency made arrangements with Ralph's Market in La Jolla to obtain kosher cuts for the corner market. Provision of kosher meat will help not only the couple in question, but other JFS clients who observe the dietary laws.

Welcomed to the speaker's podium with a standing ovation from donors, staff members, and community partners, Joan and Irwin Jacobs kept their remarks brief.

"I think Irwin puts my name first on these buildings because he wants me to speak first," Joan Jacobs quipped. "You know a building is a wonderful thing to have but it is so important to have the right people running the organization that the building is in. That is one of the reasons that Irwin and I are so fond of JFS. We have always admired the work that is done here, and in the community, and that is why we are really happy to support this building and all of you here to carry on the great work that you are doing."

Irwin Jacobs noted that nobody knew initially that the building at 8788 Balboa would come up for sale, but when it did, JFS's staff and supporters launched themselves into action. "In business I have always been a great believer in being optimistic," he said. "An opportunity comes up and even if you didn't plan that far ahead, let's be in a position to move quickly."

The Qualcomm co-founder said that providing food for the needy is an important cause for him. He and Steve Cushman have jointly funded the Jacobs and Cushman San Diego Food Bank, and Jacobs said that "one of the things I checked there was that they work closely with JFS."

He added: "There are still many things that need to be accomplished, but it is great to see the kind of support, activity and leadership addressing the problems." He added that he planned to be associated with JFS for the long term.

Meg Goldstein, the chair of the JFS board, commented that, "Like any large construction project, this undertaking is still a work in progress. Though the staff have actually been serving our clients here for more than two months, we are still waiting for building and donor signage . . . and even some of our furniture."

Hopkins, saying it's always a challenge to find a gift for people who already have everything, presented the Jacobs with a plaque simulating the marker that will identify the Jacobs Family Campus. Besides the "Jacobs Family Campus" name, the plaque bore the inscription: "In gratitude for your leadership and partnership."

Israeli Rain Barrel System on Trial at 3 Schools

San Diego Jewish World,
February 1, 2016

Fifth graders at the Benjamin Franklin STEAM Magnet Elementary School on Monday, February 1, helped to explain to the news media how a low-tech Israeli invention will help their school conserve rainwater, and may prove to be an important tool in California's fight against periodic droughts.

STEAM is an acronym for Science, Technology, Engineering, Art and Mathematics, and Benjamin Franklin Elementary—named for the 18th Century American statesman and inventor who did some playing in rain himself—caters to students who are interested in developing their skills in these areas. The U.S. Israel Center on Innovation and Economic Sustainability at UCSD's Rady School of Management helped arrange for Franklin Elementary to become one of three pilot sites in San Diego County for a rain barrel system that separates water from sediment and other debris, thereby clarifying the water sufficiently to be pumped to toilets for flushing.

Rainwater-using toilets could be a possibility in the future of Franklin Elementary School and Pacific Beach Middle School, but for the time being at least, the roof runoff water will be used to irrigate vegetable gardens maintained by students on the campuses. At the Encinitas School District Farm Laboratory, which is the third pilot school in San Diego County, indoor plumbing has been configured to permit the rainwater to be used for toilet flushing, according to Susan Lapidus, executive director of the U.S. Israel Center.

"We have been learning about water and water conservation for the last month or two," commented Ben Kleinpastor, a 5th grader. "It's really important to conserve water because we are in a drought currently. We want to conserve water so we don't run out of water."

His classmate Scott Impham added: "I think the rain barrels are a really good thing for our school . . . . Like in the slideshow that [Israeli inventor Amir Yechieli] showed us, there was really dirty water, so he created this rain barrel which helps our school and helps us conserve."

Besides involving the students with problem-solving water technology, the three large rain barrels installed at the school in San Diego's City Heights neighborhood will serve as canvases for water conservation-oriented student art projects.

Ethan Le, another fifth grader in the class taught by faculty member Rick Froehbrodt, explained that the students intend to paint on one a waterfall, on another a pond where animals come to drink, and on the third a scene evoking the time and effort people in some developing nations must expend just to fetch water.

Yechieli, an Israeli inventor who has installed his rainwater system in more than 150 Israeli schools, said that whereas rain barrels have been in use for centuries, the problem always has

211

been that they collect sediment and debris and eventually become unusable. He said that instead of a flat bottom, the barrels or tanks that he has developed have a "very efficient" round bottom.

"The round bottom tank with an outlet at the bottom proved to be a very efficient way to remove all the sediments that accumulate in the tank," he said. "The tank never, never gets dirty. After two or three days when you flush out the dirt, the column of water in the tank is totally clean and suitable for indoor [toilet] use."

He added: "you can refill the tanks as many times as rain comes during the winter."

Yechieli said that at Israeli schools, and probably at American schools as well, 90 percent of the water usage is for flushing toilets, and only 10 percent for handwashing or drinking water or other uses. If systems are used in which rainwater is cleaned to government-required levels for flushing, a tremendous amount of water can be saved. For the 150 Israeli schools now using the system, he said, this "amounts to millions of cubic meters per year."

Don Whisman, the principal of Franklin Elementary (who occasionally dresses up as Benjamin Franklin to dramatize a lesson), said the mission of his school is to teach its students "critical thinking, problem solving, and how to solve real-life situations. And we try to use 'design thinking' in our learning here. Amir has modeled for them how to use design thinking to solve a problem we have here in California, and they have in Israel."

Whisman added that the pilot project "aligns well with the Next Generation Science Standards which our school district is one of the first in the state to implement. . . . A lot of the fifth-grade standards have to do with water conservation and human impact."

Froehbrodt commented that the students in his class have been "focused in on the understanding of the effects of pollution on our watershed, and the effects of water scarcity around the world." The rainwater project enables his students to "see first-hand how we can collect water, how we can conserve and reuse the water that is available to us, and give them a tangible project . . . ."

Whisman noted that UCSD graduate students "helped develop curriculum to go with the rain barrels which Mr.Froehbrodt will use in class. We are doing surveys pre and post to see how their (the fifth graders') attitudes change. We're also doing surveys at control schools to see how our kids compare to those in schools that don't have a rain barrel system."

Yechieli told *San Diego Jewish World* that roof runoff systems for an average size school cost approximately $10,000 U.S. to build and install.

Gravitating to the Familiar at the Fleet

San Diego Jewish World,
April 6, 2017

While I gravitated on Wednesday, April 5, to an exhibit featuring the image of Albert Einstein and another portraying the cells that I imagine Jonas Salk grappled with while developing the vaccine against polio, my grandchildren—Sky, 10, Brian, 8, and Sara, 6—were transfixed by a room filled with toys patented in the late 1950s by the Kristiansen/Christiansen family of Denmark.

For well more than an hour, I wondered if my grandchildren would get around to exploring anything else at the Reuben H. Fleet Science Center in Balboa Park, so happy were they fitting regular-sized LEGOs together on kid-sized tables or jumbo LEGOs on the floor in the "Fit-A-Brick Build Zone."

With their grandma, and Sara's and Brian's mom and dad watching the children at their creative play, I visited the other exhibits and then came back to find my grandchildren still absorbed in their activity. I marveled at this because there are plenty of LEGOs at Brian's and Sara's house, as well as at Sky's, so fitting the bricks together was no novelty for any of them. Yet, the LEGO's had a near magnetic allure.

While they concentrated on what was both enjoyable and familiar, I studied a series of images that had been taken through an electron microscope, and later enhanced, that introduced viewers to the structure of viruses, how they wreak their havoc inside the human body, and how the body's immune system try to fight them off. The large, colorized photographs, isolating these phenomena almost seemed as if they belonged in an art museum, rather than a science museum, but more and more today these disciplines seem to complement each other.

In an explanatory panel for one photograph, written by Arthur J. Olson of the Scripps Research Institute, viewers are informed that "four different components combine to form this hollow shell of poliovirus. The four components, colored blue, yellow, red and green in this picture, assemble in a very ordered way to form the virus particle.

The storyboard continued: "The bumps on the outer surface match up with proteins on the surface of the cells the virus infects. Once drawn into the host cell, the shell opens up to release the genetic material carried in the central cavity. The viral genes take control of the host cell, turning it into a virus-making machine. The infected host cells stop performing their normal job and symptoms appear in the infected person; the infected cells eventually die. This virus causes poliomyelitis, a rare and dangerous disease . . . ."

Not far away, a light portrait of Einstein—created by punching holes into dark material to allow a light source to shine through—offered a lesson about perception.

If one looks at the Einstein picture up close, one cannot make out his face; all one sees is an undifferentiated series of dots. But stand back some feet, and Einstein's face–comprised of 1200 pixels ranging from white to black with seven shades of gray in between—becomes quite evident.

A storyboard explained:

"Computer monitor screens that convey vast amounts of detailed information, have anywhere from a few hundred thousand to over a million pixels, and each pixel can have 256 levels of brightness. Compare this with the information contained in the Einstein portrait made of holes; 1200 pixels, each with 9 levels of brightness. That we can recognize Einstein's face with so little information points out how remarkable are the human powers of pattern recognition.

"How does our brain process so little information and come up, instantly, with a detailed representation of a particular face? The prevalent model is that the brain functions much like a computer that passes information simultaneously along a large number of connections among brain cells. Our brain has 10 to the 11th power cells (100 billion) and each cell has about a thousand connections to the other cells. These connections, which can have varying levels of strength, characterize the working of the brains. The simultaneous (also called parallel) style of computing of the brain is different and faster than the sequential (or serial) operation of ordinary computers."

On reflection, my activity and those of my grandchildren were not so different. They happily focused on something they knew and enjoyed—LEGO's—and I did the same thing, gravitating towards stories with a "Jewish angle." Einstein and Salk were both famed Jewish scientists.

Eventually, our family migrated together to the Science Center's IMAX Theatre where, on its 76-foot wraparound screen, we watched *Dream Big: Engineering Our World,* in which we learned how engineers help us solve many of the problems we face in this world. For example, we saw a bridge being built over a wild river in Haiti that enabled children to go safely to the school in the next village; learned that spiraling construction on sky scrapers can increase wind resistance; and were educated about making structures earthquake resistant in the San Francisco Bay Area. Along with

216

this, we watched as a robotics team from an Arizona high school, using only the simplest materials, was able to build an underwater robot that outperformed one assembled by students at the Massachusetts Institute of Technology (MIT).

The movie perhaps motivated the younger set of our family to explore other exhibits, including one extensive one in which visitors go from room to room to solve a Sherlock Holmes mystery. As for the oldest guy in the bunch—me —I was content, following a bite to eat, to sit at the outdoor tables of the Science Center's café and watch other visitors to Balboa Park ride in vintage electric carts near the large Bea Evenson Fountain.

San Diego Schools Salute Conductor David Amos

San Diego Jewish World,
April 27, 2017

D avid Amos, who is best known to the Jewish community as the conductor of the Tifereth Israel Community Orchestra and as a music columnist for *San Diego Jewish World,* on Thursday evening received a plaque naming the orchestra pit at Patrick Henry High School in his honor, and became the namesake for an annual award that will be given each year to a qualifying orchestra or band teacher in the San Diego Unified School District.

Amos was the first music teacher at Patrick Henry High School, serving from 1968 to 1971 in classrooms and in what some people called the "cafeterium" but which he dubbed the "auditeria"—a cafeteria with a small stage appended to it, on which musical and dramatic programs were presented until a performing arts center was inaugurated last November at the high school.

David Berman, who headed a drive with his wife Sharlene to raise $20,000 to have the orchestra pit named for Amos, presented to Amos a plaque that read in part: "In recognition of lifetime achievement in conducting symphony orchestras around the world and producing great recordings in classical music and imparting musical knowledge to the youth of the community, his friends and admirers present this tribute on the occasion of the dedication of the PHAME concert hall orchestra pit named in his honor on April 27, 2017."

Kevin Beiser, a trustee of the San Diego Unified School District, also announced that "the board of education is going to be honoring David Amos's legacy with an annual award to a band or orchestra teacher every year that embodies the values and passion of David Amos.

"The David Amos Music Award will be a district wide recognition to keep his legacy forever," said Beiser.

The awards were announced at a reception for donors at the school's new performing arts center in ceremonies that also included the school's principal Listy Gillingham and former school board trustee Katherine Nakamura, who now serves as president of the Cowles Mountain Community Foundation which to date has raised $400,000 for the PHAME (Patrick Henry Arts, Media and Entertainment) Performing Arts Center.

The current, 20-year director of instrumental music at Patrick Henry High School, Matthew Kalal, led the school's band in a rendition of Charles Carter's "Sonata for Winds," and later conducted the high school musicians in renditions of the school's alma mater and fight song, both of which were originally composed by Amos and given a new arrangement by Kalal 10 years ago.

In his response, Amos mixed humorous anecdotes with a plea for more support for music in the schools.

He told how in the early years of the school's music program, band members sold light bulbs to illuminate the need for music. An incentive to sell as many light bulbs as possible was allowing the winner of the contest to push a cream pie right into Amos's face.

Recalled Amos: "The trouble is two or three things went wrong. First of all, I had a beard. Second of all, they kept the can for the spray of the cream at the school during the weekend, so it rotted, because it needed to be refrigerated. I got this stinking mess on my face at the same hour that my daughter was being born at the hospital. I had to go home and take a shower, but I continued to smell for three days—that stuff wouldn't go away!"

On a more serious note, Amos said that ever since Californians enacted property tax cuts in the form of the Howard Jarvis Initiative (Proposition 13) in 1978, schools have been hard-pressed to support music programs. This, he added, led to a generation of adults who never received music education, and whose children are now in school. Amos said many of these adults, never having benefitted from music programs, don't understand the value they can be to their children.

"So, we have to try to close that gap by making good music and making it available so youngsters in junior high and high schools have instruments, have good instrumental and choral music education and that they can create love for it [music] for the future. This country, in general, will have less problems, less crime, more respect for the arts, if we give music its proper place!"

Amos said he treasures his time at Patrick Henry as much as he has valued subsequent stages of his career, including conducting the Jewish Community Center Orchestra, which later became the Tifereth Israel Community Orchestra; and making numerous CDs with professional orchestras around the world, among them the London Symphony and the Israel Philharmonic.

Nakamura mentioned that one upcoming expense will be for "a net" to cover the orchestra pit so no one falls into it from the stage. This prompted Amos, a notorious punster, to comment the program already had "Annette"—a reference to actress Annette Bening, a Patrick Henry High School graduate and contributor to PHAME.

220

Jewish Community Day with the Padres

San Diego Jewish World,
August 20, 2017

The Jewish community day at Petco Park would have been better if the Padres had won instead of losing 4-1 to the Washington Nationals, but still there was much to enjoy: New hats with Padres inscribed in Hebrew and the Flag of Israel emblazoned above the bill; kosher hot dogs, and lots, but lots, of schmoozing.

There were a few special moments, such as when Rabbi Leonard Rosenthal, the emeritus spiritual leader of Tifereth Israel Synagogue, raised his hands and bestowed the three-part rabbinic blessing on the Padres Swinging Friar, a character made out to look like one of the Franciscan monks who used to habituate the San Diego Mission.

And there was the opportunity to see the new national president of Jewish National Fund, Sol Lizerbram, and his wife Lauren, take a seat in the upper stands in right field. On Monday evening, Lizerbram will have pre-inaugural ceremonies in San Diego to celebrate his forthcoming installation as JNF's first president to be elected from any city on the West Coast. He lives in San Diego County.

Other high points included a group of Jewish synagogues and institutions handing out literature and souvenirs at the "park in the park"—an area where kids can roll down the grass, and visitors can take photos of a statue of the late Hall of Famer Tony Gwynn, who played his entire Major League Baseball career in a Padres uniform.

Jewish men passing the Chabad tables were offered the opportunity by Rabbi Zalman Carlebach to don *tefillin* if they hadn't already. Carlebach led those who accepted—including this reporter—in the traditional prayers.

Various kinds of swag were offered at other tables. Beth Jacob Congregation offered *tzedakah* boxes. So did the Jewish National Fund. StandWithUs had pens, sunglasses, keychains, and various useful trinkets.

At all the tables, it seemed, there were pamphlets and brochures.

Nancy and I met the red-shirted members of the Tifereth Israel Synagogue Men's Club before the game and we all sat together in a block of seats. Our synagogue's new rabbi, Philadelphia Phillies loyalist Joshua Dorsch, and family joined us. Our grand-niece Jessica met the blue-shirted group of 20-somethings who recently had gone on a Birthright/Taglit trip to Israel.

Other groups in our immediate vicinity included members of Chabad of La Costa and Adat Yeshurun Synagogue. Among the latter group, I saw Jack Forman sitting with his Jewish Little Pal.

La Jolla Walkway Named for Walter Munk, 100

San Diego Jewish World,
October 18, 2017

Famed oceanographer Walter Munk predicted that a beach walkway named for him October 18, 2017, on the eve of his 100th birthday won't survive as long as he has unless nations cooperate to fight climate change by converting fossil fuels into renewable energy.

At a ceremony in Kellogg Park at the La Jolla shore, Munk, whose centennial birthday was October 19, 2017, predicted the beach and walkway along La Jolla's prime coastline will be inundated by rising seas if matters continue as they are. This scientist who successfully predicted wave heights in time for Allied landings in North Africa and subsequently at Normandy during World War II said that just as military officials and scientists of Allies working together produced the miracle of the successful landings, so too must scientists and political leaders forge a miracle of cooperation to stave off rising seas caused by climate change.

Similarly, Munk noted, scientists had worked together "to understand the acoustics of the ocean" to develop protective programs for warding off Nazi German submarines—another project in which he was a principal.

"We had cooperation between different parties of the United States; we had good relations with our Allies. We need to do the same kind of thing now to get a similar miracle," added Munk, who is known popularly as the "Einstein of Oceanography."

Like Einstein, Munk was a Jewish refugee from Nazi-controlled Europe. He left his native country of Austria, first for Norway, and later for the United States, arriving in La Jolla 75 years ago.

"On the scientific side, we need to learn how to convert fossil energy to renewable energy," Munk continued in a brief talk preceding the unveiling of a Walter Munk Way sign on the walkway. "It's a tremendous job but I really believe it can be done with a similar effort that we had in World War II." He added that a spirit of bipartisanship is essential in the United States, and, "We need to have good relations with the United Nations and our Allies."

Munk concluded his remarks by stating that it is his "fervent hope" that there will be a 100th anniversary for the new Walter Munk Way.

On the dais to celebrate Munk's lifelong accomplishments were three elected officials and two higher education administrators. The elected officials were San Diego City Councilwoman Barbara Bry (whose district includes La Jolla); State Assemblyman Todd Gloria (D-San Diego), and San Diego County Supervisor Ron Roberts. Education officials were UC San Diego Chancellor Pradeep. K. Khosla, and Vice Chancellor Margaret Leinen, who serves as director of Scripps Institution of Oceanography, with which Munk still is formally affiliated. Munk's second wife, Mary, who is heading a project to create a large outdoor display of the sea life that lives in the underwater La Jolla Grand Canyons, also spoke briefly.

Bry led off the parade of accolades for Munk by noting that the oceanographer participated in a 2015 study by the Vatican that led to Pope Francis's encyclical decrying man-made climate change. She noted that Munk has been a leading scientist in humanity's understanding of "ocean currents, tides, deep ocean mixing, wind waves, tsunamis, seismic waves, and the Earth's rotation" and related that his former students recently discovered pygmy devil rays in the Sea of Cortez which they gave the scientific name of *Mobula munkiana* in his honor.

While Munk basked in the accolades and the warm California sun, Chancellor Khosla related three brief anecdotes that he said typified the oceanographer. On one occasion, he said, Munk had discovered new information on an oceanographic matter that he wanted to add as a correction to a previously written paper. The problem, said Munk, "I don't know if people take corrections after 40 years." He was the only surviving author of the paper that had been co-written with other scientists. Khosla suggested Munk's desire to keep improving upon knowledge is one of many strong points.

A second anecdote concerned a time Khosla made a trip to Arizona, where he met a 91-year-old retired physicist. Inquiring if the physicist knew of Munk, the physicist responded that not only did he know of him, but that back in his student days, he already had regarded Munk as an icon in his field.

The third anecdote concerned Dartmouth College's desire to present Munk with its highest academic honor. Munk shyly said there might be a problem with that: Dartmouth had awarded him the same honor 40 years previously.

Dr. Leinen, the current director of Scripps Institution of Oceanography, recalled that it was *The New York Times* that had dubbed Munk the "Einstein of Oceanography." It was his wave predictions that helped the Allies land safely at Normandy, his studies that developed warning systems for tsunamis, and his tenacity that gave World War II Allies the edge in submarine warfare. Munk personifies the concept of a "living legend."

Assemblyman Gloria said that in the Legislature, elected officials like to play the game, "Who is the most famous person in your district?" In cities to the north of San Diego, members of the Legislature mention Facebook's Mark Zuckerberg, television personality Oprah Winfrey, and various Hollywood celebrities. Gloria said he proudly claims Munk as his most famous constituent. He added that the state of California is inspired by Munk's vision, having set for itself a goal to be powered 100 percent by renewable energy.

Supervisor Roberts commented that there already is a Neptune Street in La Jolla. It's only appropriate that there be a Walter Munk Way because "he's done a lot more for the oceans than Neptune!" Roberts quipped.

Munk took home from the ceremony a collection of plaques and resolutions from the U.S. Senate (Dianne Feinstein), U.S. House of Representatives (Scott Peters), California State Senate (Toni Atkins), Assembly (Gloria), County Board of Supervisors (Roberts), and City Council (Bry).

He also was serenaded as an "elder of the sea" by Kimoteo Kupahulehua from Maui, Hawaii, who ceremonially blew a conch shell in his honor.

Tifereth Israel Prayer Space Named for Aaron Gold

San Diego Jewish World,
March 11, 2018

The prayer space within the Tifereth Israel Synagogue sanctuary that the late Rabbi Dr. Aaron Gold helped to design and where he spent much of his life leading prayer services, now has two new names. One is *Ohel Aharon,* or the Tent of Aaron; the other is "The Rabbi Aaron S. Gold *Beit Tefilah,*" meaning the Rabbi Aaron S. Gold Prayer Space.

While the prayer space is named for Gold, the overall sanctuary still is named for previous donors, the late Charles and Ethel Silverman.

The names honoring Gold were announced during the Conservative synagogue's annual Abraham and Anne Ratner Scholar-in-Residence Weekend during which Cantor Hanan Leberman, an American who made Aliyah to Israel, spoke and chanted during Friday evening and Saturday morning Shabbat services, then concertized with Hebraic, Broadway, and operatic tunes on Saturday evening, March 10.

Rabbi Leonard Rosenthal, who succeeded Rabbi Gold as spiritual leader of Tifereth Israel Synagogue, and is now himself retired, said Gold's widow, Jeanne, told him she would like to make a substantial gift to the synagogue, located at 6660 Cowles Mountain Boulevard.

"We searched for an appropriate way to honor her gift and Rabbi Gold's Legacy and concluded that his presence was most felt and he affected the most people here in this sanctuary," Rosenthal said. "It was here that he most shared his insight, knowledge, analysis, warmth, and love. This sanctuary was his spiritual home."

Rosenthal added that, "We will no longer refer to this space as our 'sanctuary,' but rather as 'Ohel Aharon' or 'The Rabbi Aaron S. Gold Beit Tefilah.' I cannot think of a more beautiful way to acknowledge, remember, and celebrate his legacy."

Further, said Rosenthal, "Tonight [March 9, 2018], for the first time in *Ohel Aharon*, may all of us be inspired to be disciples of Aaron, loving peace and pursuing peace, loving humankind and bringing them close to Torah."

In response, Jeanne Gold paid tribute to Cantor Leberman; to Rabbi and Judy Rosenthal, who chaired the weekend; to Rabbi Joshua Dorsch, who is her late husband's second successor, and to synagogue senior staff members Lori Kurtz and Beth Klareich, who handled the many internal arrangements to make the weekend possible.

In an interview afterwards, Jeanne Gold said her gift, part of which was immediate and part of which is reserved for the synagogue after her death, will help to underwrite the salaries of rabbis, and generally to help in the running of the synagogue. "It is a gift in perpetuity, an endowment," she said. Previously she had established in Rabbi Gold's memory a scholarship fund enabling students Tifereth Israel teens to travel to Israel.

"The phrase 'Ohel Aharon' is so beautiful to me; it's an idea that evolved," Jeanne Gold said. "A few months ago, it simply would have been the sanctuary dedicated in memory of Aaron Gold." She said the new name will be placed on a double-door entrance to the *Ohel Aharon*, and also on a plaque inside.

She recalled that her husband had been very much involved in the design of the sanctuary, which seats some 300 persons but can be made into a much larger space, seating up to 1,500, by opening the movable wall between it and the social hall. He was particularly proud of the stained-glass windows depicting the Burning Bush behind the pulpit that were designed by artist Leslie Perlis and of a special cabinet containing a Holocaust Torah, which Jeanne played a role in transporting.

She said that while she was working at Ryan Aircraft she received a call from her husband, the rabbi, saying that a Torah once seized by the Nazis and later liberated to a synagogue and museum in Westminster, England, was soon to land at San Diego International Airport. Would she please pick it up. "Having it in the back seat of my car was a very moving experience," she said.

Today, the Torah is covered in a special mantle designed by the artist Jackie Jacobs, depicting butterflies rising from a darkened field surrounded by barbed wire into the sunlight of freedom—an homage to the poem 'I Never Saw Another Butterfly' by Pavel Friedmann, who was incarcerated at the Theresienstadt ghetto and concentration camp.

Of her late husband, she said, "He was a visionary, so creative, always looking for something else, something beautiful, something meaningful."

The ceiling of the sanctuary is made of cedar, recalling the Cedars of Lebanon of the Bible.

In that sanctuary, she said, Rabbi Gold celebrated his 13th or bar mitzvah year as a rabbi, in a ceremony attended by some of his Orthodox relatives from the East Coast. One member of the family, she remembered, sat in Gold's office during the service rather than sit with the congregation because it had mixed seating for men and women.

"I remember the special celebrations at our synagogue as well, for example, the time that Ezra Taft Benson, head of the Mormon Church came to visit; and another time when Aaron exchanged visits with (Roman Catholic) Bishop Leo Maher."

Maher delivered a sermon in the Ohel Aharon, and Gold preached a return sermon at the Church of the Immaculata on the University of San Diego campus.

Because the dedication ceremony was held during the intermission of Leberman's concert, Gold modestly decided not to take too much time in her remarks, but had she more time, she said, she would have retold the story of how she met the rabbi.

She said her Aunt Rose and some of her friends had formed a "Let's Get Jeanne Fixed Up" fan club, and told her about Rabbi Gold, who then was serving as an associate rabbi at Tifereth Israel's previous home at 30th and Howard Streets.

"I waited a few weeks and he never called, but one night, while I was on my way to a meeting, he called me," Jeanne related. "We talked several hours, and he told me how busy he was—even reading his schedule. That Friday night I went to his synagogue with my friend Sharon, and that happened to be the ORT Shabbat [ORT is a Jewish organization specializing in job training] so there were many women there who weren't members. An elderly man, Cantor Eugene Goldberger, came on the pulpit, and I thought to myself, 'He's too old for me,' but then a younger man came on, and I thought he was gorgeous. At the end of the services, there was a receiving line, and I waited until the end of the line. I said, 'Hello Rabbi, I'm Jeanne Weissbuch,' and Joel Sucov who was behind me joked, "And I'm her chaperone." The rabbi said, "Can I take over for the evening?" He told me during the Oneg Shabbat that he was expected to mingle with the congregants so when someone came up to talk to him, I would walk away. When the evening closed, he asked me out for the following night, Saturday night, after Shabbat."

They went with some friends to an engagement party, where, after being asked to do so, Gold gave a toast to the newly engaged couple. "He gave a glowing toast after which they all applauded, and I was totally impressed. I said to him, 'You know Rabbi, I would like you to officiate at my wedding.' And he said, 'How do you know, I won't be the groom?'"

They met before Thanksgiving, they became engaged the following Valentine's Day, and were married in June, time enough for Jeanne to observe the planning and dedication that went into the creation of the synagogue and education center on Cowles Mountain.

Gold's father composed liturgical music, and according to Jeanne, the son would frequently sing or hum it as they drove together in a car. The evening in which Cantor Leberman, occasionally in duet with soprano Carolyne DalMonte, and accompanied on piano by Janie Prim, was in Jeanne's estimate "the perfect occasion" for the dedication. "Aaron would have loved it."

Gold served the congregation for 18 years, becoming its emeritus rabbi in 1992.

Unable to stay retired, he subsequently served in the pulpits of Ner Tamid Synagogue in Poway, Beth Sholom in Chula Vista, and Beth Emet in Anaheim. He died in 2001 in the San Diego suburb of La Mesa, where he and Jeanne made their home.

Community Says Farewell to Gussie Zaks, z"l

San Diego Jewish World,
March 13, 2018

At a packed funeral service Tuesday, March 13, at Tifereth Israel Synagogue, the community bade a final farewell to San Diego's First Lady of Holocaust Survivors, Gussie Zaks.

The longtime lecturer, organizer, and educator—who had told her story of survival countless times to students, club members, law enforcement, and numerous disparate groups—died at Seacrest Village on Sunday, March 11, at the age of 92, leaving two children, four grandchildren, and seven great-grandchildren.

According to her daughter, Marcia Rosenberg, "Gussie," as everyone knew her, considered each one of her descendants, and their successes, her "revenge against Hitler."

The service was conducted by Rabbi Joshua Dorsch of Tifereth Israel Synagogue, with assistance from retired Rabbi Emeritus Martin S. Lawson of Temple Emanuel and Rabbi Emeritus Leonard Rosenthal of Tifereth Israel Synagogue. The latter rabbi delivered the main eulogy, which was followed by emotional goodbyes to their mother from Rosenberg and Jack Morgenstern. Later, Gussie was buried besides her late husband and fellow Holocaust survivor, Mike Zaks, at El Camino Memorial Park.

Rosenthal told of the legend of the *lamed vavniks,* the 36 people upon whose good deeds the world continues to exist. They are not aware that they are among the 36, Rosenthal said, and "we may not assign individuals living in our midst to this rare company of spirits, but we do recognize that there are people who possess a certain quality of personality which creates a climate about them, and helps to sustain the community of which they are a part. Our beloved Gussie Zak . . . was such a person."

Born in Klobuk, Poland, Gussie suffered from anti-Semitism from an early age, Rosenthal said. "When she was in school, there were only two Jewish kids. She remembered how the teacher singled them out and wouldn't let them sing, because they were Jews. . . . In nearby Czestochowa, there was a shrine to a painting known as the Black Madonna. Every year there was a festival and all of the school children would go up to the shrine and celebrate. But not Gussie, and her Jewish friend. They were made to attend school that day, which consisted of them waiting by themselves until everyone else returned from the celebration."

The experience that Gussie and her husband had at the hands of Poles "puts the lie to the Polish government's recent attempt to white wash the participation of Poles in the Shoah," Rosenthal declared. Furthermore, he said, "When Mike and Gussie took their family back to Poland in 2003 to see the place in which they grew up (Mike had also lived in Klobuk before moving to Czestochowa), she insisted on visiting the church with the Black Madonna. She told her family, 'before I die I want to see that damn black Madonna.' She went into the church and saw a reproduction painted on black velvet, the original having been returned to Mexico. She walked in among the tourists, gazed at it, walked out, and said, 'Now I can die in peace.'"

However, anti-Semitism continued to dog her steps on her visit to Poland, Rosenthal reported. The owner of Gussie's previous home refused to let her see it, maintaining falsely that Gussie had never lived there. A neighbor, however, said she remembered Gussie and her family very well. "One of the last stops on the trip was Krakow, and as was her custom each week, Gussie wanted to have her hair done. Marcia and Jack dropped her off and went off to a local square to have coffee. When they came back, they found Gussie screaming in Polish at the other clients. The woman in the shop had asked her why she was visiting Poland. She told them she wanted to show her children where she grew up. The woman said to her, 'You will find that everything is much better now, now that we have gotten rid of the Jews.' Having experienced Polish anti-Semitism early in her life, Gussie was not going to tolerate it now and gave those woman an earful."

On that same trip, Gussie visited Treblinka where she understood that her parents and most of her six siblings has been murdered in the gas chamber. Gussie, youngest in the family, had been sent to a work camp—a "miracle," that she believed had enabled her to survive. Later she was among 1,000 women who were marched for 12 weeks through the frigid European winter and "then loaded onto box cars for the ride to the Bergen-Belsen death camp," Rosenthal said. "She was emaciated, weak, and only survived because other women propped her up to make her look taller and healthier than she was. Right before she was liberated by English soldiers, she said she was 99 percent dead. 'Nobody could react when the English soldiers came to our barracks to tell us we were free.'"

In the aftermath of the Holocaust, she contracted typhus which killed four of her hospital roommates, but somehow survived. She moved to Sweden where she further recuperated and learned that an Aunt Karola in Belgium still was alive. Karola adopted Gussie, and the two women remained close until Karola's death a few years ago.

Gussie's first marriage was to Abe Morgenstern, another Holocaust survivor. Their son Jack was born in Europe. After learning that she had a cousin in New York, the family was able to resettle in the United States in 1951.

At that point, said Rosenthal, "Life was not easy for Gussie. She didn't know the language or the culture. She worked in a sweat shop to help support her family. Before Marcia was born, she put Jack in a yeshiva. After work she would pick him up, and then go home to make dinner. It was a lot for her, but she rejoiced in being alive and raising a family.

"She was very insecure in those days, especially since her English was not very good," Rosenthal reported. "When she saw Marcia's second and third grade workbooks, she asked Marcia to use them to help teach her English."

Abe and Gussie were divorced, and later Mike Zaks, living in Los Angeles, also divorced, watched a cousin's home movies in which he saw Gussie wheeling Marcia in her baby carriage. Mike recognized Gussie as a childhood friend. He traveled to New York for a bar mitzvah, searched for her, and they were reunited. Married in 1963, they were together for 45 years until Mike died.

Rosenthal related that "Gussie could not believe what a good man Mike was. He was easy going, optimistic, fun loving, and he loved her kids and they loved him.

They settled in a home that Gussie bought for $16,000. Mike soon began to find success in business, and one day came home from one of his walks to tell Gussie that he had just found and purchased the perfect home for them in the Del Cerro neighborhood. Gussie couldn't believe it, but when she saw the home . . . she knew he was right and she knew that Mike had bought it for her."

Mike and Gussie divided their communal responsibilities. Mike became president of Tifereth Israel Synagogue, while Gussie excelled as the president of the New Life Club of Holocaust Survivors, which had parties, gatherings, and social occasions together. She also became a noted speaker about the Holocaust, her efforts winning acclaim and recognition. The family has boxes and boxes of her awards.

Mike died 10 years ago, and although deeply pained, Gussie soldiered on, continuing to preach messages of tolerance and "never again" to many audiences. However, six years ago she could no longer live on her own and moved to Encinitas' Seacrest Village, which is the successor to the San Diego Hebrew Home. "While it took her a couple of years to adjust, Gussie was, afterall, Gussie, and soon became everyone's friend, a natural leader, and an advocate for other patients," Rosenthal said. "If someone was left out in the hallway too long, it was Gussie who called it to the nurse's attention."

Towards the end of her life, Gussie was "bedridden and could no longer do the things she loved," Rosenthal said. "She knew it was her time, said her goodbyes, and stopped eating and drinking. She died peacefully, an end she richly deserved."

Daughter Marcia Rosenberg filled in some additional parts of Gussie's life. At first, "She felt uncomfortable socializing with other Americans because of her heavy accent. With encouragement from Anita Shonbrun, she joined Sisterhood at Tifereth Israel. With Sisterhood's warm acceptance and hospitality, and obviously with always a need for volunteers, her passions were ignited for community service." Gussie rose to vice president and then president of the Sisterhood.

However busy Gussie was –and she was very busy—"family was always first in her heart," said Rosenberg.

"Mom surprised me on my 17th birthday. She acted as if her day was very busy but she would make time for lunch with me when she was done with her meetings. Me, being a typical teenager, was a little put off that I had to adjust my day to her schedule. When she came home from her meetings, I begrudgingly jumped in the car with her. She drove to Tom Ham's Restaurant—Surprise! Inside all my girlfriends were gathered at a huge table decorated with balloons and banners and gifts. Her mind was civic—but her heart was all family!"

She added: "Gussie and Mike were always about family and bringing everyone together for important holidays, lavish meals that she started cooking days in advance."

Gussie's son, Jack Morgenstern, said his mother had four main passions: the synagogue, Holocaust remembrance, the New Life Club, and her family.

The family joined the Conservative synagogue in 1963 before its move from 30th and Howard Streets to 6660 Cowles Mountain Boulevard. Over that period, they were befriended and inspired by four rabbis—Monroe Levens, Aaron S. Gold, Rosenthal, and Dorsch. "We have been members here for 55 years and all that time my mother was in charge. She loved to do the seating arrangements for all the synagogue events. My mom and dad along with Hal and Helen Cohen started the biggest fundraiser the synagogue ever had—Carnival. There was never an event that my mom and dad missed. Look out to the fifth row in this sanctuary and that's where they sat for every event . . . ."

To tell the story of the Holocaust—and to impress upon her listeners the lessons of tolerance—Gussie would "some days speak at three schools," Morgenstern related. "Here would be this little Jewish lady in a big white Cadillac going about 80 miles an hour. I was scared to drive with her. No GPS in those days but she got to every school in plenty of time. . . . She confronted skinheads many times in the schools but she never backed down. Students in the classrooms called her 'Gutsy Gussie.' One of her joys was taking busloads of students to Los Angeles to visit the Museum of Tolerance along with her good friend Pearl Recht and other survivors. She became friends with the famous author, Elie

Wiesel, who wrote many books on the Holocaust, and also Benjamin Mead, president of the U.S. Holocaust Association."

The New Life Club grew out of the desire of Holocaust survivors to socialize with people who had similar experiences. Initially, "Survivors on every Sunday with their families went to La Jolla Cove and we had a great time there. One Sunday, Nazis marched down to the Cove carrying their flags. We left and vowed never to go back. So, on Sundays, the survivors went to Ruben Recht's house in Del Cerro to play cards, eat, and swim in the pool.

The Zaks family joined the New Life Club in the mid-1960s, and "my mom quickly became a leader in the club. She was President a few times. They would have a New Year's Eve party here in the synagogue. They had a beach party picnic at Mission Bay for the members and their kids."

Back then, there were some 300 members of the New Life Club; today there are about 30 led by Rose Schindler. Only last week, another New Life Club member Agathe Ehrenfried, "a very good friend of my mom," died.

Gussie's fourth passion was family, according to Morgenstern. "For almost 30 years she would cook for Passover and Rosh Hashanah for 40 people in her house. . . . My mom was a great cook. . . . Getting up in years, she could no longer tolerate all the work. So, my sister-in-law Linda Okmin took over the holiday cooking and had 40 people in her home and did a great job for many years."

Morgenstern concluded his remarks by asking the hundreds of attendees to do him two favors: "Please remember my mom as she was 10 or 15 years ago, when she was a classy, beautiful, elegant woman. Also, my mom would like you to, when you go home today, hug and kiss your parents and grandparents, kids and grandkids, and maybe this world would be a better place."

JFS, Looking Back a Century, Recalls Rose Neumann

San Diego Jewish World,
April 8, 2018

When the eight women who will be honored at the Jewish Family Service gala on April 21 posed for portraits, they all wore roses—a fitting tribute to the woman who started it all 100 years ago, Rose Neumann.

Up until the current executive director Michael Hopkins broke the pattern, Jewish Family Service has been led by female executives throughout its century. Neumann was followed by Jeanette Tobias, who in turn, was followed by Henrietta Rubenstein, Marianne Kaye, and Jill Spitzer, the latter being Hopkins' most immediate predecessor.

Spitzer, who served as executive director for 26 years, is one of the eight women honorees whose ages span several generations and who represent the continuing leadership provided to JFS by donors, volunteers, and staff members. In addition to Spitzer, the honorees who will be feted at the Hyatt Regency La Jolla at Aventine are Marsha Berkson, Jenny Daniel, Estee Einhorn, Inge Feinswog, Kira Finkenberg, Evelyn Rady, and Lois Richmond.

Recently, Jewish communal historian Joellyn Zollman discussed with *San Diego Jewish World* some noticeable themes throughout the 100-year history of Jewish Family Service. She paid tribute to Neumann, the hard-working, original leader whose priorities of case work, refugee assistance, and help for the elderly have remained essential elements of the Jewish Family Service mission.

Zollman, a Brandeis University PhD in Jewish Studies who curated the exhibit on San Diego's Jewish community that is currently on display at the San Diego History Center in Balboa Park, recently compiled a history of JFS that will be published in the upcoming Spring/Summer issue of the *Western States Jewish History* quarterly.

One of the things that she noticed at JFS "from beginning to end is female leadership," she commented. "I joke that there are the four founding mothers of JFS—the Hebrew Sisterhood, the Jolly 16, the Junior Charity, and the Ladies Hebrew Aid Society. These were four Jewish benevolent societies in San Diego that came together in 1918 and realized that they were essentially doing the same thing in the community, and that it didn't make sense to repeat the work of another organization in a town this small. So, they came together to better serve the community."

Neumann, who had been affiliated with the Hebrew Sisterhood at Tifereth Israel Synagogue (which then was Orthodox, but today is Conservative), was chosen to head up the consolidated organization. "She was the real force behind JFS," Zollman commented.

During its 100-year history, JFS had four names. It began as Federated Jewish Charities, continued from 1936 to 1952 as the Jewish Welfare Agency, morphed from 1952 to 1962 into the Jewish Social Service Agency, and since 1962 has been Jewish Family Service. To simplify our discussion, Zollman referred to the agency as JFS, no matter which era in its history she was discussing.

"I sometimes joke it should be called Jewish Female Service because you have Rose Neumann right at the beginning of this, and then you have this continuum of women—most recently Jill Spitzer from 1986 to 2012," Zollman said. "One of the things that makes San Diego unique is that in other towns and cities, usually around the time the Jewish Welfare Agency came into being, around 1936, social work became professionalized and usually that meant men coming in and taking over. As long as women were at the fore, in those other cities, JFSes were volunteer organizations, with women being what one historian called 'caretakers of the larger house of Israel.'" In San Diego, professionalization did not bring with it male leadership. "I could not say for sure why, but I guess it was a combination of the force of some of the female personalities here in San Diego, and the fact that the community was small and there might not have been professional Jewish male social workers around. A combination of these factors led to women being in charge . . . ."

Neumann, indeed, was a force to be reckoned with, said Zollman admiringly. "She seemed to have an unending amount of energy. She came here in 1911 from Brooklyn, and obviously found a very different community here in San Diego. She came with her husband Al, who had a furniture business, and she was shocked at how little the Jewish community was doing here. She set out to make it her mission for the rest of her life to build a really vibrant Jewish community in San Diego. She was involved in a lot of organizations, but she spent most of her time running JFS."

Two letters that Zollman found in archives help to portray Neumann. One was an answer to a rabbi in Sacramento, who asked her to explain just exactly what her agency did. "She told him that it was primarily casework helping people solve their individual problems. One of the main issues they had was what they called 'transients.' Lots of people came to California to escape money problems, to make a new start, or for whatever reason. Maybe they were not on good terms with their families. So, Rose Neumann would get a telegram from the Jewish Welfare Society of Cleveland, for example, asking "Have you seen Mr. Goldberg? This is what he looks like and we think he came to your town.' She would go knock on doors and say, 'Are you Mr. Goldberg?' She was pretty fearless. Sometimes she would describe situations like 'I went down to a sketchy neighborhood where there is a woman recovering from tuberculosis, and her husband wants her to come home. I knocked on her door, and she doesn't want to go.'" She did this kind of case work herself. She didn't send other people to do it, although sometimes members of the Jolly 16 (which began as a Jewish sewing circle) would go with her, and perhaps take their husbands.

"They were also helping people who didn't have enough to eat, or needed a place to live," Zollman continued. "San Diego wasn't a big enough town then for there to be a Jewish hospital or even a Jewish Home for the Aged, and so they would drive old people to doctor appointments, help them make those appointments, and even pay for those doctor appointments, if they needed that. They would visit people in the hospital, and provide those kind of services that make you feel connected to the community."

Today Jewish Family Service serves thousands of clients, 85 percent of them not Jewish. But in Neumann's day, JFS dealt with Jews, Catholic Charities dealt with Catholics, and the YMCA served primarily Protestants, Zollman said.

The organizations that formed Jewish Family Service were drawn from the only two congregations in San Diego at the time—Beth Israel and Tifereth Israel—as well as secular organizations. There developed a sense of "peoplehood" that regardless of whether people were Orthodox or Reform (the Conservative movement came later), or not at all religious, they were all part of the Jewish people, who needed to be served. So as not to become identified with any single religious movement within the Jewish community, JFS had informal rather than formal relationships with rabbis, Zollman said. Traditionally, no rabbi served on the board of Jewish Family Service, but rabbis as individuals and JFS often cooperated.

For example, said Zollman, Rabbi Jonas Wrottenberg of Tifereth Israel Synagogue, which then was located on 18th Street downtown, "would go down in the morning to the harbor with an assistant, perhaps a newly arrived immigrant, and he would buy fish from a fisherman at a really cheap price. He would wrap them up in newspaper, give them to the assistant, who would take a trolley to take them to Rose Neumann, who lived in North Park. All the trolley operators knew to say, 'All beards off here,' at Rose Neumann's stop because religious Jews wore beards, and then Rose would clean the fish and distribute them to hungry people in the community."

In an aside, Zollman said that Michael Hopkins, the current CEO of JFS, loves that story, once exclaiming, "We do the same today; we have fishermen who donate fish to us here." Hopkins showed Zollman a freezer full of fish. "He loves this story because it is an example of continuity, of what the mission has been."

In addition to individual casework, JFS has had an historic interest in helping to settle refugees. Other correspondence uncovered by Zollman detailed the trouble that Neumann had in awakening the rest of the Jewish world to the plight of destitute Jewish refugees in San Diego's next-door neighbor city of Tijuana, Mexico.

"In the 1920s, Jewish immigration to the United States slowed to a trickle because of strict immigration laws passed by the U.S. Congress," Zollman said. "Yet, Jews increasingly were needing to get out of Europe. It was much easier to get into Mexico than the United States and that is why we saw increased immigration to Mexico in the 1920s. Some of the Jews who went there hoped to use it as a stepping stone to the United States, and a portion of that community settled right on the border in Tijuana, hoping that as soon as the U.S. eased the restrictions, they might be able to come over."

However, Zollman added, "A large number of them were extremely destitute and Rose Neumann became very concerned about this community. She had a problem, though, which was that the

243

money she raised for Federated Jewish Charities was for the San Diego Jewish community, so she could not in good conscience spend it on Jews in Tijuana." Neumann wrote to the B'nai B'rith organizations in Los Angeles, San Francisco, and New York City hoping to find help, but each organization, in essence, responded, this was not their problem.

In one letter, Neumann told "a particularly compelling story of three sisters whom she was sure would be forced to turn to prostitution if they could not get jobs to feed themselves and get clothing and decent housing." At one point, Neumann took a train up to Los Angeles to plead for assistance with various rabbis of that community, all to no avail. "She was outraged," Zollman commented. "She came back to San Diego and decided she would have to create an organization herself, which she did, naming it something like the 'Tijuana Jewish Relief Association.' Then, she wrote letters to what seemed like every Jewish business owner in San Diego as well as to anyone who might have a business interest in Tijuana to try to get these Jews jobs."

Zollman commented that this episode illustrates that "Rose Neumann in the outpost community of San Diego saw herself as a link in the larger web of the Jewish world. She was saying, 'this is what we do, we take care of each other. I might be here in San Diego, but you in Los Angeles, San Francisco, and New York should be interested in this because Jews take care of one another.' They weren't interested, and it tells a lot about her character that she just went out and solved that problem herself."

Neumann retired in 1947, but her programs for aiding the Jews of Tijuana paved the way for JFS, under the leadership of Jeanette Tobias and Henrietta Rubenstein, to help resettle Holocaust Survivors following World War II. This process involved helping the refugees to find housing and jobs in San Diego, and additionally to acclimate them to American culture.

That experience in turn led to JFS participating with the national Hebrew Immigrant Aid Society (HIAS) in the resettlement of Vietnamese refugees who were airlifted to Camp Pendleton in 1975 following the fall of Saigon, and also in the resettlement in San Diego of Jewish refugees from the Soviet Union. Today, JFS remains involved in resettlement services, helping people from all over the world, including currently, refugees from Iraq, Afghanistan, Burma, and the Democratic Republic of the Congo.

A third area of continuity in the JFS story was help for the elderly. In 1944, the community established in a residence a home for the aged that housed ten residents. Eventually it expanded to the Hebrew Home for the Aged which in the late 1950s was built on 54th Street on a bluff overlooking the Jewish Community Center. This complex eventually was sold to help finance the transition to the more modern Seacrest Village Retirement Communities in Encinitas in 1989 and in Poway in 1996.

Early on, JFS recognized the need not only to provide institutional care for the elderly, but also to provide social and recreational opportunities for elderly people still living in their homes. "Under Marianne Kaye, the first senior center opened in 1973," near Beth Jacob Congregation's previous home on 30th Street in the North Park area, Zollman related. Over a short period of time, this "Drop-In Center" served over 500 seniors. A nine-passenger automobile, which, eerily, had been converted from a hearse, was used to transport seniors from their homes to the center. Additionally, during this period, another senior center was opened in North County, Zollman commented.

Subsequently, JFS opened older-adult centers in the College area, near San Diego State University, and at JFS's main campus on Balboa Avenue in the Kearny Mesa area. Transportation for seniors continues to be an important aspect of JFS service with the "On The Go" Service regularly transporting older adults not only to these centers, but to doctor appointments, grocery stores, shopping centers, and other venues.

Although JFS has greatly expanded in the many years since Rose Neumann's administration—going during Jill Spitzer's administration from a budget of $500,000 in 1986 to $20 million, with 300 employees staffing more than 50 programs, in 2012—the basic missions remain the same, Zollman emphasized.

Today, JFS continues to help families in crisis, providing both material assistance and psychological counseling. It comes to the aid of refugees, acclimating them to life in San Diego County. And, it is a good friend, advocate, and companion to the elderly.

Sea World Encounters on World Penguin Day

San Diego Jewish World,
April 26, 2018

I f I had gone into the place blind-folded, I might have thought I was in the sanctuary of a synagogue—a very cold sanctuary—listening to the sounds of shofars being blown in celebration of Rosh Hashanah.

The blasts were reminiscent of the *tekiah* call of the shofar, and one mighty one even sounded like *tekiah godol.* The temperature in the room made me reflect back to the time that I had served my congregation as religious affairs vice president, which on Saturdays consisted mainly of handing out Torah blessing honors, and trying to find a balance between those congregants who thought the sanctuary too hot and those who thought it too cold. In this instance, I definitely would have agreed with those who thought it too cold. It was 25 degrees Fahrenheit.

The occasion wasn't a Jewish holiday, but rather it was a secular celebration. April 25 was World Penguin Day, the day when penguins in Antarctica typically begin migrating towards the northern part of the continent. To mark the occasion, photographer and grandson Shor M. Masori and I took a "Behind the Scenes" tour of the Penguin Encounter at SeaWorld. Shor's classmate, Fausto Baltazar, for whom penguins are a major interest, joined us—his penguin-themed T-shirt attracting several favorable comments from SeaWorld staff members Booker Crenshaw Jr. of the marketing department and Paige Silva, an aviculturist. What the penguins thought of it, I couldn't tell, but the way one of the penguins nestled onto Baltazar's lap, surely it didn't disapprove.

Those shofar-like blasts were the "trumpet" calls of the Emperor Penguins, largest of the penguin family.

To begin our tour, we stepped in a tray filled with solution to prevent our shoes from tracking in contaminants. We were next met in the kitchen area of the Penguin Encounter by aviculturist Silva, who dimmed the lights in the room, and then brought out a Macaroni Penguin, so-named because it has on its head yellow feathers that somewhat resemble the pasta favorite.

This particular Macaroni didn't have a nickname yet, but seemed to respond well to its breed and number, Macaroni 221, whenever that name was cooed by Silva, an eight-year employee of Sea World, with the last two years in specialization at the Penguin Encounter. "A lot of the birds get nicknames—this one doesn't yet, but you will see several upstairs [in the exhibit area], for example, Stephen, Princess, and Vlad," she commented. "Princess, an Emperor Penguin, was so named because she has a regal air about her. Stephen, a King Penguin, was named for the author Stephen King. As for Vlad, Silva said, "He is a bird that came here as part of SSP— Species Survival Plan. They want to make sure that all the genetics aren't bottlenecked in one location. Vlad came here from Cincinnati and he had a different name when he came. But we noticed that he had a behavior that was very stabby, and he has a long beak. So, he was named after Vlad the Impaler," the 15th Century Romanian prince who used to dispatch his opponents by impaling them. "To be honest," Silva hastened to add, "he is a super sweet bird, but it's like he walks around with a little sword."

If I were naming Macaroni 221, I might call him "news hound" or perhaps "news critic," because while I was interviewing Silva, and not paying strict attention to 221, he waddled across a kitchen counter and tried to take a bite out of my reporter's notebook. Silva said penguins are naturally curious animals, and that they love to play games and have fun. Probably Macaroni 221 was attracted to the spiral rings on the notebook, as penguins like shiny objects.

I wondered if penguins minded the constant stream of visitors who ride along a motorized sidewalk along the glass viewing area of the Penguin Encounter.

"I think it is white noise to them," Silva replied. "It doesn't bother them. If anything, it can be a type of enrichment for them. When we walk out along the glass, and I kneel down to the water level [where the penguins swim], the Gentoo girl [one of her favorite penguins among the 400 that populate the Encounter] and a bunch of others come right over, and it's a game, enriching, different, and exciting for them."

"Penguins are very easy to entertain," she added. "The fresh snow that we provide every day is like Christmas for them. When you are blowing snow in there, they get all excited and they do snow angels, and they are tobogganing, and sometimes we give them a hill to climb over. On another occasion we gave them tunnels by putting snow over buckets, and after the snow freezes, pulling the buckets out, creating a frozen igloo, and they go running in and out of it. We have made slides into the water, and even if you throw chunks of ice with krill and other types of fish, it is enriching for them to play with in the water. We've given them a tennis ball and they chase it around as if it were an egg that they can try to steal from each other."

Machines like those that make snow cones, but on a far more giant scale, provide 400 tons of snow each day that is blown into the Penguin Encounter through a lengthy, fat hose than can be extended through the exhibit. Between 700 and 1,000 pounds of fish are provided daily to the collection of 400 penguins, through three methods of feeding. Some penguins accept fish given to them by hand. Others prefer to scoop it out of feeding stations that look like little huts. Others prefer to catch the fish in the water. SeaWorld makes it a point to keep enough fish on site so that none of the penguins go hungry.

Prior to the breeding season. penguins will eat more fish in anticipation of the fact that while they are hatching eggs, they won't be able to move much from the nest. Being so stationary, the penguins survive off the fat stored in their bodies.

Silva said the Penguin Encounter is darkened, as was the kitchen where we entered, because SeaWorld carefully simulates the light conditions of Antarctica and the Southern Hemisphere. Being that the seasons of the Southern Hemisphere are reverse of those in the Northern Hemisphere, winter is approaching back in Antarctica, even as summer is approaching here.

From the back side of the exhibit, one can see a lot of lights on the ceiling. "We are gradually dimming those lights so that every day they get lower and lower, and eventually it will become dark 24 hours a day," Silva said. "We even simulate a sunrise and a sunset. Tonight about 5:30 p.m., I will go and change the lights, and that will signal to the birds that the sun is going down. At night, the lights go out, and then in the morning we simulate a sunrise. As daylight gets shorter in the Southern Hemisphere, the period of light here will also get shorter."

Silva said every penguin is banded with a number code that corresponds to a numbered computer file, so that such information as the penguin's date of birth, parentage, current weight, and medical history is easily accessible. As the differences between male and female penguins do not meet the eye, the files also include the penguin's gender. "Generally, we get that information from blood samples; either when the blood is drawn and tested, or if they have hatched here, you can take their egg shell and you can extract DNA."

She said she thinks Macaroni 221 may be male, but that she tends to personify all of them as females. "The beak is pretty," she explained. Macaroni 221 is just two years old. "The Macaronis really like to explore things," she said.

Penguins are soft to the touch, possibly because of the density of their feathers. "They have 70 to 100 feathers per square inch, so they are extremely well insulated for their environment," Silva said. "It's like wearing a wet suit. They are the densest birds, in terms of feathers. A chicken, for example, has only 12 to 15 feathers per square inch."

Birds like gulls and sparrows have relatively hollow bones, because "they want to be very light to be able to take flight," said Silva. Heavier-boned penguins are divers, and "they are depending on that weight to help take them down into the ocean."

Silva said World Penguin Day, April 25, is useful for explaining to people that it's important to protect the oceans from pollution and global warming. Penguins are an "indicator species for the ocean," she said. "Their ovulations, their breeding sites, their access to food—all are parts of knowing what is going on in the ocean."

Having been assigned for two years to the Penguin Encounter, Silva has developed a fondness for a number of the birds. Among others, she likes Macaroni 221, "Princess," and Gentoo 358, whom she calls "Baby Girl."

"I can come here and say, 'Baby Girl,' and she will come running over," Silva said. "She is only a couple of years old, compared to this lady here, Gentoo 31, who is 34 years old."

A mark of distinction for SeaWorld are its Emperor Penguins, whose calls are like the sounds of a shofar. "We are the only institution in the Western Hemisphere that has Emperors, so I tell people who take the Behind the Scenes tour to take a deep breath when you are around them because it's probably a once-in-a-lifetime opportunity. I don't know of any place except the Antarctic where you can get this close to them. We were originally built as a facility for scientists to research cold weather penguins, so we are very fortunate."

Second in size to the Emperors are the Kings, followed by the Gentoos. Smaller penguins in the Encounter include the Macaronis, Chinstraps, and Adelies. The Chinstraps are so named because of a dark band below the white portion of their faces; The Adelies have a white ring around their eyes.

"Emperors are very sweet," Silva commented. "Princess will fall asleep in your lap, but it is always on her terms."

Lag B'Omer at Kumeyaay Lake Campground

San Diego Jewish World,
May 3, 2018

Two ancient traditions briefly were juxtaposed on Thursday, May 3, as Chabad of East County celebrated the Jewish holiday of Lag B'Omer at the foot of Kwaaypay (Chief, Headman) Peak at the Kumeyaay Lake Campgrounds in Mission Trails Regional Park.

When the indigenous Kumeyaay were a semi-nomadic people, they followed the San Diego River from the beaches to the mountains, from which they took side trips to the desert—and then, they came back the way they came, camping during the winter at sites along the river in today's Mission Trails Regional Park.

Ranger Heidi Gutknecht, whom I interviewed the day before Lag B'Omer, commented that "Next door to the San Diego River there is an historic grinding rocks area where you can see worn away basins," created by Kumeyaay women who pounded acorns with their pestles, known as "morteros."

The reason the Kumeyaay chose what is today, Mission Trails Regional Park, Gutknecht said, was "where there is water there will be plants and animals. Mother Nature was like their Walmart, their store, to get everything. . . . We have mule deer here, a prize prey for the Kumeyaay who never let anything go to waste. They not only ate the meat and kept the fur but they saved the antlers which could be used as tools; and bones, hoofs, and rattles for ceremonial purposes. The Kumeyaay didn't play drums like other tribes; they played rattles—primarily gourd rattles from wild squash. Deer toe rattles were for more special ceremonies. Gourd rattles were for regular song cycles, songs that told their stories in the oral tradition, as they had no written language."

Chabad Rabbi Rafi Andrusier stood on a log on Thursday and spoke to an assemblage of parents and children, who had enjoyed at their campfire not the acorn meal and mule deer meat beloved by the ancient Kumeyaay, but toasted marshmallows, hamburgers, hotdogs, and various salads, all kosher, of course.

He didn't sing the song of his people's history, accompanied by the sound of gourd rattles, as the Kumeyaay might have, but he did tell the story of Lag B'Omer, thereby transmitting Judaism orally.

Rabbi Andrusier pointed out that this is the time of the Omer, the counting of the 49 days between Pesach and Shavuot, and that the 33rd day of the Omer is a special day. Sometimes, he quipped, people say "lag sameach" rather than "hag sameach." The latter expression means "happy holiday." The word "lag" in Hebrew is a contraction of the letters lamed, which stands for the number 30, and gimel, which stands for the number 3. Together, they represent the number 33, thus the name "Lag B'Omer."

He told of Rabbi Akiva, a wonder rabbi who lived in Israel during the second century. Like the Kumeyaay, for the first 40 years of his life, Rabbi Akiva was a man of the land, who earned his living tending sheep. He married the daughter of a very wealthy family. His bride's father was incensed that the daughter would pick such a man, who was unlearned and poor. He disinherited her.

"But," Rabbi Andrusier instructed, "she had confidence and faith in her husband that he could become a great sage and a great scholar. Eventually he did. One day, he was out shepherding the flock and he passed by a stream." He noticed that water dripping drop after drop on a stone had begun to wear an indentation in the stone.

In contrast to the pestle used by the Kumeyaay to pound the acorns on the grinding rocks, the indentation that Rabbi Akiva saw was created by water. "He thought if something as soft as water can penetrate something as hard as stone," then perhaps Torah learning could even penetrate his brain. So, at the age of 40, Akiva started to learn Torah, sitting in a cheder with little children to learn the Hebrew alphabet. "Eventually he became one of the greatest Torah scholars."

However, the thousands of students whom Rabbi Akiva accumulated did not pay respect to each other, and a plague caused the death of 24,000 of them—one reason why the period of the Omer is such a mournful time. But on the 33rd day, the plague stopped, so it was a cause for celebration.

"But more than that," Andrusier told those seated near him around the campfire. "One of the surviving students of Rabbi Akiva was Rabbi Shimon bar Yochai, who was the author of the *Zohar*, the first Kabbalistic work that we have. He said that 'on the day I die, it should be a day of celebration.' Who celebrates on the day someone dies? We make a *yahrzeit*; we don't go out into the field and make a fire. So why do we have a bonfire on the day of Rabbi Shimon bar Yochai's passing?"

He answered his question saying, "He was a mystic, a man of great soul and great spirit. Fire is like the spirit, and he looked at the world in a different way than most people. He saw infinite potential in every moment of existence, and he lived and breathed that." The final day of his life "was the culmination of his work; it was when all the pieces came together. So, he said, 'The day of my passing is not a sad day; it is a wonderful day,' and ever since, it has been a tradition to have a bonfire on Lag B'Omer and to celebrate.

Rabbi Andrusier told one more story, standing there on the log at the campfire. It seems there was a couple in Israel who desperately wanted to have children, but after years of marriage, still no children came. Perhaps, said the husband, they should divorce because they want children but can't have children with each other. So, they decided to have a 'divorce party,' which their friends attended, so amicable was their relationship. The husband, who was wealthy, declared that his wife may take any treasure in his household, no matter what it might be. And the wife, a wise and clever woman, declared that the one single thing that she wanted was her husband.

The couple decided to stay together, and they went to the town of Meron, where Rabbi Shimon bar Yochai is buried, and prayed there for the blessing of a child. The blessing was granted, after all those many years. Today Rabbi Bar Yochai's gravesite is a place of pilgrimage—especially on Lag B'Omer.

The Kumeyaay and the ancient Jews were very different people, with very distinct lifestyles and beliefs. But every society has points of intersection with every other.

Evangelical Christian Directs StandWithUs in San Diego

San Diego Jewish World,
May 13, 2018

Sara Miller, 33, director of the San Diego chapter of StandWithUs, is a descendant of a long line of evangelical Christian ministers associated with the Assemblies of God denomination. A great-grandfather was one of the denomination's original missionaries to India; her grandfather preached in Iran during the Shah's regime; her grandmother composed one of the praise songs found in a denomination hymnal, and her father, Jonathan Schoonmaker, occupied pulpits in Hawaii, Missouri, and Maine.

As a high school and college student, Miller participated in youth missions to such countries as Ukraine, Nigeria, Australia, and South Africa. Today, along with her husband Mark Miller, she is an active member of the Skyline Church in Rancho San Diego.

StandWithUs is a growing, dynamic, grassroots, pro-Israel organization, that, on campuses throughout North America and other parts of the world, fights an ideological battle with anti-Israel demonstrators who call for boycotts, divestment, and sanctions (BDS) against the Jewish State.

"One of my dreams has been to help create a lasting bridge between the Christian and Jewish communities," Miller told this interviewer. "I know that there is a plethora of organizations that already do that, but I see myself as the hands as well as the feet on the ground, essentially getting myself completely immersed in Jewish culture while staying true to myself and my own beliefs. I am what you see: I am a passionate Christian who cares about the Jews and cares about Israel."

As a fundamentalist Christian working in an organization whose membership and leadership is predominantly Jewish, Miller must adroitly navigate some potential controversies. For example, some church leaders that she would like to recruit to Israel's cause take issue with Israel's liberal values—such as its embrace of gay rights. On the other hand, some Jews are wary of Christian evangelicals' desire to convert Jews to their religion.

"As a professional with StandWithUs," Miller says, "I don't practice my faith in my job. I can say that I am a Christian and I can act like a Christian, but it is not even an option to try to convert someone, or share (her faith) with them, unless they ask me a [sincere] question . . . ."

While this means separating her job from some of her personal beliefs, Miller says, "I have been able to compartmentalize pretty well. The nice thing is that StandWithUs employs Christians; it is considered a positive thing. We represent diversity. We're bringing in evangelicals who are very interested in Israel and the Jewish people, so, that means added support for Israel. For me, I feel very accepted and welcomed as a Christian StandWithUs staff member. I'm an unabashed Christian, proud of my faith, but I have no desire to make anyone uncomfortable and I understand that there is a clear boundary there."

Miller started with StandWithUs on October 8, 2015, in a higher position than the one for which she originally had been hired.

While obtaining a master's degree in Islamic Studies at Hebrew University in Jerusalem, she interviewed via Skype for a job as an event planner in the San Diego StandWithUs office. However, the previous director, Nicole Bernstein, had resigned, so Roz Rothstein, the Los Angeles-based CEO of the organization, asked Miller to step up to the position of associate director. Miller, then still known as Sara Schoonmaker, became the only paid professional in the San Diego office. She had a steep learning curve.

"The first year was all brand new, challenging, and scary. It was like swimming in shark-infested waters," Miller recalled in our interview. "I still consider myself very ignorant of Jewish culture because I spent only a year in Israel and wasn't even studying Jewish culture. I was studying Islamic Studies—so, how does that make me an expert? So, there was this incredible pressure to learn as much as possible as fast as possible."

She set about studying the history of Israel, all the while trying "to learn the San Diego Jewish community, where everyone falls in the spectrum, and who is who. I had never heard of BDS before I started with StandWithUs. I literally had no background, but I think Roz saw that I was really a hard worker, and that I would put my heart and soul into it. I think she appreciated the fact that I was a Christian and that I came with a different perspective. Basically, I fit into my shoes after a while. I became more comfortable and got promoted to director about two years ago."

Although she didn't have a paid staff, Miller had some knowledgeable, well-placed Jewish community members who were her combination advisors and support system. Among others, these included Nina Brodsky, Jenny Josephson, and Mitch Danzig, the latter an attorney who currently is the chapter president.

There were grassroots activities and chapter-building activities that kept Miller quite busy in her first year. The very first week that she was on the job, anti-Israel activists announced plans to demonstrate outside Target and call for a boycott of SodaStream, an Israeli product which allows users to carbonate and flavor their water, thereby making sodas at home. At the time, the company had its factory in Ma'ale Adumim, a community beyond Israel's 1967 borders. The campaign against the factory resulted in the company deciding to move to a location within Israel's pre-1967 borders. This, in turn, resulted in hundreds of Palestinians losing their jobs, being unable to commute to the new factory.

Not long afterwards, the Sufi Mediterranean Restaurant on Balboa Avenue was the venue for a dinner at which an anti-Israel film and a variety of anti-Israel speakers were featured. "We stood outside and handed out pamphlets to respond to their charge that Israel and the IDF were child killers. The booklet directly answers those accusations. It talks about how Hamas and the Palestinian government use children as human shields and as workers in tunnels that collapse. It talks about how Hamas [in Gaza] withholds needed infrastructure, with no educational materials, and hospitals going unfunded because everything is diverted for war purposes."

Miller also helped to organize, in the span of a week, a rally in Balboa Park protesting Iran's nuclear program, and cautioning against the proposed nuclear pact with Iran from which, just this week, President Trump formally withdrew the United States. "I think that event connected a lot of people in the community together," Miller said. "I know that we brought Pastor Jim Garlow [of Skyline Church] to speak, Mitch Danzig spoke, and [columnist] Caroline Glick spoke, and since then there have been a lot of alliances. I feel good about that."

Meanwhile, Miller also was building the StandWithUs organization. A Herzl Club, named for Zionist leader Theodor Herzl, was founded for donors of $5,000 annually or higher. Herzl Club members are invited to four functions a year, typically a catered dinner at a private residence or hall, at which a prominent speaker is featured. An upcoming Herzl Club meeting on May 31 will bring Capt.

Elgen M. Long, who helped fly Jews from Yemen to Israel in a secret airlift operation in March 1949. For donors of amounts between $2,500 and $5,000, there is a Guardians of Israel Club which will have similar activities, only twice a year. Lunch-and-learn get-togethers with speakers are scheduled twice a year, typically at the Mintz and Levin Law Offices, where Danzig is a member.

"We also have a StandWithUs Campus Crash Course for graduating high school students going into college, and their parents, grandparents, and any other adult who is invested in that child's life," Miller said. We basically do three to four hours of really important topical studies like, "know your legal rights on campus," which Mitch Danzig teaches, or an introduction to the Israel clubs on campus. We also have some fun stuff like Krav Maga (an Israeli martial art) to keep the kids entertained. It is a time for us to meet with the students, to give them an overview of what they can expect at college, and to know that StandWithUs is a huge resource. . . . It is a great launching pad for them if they want to be outspoken advocates for Israel on their campuses. They have this entire organization backing them."

The national StandWithUs organization helps select Emerson Fellows to become lead advocates for Israel on various college campuses. In San Diego, there are Emerson Fellows at both San Diego State University and UC San Diego. There also are a few high school interns in the county, having been chosen for the upcoming academic year at Torrey Pines, Canyon Crest, and Southern California Yeshiva (SCY) high schools.

Within the last several weeks, Miller has been joined at the San Diego office by another professional, Yael Steinberg, a Jewish community member who has taken the position of associate director. Like Miller, Steinberg obtained a Master's Degree at the Rothberg International School at Hebrew University. Her major was Non-Profit Management.

Miller was born on the island of Maui after her father accepted a pastoral position with the King's Cathedral, founded by the Rev. James Morocco. Eventually, he was asked to establish an extension church on the island of Lanai, which today is 98 percent owned by Oracle founder Larry Ellison. At that time, the Schoonmaker family consisted of Sara and her sister Rebecca; two daughters born to their father's previous marriage, Julie and Jenny, and one daughter born to their mother Kathleen's previous marriage, Rachel. The combined family boasted five daughters in all. While Sara's father had grown up in a missionary family, her mother's family was secular. An entrepreneur, Kathleen purchased an air freight company at the age of 19, and added a figure salon to her holdings at age 22. She became a religious Christian after her marriage to Pastor Schoonmaker.

Although Lanai is a tourist's paradise, with two large Four Seasons Hotels on either end of it, it proved a challenge for young Sara, who along with her sister Rebecca, suffered bullying as she walked to the island's only school. One day children sitting on an embankment threw stones down at them, while taunting them as *haoles,* which though often taken as a synonym for "white mainlander" is also an insult in the Hawaiian language that means a person who has "no breath, no life," Miller said.

Her father was able to rent a local theatre in which he fashioned a one-room church school called Ka'ahumanu Hou, into which Sara happily was enrolled. "He was a natural teacher, and this was in addition to his pastoral duties," Miller said. "That first year we had between 20 and 30 students, which was pretty good for the first year. . . . The education was tremendous; they had a lot of geography, and my father was a bit of a linguist, so he taught the kids proper grammar. My mom loved to get the kids together to sing and we would have a worship service in the morning. They gave us harmonicas to play, so we learned that. It was a very special time; all the kids improved academically, and it was a very positive experience."

From Lanai, the family moved to Springfield, Missouri, where Sara's grandparents, Pastor Paul and Harriet (Williams) Schoonmaker, had retired, and where, after Paul's death, his widow married Sydney Bryant. Sara's family didn't stay there very long because a brother-in-law of Sara's father appealed to him in 1997 to serve as a co-pastor at a church in York, Maine. "I was just going into seventh grade; and public school was a rude awakening. It was a very secular, liberal school, and I had a difficult time adjusting there, but I eventually made friends."

Until then, she reflected, "I really had been sheltered, brought up in a very conservative environment. To go from that, where you are protected, and to be completely thrown into that environment, I didn't know anything about pop culture which the kids were talking about. I didn't have any of the same experiences that they did, and I was dressed as a tomboy, whereas the girls in seventh grade were into hair and makeup."

Nevertheless, Sara was an all-around athlete, playing tennis, basketball, soccer, and track. She also played the saxophone, joined a band, and served on the student council. She made friends.

When she was 15, she participated in her first overseas youth mission. It took her to Kiev and Dnepropetrovsk in Ukraine, where the Christian cadre set up and managed basketball camps and preached the Gospel. After that segment of the trip, the youth mission traveled to Amsterdam, Holland, where they visited the Anne Frank House. "I remember just being in awe there," Sara recalled. "I remember seeing some of the letters on the wall there, and how impactful that was." She has returned to the site twice.

The mission inculcated Sara with a love for travel. The next mission she went on was to Lagos, Nigeria.

"We went to different churches where they had the most gracious welcoming for us," she recalled. "We would take a canoe and go down the Niger River and visit these tiny, little, remote villages on the riverbank that were just covered in trash. Half the villagers didn't have any clothes on. They would be so warm and gracious and excited that American missionaries were coming to spend time with them. I remember distinctly going into one straw-thatched building. It was missing its walls, but it had a roof over it. There was a whole parade of people coming in and they put in front of us a few bushels of plantains and some live catfish as an offering. We were just a bunch of kids; it was exciting to be honored by such a warm and hungry people."

The young missionaries stayed in the homes of local hosts, ate breakfast with them, then went off to various assignments, such as to the local hospital where "we would visit people and ask them, 'Is there anything we can pray for you for?' Some people would say no, and others would say, 'Sure, you can pray for my leg,' or 'You can pray for my daughter,' and then there would be a few persons who would just gather around that person to pray. There would be a translator there. I would stand at the foot of the bed, and if they had a blanket on, I might touch that, just so that there was contact, and say, 'Lord, thank You so much for so-and-so; thank You for giving us the opportunity to pray for him/her. God, You know this person's heart. You know his situation. You know that only You can provide healing, and we ask that You intervene, that You touch this person and that You heal him. . . . We thank you, in Jesus's name."

Miller told me that she personally believes in healing: "I have seen people heal right in front of me. I think that it ministers to people in more ways than just being prayed for. I think when they see young people in faith, that is an encouraging aspect of prayer."

On another occasion, Miller said she encountered real "evil" while participating in a prayer service in a church, which had undependable electricity. "When the lights would go off, the whole room would fill with screams—a lot of screams came from the local 'witch doctors' who had come into the building to curse the missionaries while we were there. I will never forget that moment when we were in the church building. We were all praying and there was great faith in the room, and the lights went off and there was this horrible screaming and cursing from these witch doctors. Then the lights went back on, and it was silent again. I remember the power, the fear, and it felt like a direct confrontation with the supernatural. I definitely experienced what I considered to be demonic forces there, and seeing eyes with completely glazed over pupils, things that really frightened me. I think my faith was really developed after those encounters, knowing that there is a God and there really is evil; there really is healing; and that there really are forces fighting that."

From Nigeria, the youth mission traveled onto England. In London, they "visited a series of churches, ministering to the people, which meant that we would pray for them to get healed, or for God to give them a better life."

Miller enrolled at Evangel University in Springfield, Missouri, where she majored in International Studies. "I knew that I loved missions, loved traveling, and really had found politics interesting. So, I thought I might become some sort of minister, or government worker, or maybe join the Peace Corps, but do something that was service based."

Between her sophomore and junior year, she took a year off from formal studies to go to Australia as part of a group called Youth With A Mission—or Y-WAM—which was another Christian evangelical group. For three months, her group sat in a classroom in the Rooty Hill suburb of Sydney, to learn "about the character of God; who is God?; What are His attributes?; What are His characteristics?; How can we know Him better?"

Later in the program, the group traveled from Australia to Durban, South Africa, to do street ministry. "We were basically on Skid Row; we were dealing a lot with drug lords, prostitutes, lepers. We would pray for people. We would hold worship services in the street. We would visit drug houses. We would dress up in very modest, long skirts at night, and we would visit the brothels and try to talk to the girls. It was very dangerous. I remember we were walking one evening, and there was this poor, pitiful woman covered in sores, just lying in the dirt, and she literally had cockroaches crawling on her body. Her pimp was around the corner, just watching us. The lady we were with had a local ministry, and so she knew the language, and she asked if we could pray for her. I remember being terrified, and absolutely overwhelmed by her loss of dignity and the terrible suffering she had experienced."

In other encounters, the young missionary learned that children who were hungry often would sniff glue as a way to curb their appetites, not aware that this could have lasting negative impacts on their health. "We would ask them if they would trade glue for a meal and bread, and they would say 'yes,' right away, and then the second they were done eating, they would try to get the glue back. There would be mobs that would try to attack us, but we had bodyguards."

She returned to college after that gap year and was able to serve for a period as an intern in the Washington D.C. office of Republican U.S. Senator Tom Coburn of Oklahoma. As an intern, she learned "the ins and outs of how a day in the Senate works; I went to a hearing and saw Barack Obama (then a U.S. Senator from Illinois) sitting on a panel there. They taught us how to answer the phones, record constituent remarks, sort mail, attend hearings. I think I was mesmerized by the process. I fell in love with Washington D.C., the vibe of the city, and how driven everyone was to make a difference. I would say the experience enhanced my desire to be involved."

She graduated from Evangel University in 2007 and traveled back to Maui, where her sister Rebecca was living. One summer, "I contracted a real severe case of staph infection, which put me in the hospital for a week. I was close to death."

What had happened was that she had been surfing, and "I had gotten a bite on my chin from a jellyfish, and I was kind of messing with it, and it turned out to be the entry point [for the infection] because there had been some sewage spills in Hawaii that entered the waters. This was the penicillin-resistant type of staph and then I had the flesh-eating staph in my arm." Doctors called Sara's mother to prepare her for the worst, and said if Sara didn't die, she still might go blind.

"Thank God, we had prayer chains all over the country where people were praying for the girl in Maui, and I was very fortunate, I pulled through. I remember getting incredible notes and hearing that entire churches were taking a moment in their services to pray for me. I felt humbled and almost ashamed that I was the girl who was taking up people's time in church. I believe in the power of prayer; I believe that it can significantly contribute to recovery. The story is pretty amazing: my sister and I stayed up all night at the hospital, and she squeezed the infection out of my face, preventing the surgery that they were going to do."

After her recovery, she married Dan Kulp, who had played football at Evangel, and from whom she later was divorced. They lived in Missouri, where she worked at various odd jobs, including as an executive assistant for a start-up company, and at a hair salon. Then they moved to Hawaii, where she worked at a Marriott Hotel at the front desk, as a sales manager, and also managed a Starbucks. She signed up with a group from King's Cathedral to visit Israel, her first trip there, and "I was like a kid in the candy shop, so excited to be in Israel. "I think the thing that stood out was going to the pool at Bethesda, just inside the Lion's Gate, and I remember we had a worship/prayer service there and I was completely overwhelmed and emotional because I could picture Jesus being there, and the story coming to life." (In Christian Scripture, Jesus healed a paralyzed man who could not reach the Bethesda Pool, which was thought to have healing properties.)

"Another moment was walking on the Via Dolorosa where Jesus carried the Cross, and visiting the Garden of Gethsemane," where Jesus prayed with his disciples the night before his crucifixion. "I absolutely fell in love and told the pastor I was going to come back one day, but I had no idea how. I forced the pastor's wife to take a detour with me, because I desperately wanted to check out Hebrew University. I had no idea; I had an inclination. I thought it would be the most magical thing in the world to go to school there in the heart of Jerusalem and to experience it myself. So, we broke off the tour, and made a pit stop at the café right there on campus. I completely fell in love."

After her divorce, Sara decided to apply for a one-year program at Hebrew University. While the divorce was proceeding, at church, she met Mark Miller, the man who would become her second husband.

"During the divorce, I was in church one Sunday with my family, sitting in the back, grumping, and being miserable about my situation, and I looked up and saw two guys walking in," Sara remembered. "It was Mark and his father; they sat in the second row, and when you go to a church like that, you instantly know when someone new is there. So, anyway, I just observed him the entire service. I was completely astonished; it was love at first sight. I never say that, nor did I believe it, but it absolutely happened. I watched him as he interacted with his dad, watched him being very interactive and expressive during the worship service, and I watched him give an offering during the tithe-and-offering, and I was just instantly very curious. He turned around a couple of times, and we caught each other's gaze, and it turned out, at the end of the service, he came back. He recognized my brother-in-law (a sister's husband), who had been his camp counselor. . . . Rebecca knew that my heart was just jumping out of my chest, and she said, 'I will just invite him over for dinner.' It turns out he was in town for a family emergency, only his second day on the island, so the fact that we connected like that was pretty remarkable. The next ten days were a complete whirlwind; they invited him over; we talked for hours . . . I was literally on Cloud Nine."

Cautious about getting into a serious relationship so soon after the divorce, she told Mark that she planned to go to Israel for a year, and that a separation would test whether their attraction was meant to mature into something more. Except for a brief visit to Jerusalem, Mark waited back at home. When Sara completed her degree, she moved to San Diego, where Mark, who is four years younger than her, was completing his studies at Point Loma Nazarene College. She took her own apartment, and they waited an additional year-and-a-half before they were married.

Mark has a degree in business and communications, and often puts that knowledge to use as a StandWithUs volunteer. For example, recently when an anti-Israel group held a demonstration in support of Gaza protests at the Israeli border, he and Sara monitored the demonstration, which was advertised as a precursor of a nationwide protest. Sara said only a small number of people turned out, and that she relayed that information to StandWithUs headquarters, which wanted to understand what other cities around the nation might have in store for them.

I asked Sara about her goals for StandWithUs, and her personal goals. She said she would like to increase the number of Herzl Club and Guardian of Israel members, expand the Lunch and Learn program, and create more Emerson Fellowships at local colleges (such as Point Loma Nazarene, for example) and internships at high schools. She also would like to raise more money to enable the hiring of two more staff. The more staff, the more initiatives StandWithUs can take in San Diego County.

On a personal level, she said, "I have baby fever," and would like to start a family with Mark sometime in the near future. She also would like to brush up on her Arabic, learn to speak Hebrew, or at least to read and write it, to travel, and perhaps return on a program to Israel.

She added that she was thankful that her personal and career goals are complementary, and that she anticipates remaining for a long time with StandWithUs, an organization that she credits with contributing to her personal growth and increased understanding.

Curator Tells of LGBTQ+ History, Struggles, Triumphs

San Diego Jewish World,
July 10, 2018

Lillian Faderman, an historian of gay and lesbian progress and struggles in America, is the curator of the San Diego History Center's newest exhibit "LGBTQ+ San Diego: Stories of Struggles and Triumph," which will last a year, or more if attendance merits. The biographer of slain San Francisco Supervisor Harvey Milk, who was the first openly gay candidate elected to high office in California, Faderman says San Diego's LGBTQ+ community took to heart Milk's advice to "come out" and has since proved Milk's wisdom.

Although Milk was a San Franciscan, he knew San Diego very well, having served here as a Navy lieutenant, and making visits thereafter. "Coming out" was one of Milk's themes in the 1970s, according to Faderman. He taught the following: "You have to come out, you have to come out to everyone, even to the wait staff in the restaurant where you go and to the people who are the cashiers in the supermarkets where you shop. It is important that people know who we are."

Faderman said that in the 1990s, "an interesting Gallup Poll was taken across the United States, and San Diego as well, and only 22 percent of Americans said they had a close friend or relative who was lesbian or gay. In 2010, a Gallup Poll was taken asking the same question and three times as many people said they had a close friend or relative who was lesbian or gay. The difference was not that lesbian or gay people had grown in numbers but that we had come out—that made a huge difference."

"I've seen it with the groups I speak to," Faderman added. "If your son or daughter, or your aunt or your uncle, or your neighbor or coworker tells you that they are gay—or now, 'LGBT'—you can't think of those people as lurking in the shadows, ready to pounce on some 14-year-old kid, because you know that it is your son or daughter, or your best friend, or somebody you admire at work. Coming out had made a huge difference."

In the political realm in 1993, that advice paid off when Christine Kehoe, who acknowledged being a lesbian, was elected to the San Diego City Council in District 3, and subsequently was elected to the state Assembly and the state Senate. That City Council position, which represented the heavily gay Hillcrest neighborhood and surrounding areas, meanwhile, has been occupied continuously by gay and lesbian office holders, among them Toni Atkins, Todd Gloria, and Chris Ward. Atkins went on to be elected to the state Assembly, then as Assembly Speaker, and thereafter was elected to the state Senate. Today, Atkins is the State Senate president pro tempore—"a remarkable achievement," Faderman says.

Gloria went on to succeed her in the state Assembly, where he currently serves.

Whereas the Hillcrest area was the seat of gay and lesbian success, other districts also elected gays and lesbians to office. Carl De-Maio, today a radio commentator and leader of the statewide effort to roll back gasoline taxes, was elected in District 5, which includes

Rancho Bernardo, Mira Mesa, and other suburban communities along the Interstate 15. Currently Georgette Gomez, who calls herself a "queer," which Faderman said is a more fluid term than "lesbian" or "bisexual," was elected from District 9, which includes the area around San Diego State University and neighborhoods to the west along such thoroughfares as Adams Avenue, El Cajon Boulevard, and University Avenue.

The popularity of gay and lesbian candidates has also been seen in contests for other offices. Faderman noted that a fellow Jew, Bonnie Dumanis, was first elected as a municipal court judge, later as the nation's first lesbian district attorney, and today she is running for the position of county supervisor. Kevin Beiser was elected from such suburbs as San Carlos, Del Cerro, and Allied Gardens to serve on the San Diego Unified School Board, on which today he serves as the president.

Overall, suggested Faderman, San Diego probably has elected more gays and lesbians to public office than even San Francisco has.

Faderman, 78, had resided part-time in San Diego since 1994 with her partner of 46 years, Phyllis Irwin, and made her residence here permanently a couple of years ago.

She commented that it was not so long ago in California generally and San Diego specifically that both law enforcement and the school establishment were outright hostile to gays and lesbians.

The scholar and curator said that she came "out" as a lesbian in the 1950s, but that was only to her friends and relatives and not to the world at large. "I came out closeted," she said. "I went to graduate school and got my PhD, and of course I was closeted. If I had come out publicly in the '50s I couldn't have gone to a university because there were witch hunts in universities. There was no way I could have survived as a social being coming out in the 1950s and the 1960s." But in the 1970s, times and attitudes began to change and that is when she came out in a public way.

She recalled, "I started UCLA as a freshman and then I transferred to Berkeley and I did most of my undergraduate work there. I remember very well that at UCLA we were given a battery of tests, psychological tests, and I remember one question kept repeating itself, like 'Have you ever kissed a person of the same sex?' and then 10 questions later, 'Are you attracted to people of the same sex?' I knew to say 'no;' I'm sure all gays and lesbians knew to say 'no.' I couldn't figure out why that question would be on that test, and then I wrote a book in 1991 called *Odd Girls and Twilight Lovers,* I did a lot of research for that. I came across an article that had been published in 1954, four years before I started UCLA. It was written by the man who was the dean of students, and another guy who was the associate dean of students, coauthored by them. Their point was that it was the job of the dean of students to ferret out the homosexuals and either assure that they got psychiatric treatment to cure them or expel them from the university lest they spread homosexuality in the university. It was published in a magazine called *School and Society* that was for administrators of schools. I knew I had to be in hiding in the 1950s, and even when I took a job as a professor in 1968 at Cal State University Fresno, I knew that I could never make any pronouncements. By the 1970s, things had changed significantly. There was Stonewall (a well-publicized gay uprising against a police raid in 1969 against the Stonewall gay bar in Greenwich Village, New York City); the feminist movement, and everything that followed. I started doing lesbian research in 1975."

As in New York City, police in San Diego—abetted by the news media—engaged in homophobic persecution. "For instance," she said, pointing to one of the exhibits at the San Diego History Center, "this newspaper article appeared in 1974 about gay men who were arrested at the May Company. It was public shaming. Their names appeared, along with their ages, addresses, and occupations to shame them as much as possible."

Law enforcement had no mercy on those of their profession who secretly were gay. Faderman pointed to a letter written by FBI Director J. Edgar Hoover to his second in command Clyde Tolson saying, "he met this wonderful young man, just the kind the FBI should hire," named Frank Buttino. "They hired him, promoted him, he was the head of the San Diego office, and then someone outed him 20 years later. He was fired, and he fought, and he won, so the FBI can no longer discriminate against people because they are gay."

The exhibition traces some of the outrages committed against the gay and lesbian community, as well as various successes the community had in winning acceptance from the general community.

There is a memorial plaque in Hillcrest, reproduced at the San Diego History Center, for John Robert Wear, 17, who was beaten to death while three of his friends were injured by thugs who had jumped out of their car, called the friends who were walking down the street "faggots" and pounced upon them. Ironically, said Faderman, the young men were not gays.

The exhibition deals with the issue of gay marriages, with one picture showing a lesbian couple at Temple Emanu-El signing a ketuba under the proud supervision of Rabbi Martin S. Lawson. In another area of the exhibition which displays testimonies videotaped by attendees, Rabbi Laurie Coskey told of her time at Congregation Beth Israel when she was one of the earliest rabbis willing to perform for gay and lesbian couples, marriage or "commitment" ceremonies, depending on what was legal at the time. Faderman said that she and her partner Phyllis Irwin have visited a number of synagogues in San Diego and have been impressed by how welcoming they are to gay and lesbian couples. She particularly mentioned Rabbi Scott Meltzer at Ohr Shalom Synagogue and Rabbi Devorah Marcus, who succeeded Rabbi Lawson as spiritual leader of Temple Emanu-El.

Now, said Faderman, she is considering having an adult bat mitzvah, either before or in celebration of her 80th birthday, and Irwin is now considering converting to Judaism.

While together four years shy of a half century, Faderman and Irwin have had a series of legal relationships as laws regarding same-sex couples have changed.

"My partner and I had more legal relationships than anyone in the whole world," Faderman declared. "We have been together for 46 years. We have a child together. I had a child through donor insemination. He is 43 years old now, Avrom, named after my grandfather who I never met because he died in the old country . . . Avrom and his wife have a son today, our grandson. . . . In the early 1980s when our son was six or seven, I was traveling a lot because I had just published a book. I worried that if he got sick, my partner could not take him to the doctor without a note from me. If anything happened to me on my travels, she would have no legal claim to him.

"In those days in the State of California," she continued, "you could adopt if there was more than a 10-year-difference, and she is 11-years older than I am, so we did an adult adoption. So, we did that until 'domestic partnerships' became legal in California. So, we had a domestic partnership, and then it became even more legal: we got all the rights except the right to say, 'We are married,' so we did that, and then in 2008, there was a very brief period, six months in fact, when same sex couples could get married. We did it in San Diego because we spent the summers here, and it was already June. We got married in 2008 by someone at the county clerk's office, a woman. That was the first time we got married, and we were permitted to stay married—18,000 couples in California married, and they could stay married, but that November—the same November that President Obama was wonderfully elected, there was Proposition 8 on the California ballot," which voters approved, ending same sex marriages temporarily, until 2015, when the Supreme Court ruled that same-sex marriages are legal.

"In 2015," Faderman recounted, "*The New York Times* was doing an article on same-sex couples who first had an adoption as
Phyllis and I did, and then got married, and so the reporter asked in
an interview, 'And when did you undo the adoption?' and I said we
never did. We had actually gone to a lawyer here (in San Diego) in
2008, and I think she probably did her research on the Internet 10
minutes before we came in. She probably Googled "same-sex mar-
riages-adoption" and got Michigan where you don't have to undo
the adoption. I said, 'We never did,' and he said, "I think you are
wrong about that; I think you have to undo it.' I didn't pay much attention but when my book, *The Gay Revolution,* came out, I was invited to speak at the Los Angeles Public Library. After I spoke a lesbian lawyer came up to me and said all the lawyers are talking about
that *New York Times* article: 'I think you guys have to undo the
adoption and get married again.' And so, we undid the adoption by
signing some documents and in 2015 we got married again. Phyllis
unadopted me. Meanwhile, our son always had called her Mama
Phyllis. He is 43 now and has a son who is 12, and he said to her,
'But you always have been my mother, and now I have no connection to you legally. Can you adopt me? And she did. She did an
adult adoption of him. So, we have a lot of legal ties. My point is we
had to do so much to have legal ties."

The "LGBTQ+ San Diego: Stories of Struggles and Triumph"
exhibition is constructed very similarly to the recently-ended exhibition curated by Joellyn Zollman on the history and contributions
of San Diego's Jewish community, in which Zollman illustrated the
thesis that Jews have been both insiders and outsiders since they
first arrived in San Diego in 1850. Faderman said that she consulted
with Zollman on several occasions as she was designing the LG-
BTQ+ exhibition. Like the Jewish exhibition, the LGBTQ exhibition utilizes eight, 10-by-10 "pillars" in the shape of the letters S-A-
N D-I-E-G-O on which to mount photographs, video monitors,
newspaper clippings, and other documents.

Additionally, both exhibitions had a timeline covering much of a single wall, a video station for attendees to record their own experiences, and a family room where people could rest, read, and look at an assemblage of mounted photographs. The Jewish exhibition drew on the collection of the Jewish Historical Society of San Diego, while the LGBTQ+ exhibition drew on the collection of the Lambda Archives.

Although similar in presentation, the stories are different; discrimination against Jews was far more subtle than that against gays and lesbians. The LGBTQ community had to contend against hostile legislation, such as the unsuccessful 1978 Initiative sponsored by State Senator John Briggs that would have banned gays and lesbians from working in public schools. The military also did what it could to discourage, even criminalize, homosexuality. For example, there was a retired admiral, Selden Hooper, living in Coronado, whom the Navy suspected of having relationships with men who still were in the Navy. "They commandeered the house next door to spy on him and they discovered that there were men going into the house, sitting at the table, and at one point they could see two men dancing," Faderman related. "So, they forced him back into the Navy so they could court martial him and take away his rank and pension." Hooper had commanded the destroyer USS *Uhlmann* during World War II.

The first Gay Pride march was organized in 1975 in San Diego, and because police would not issue a parade permit, about 200 proud marchers kept to the sidewalk, stopping at traffic signals. But the following year, the Gay Pride parade did receive a permit, and the parade grew each year, to 100,000 participants and observers in 1997 and to 200,000 in 2016. This year's Pride parade will begin at 11 a.m., Saturday, July 14, and follow a 1.5 mile route from University Avenue and Normal Street. The parade is one of several Pride events scheduled for that weekend.

Some of the exhibits deal with the AIDS (acquired immunodeficiency syndrome) crisis, in which numerous homosexual men were stricken fatally with what up to then, had been an unknown disease. Some of the vitriol directed at the gay community was depicted by a picture of homophobic protesters wearing Hazmat suits in order to spread the lie that it was dangerous to even be in the vicinity of gay men. In actuality, AIDS is triggered by the human immunodeficiency virus (HIV) spread by the exchange of bodily fluids. A counter exhibit discussed the creation of a group known as Blood Sisters, a lesbian group that donated blood for men who were victims of AIDS, "because the gay community could not give blood, but lesbians (who had the lowest incidence of exchanging bodily fluids with men) could," according to Faderman.

As the gay and lesbian community matured, it developed a myriad of organizations that not only dealt with internal issues, but which also reached out to the larger community. Additionally, there were cultural organizations like the Gay Men's Chorus and the San Diego Women's Chorus, and the Diversionary Theatre; political organizations like the San Diego Democratic Club and the San Diego County Log Cabin Club, and chambers of commerce like the Greater San Diego Business Association. A number of these organizations pointedly refrained from identifying themselves as "gay" or "lesbian," according to Faderman, because "they were more conservative." She added, that although it was organizations such as these that flourished, earlier protests by radical groups such as the Gay Liberation Front, helped spur the community to organize.

One group that offered a double entendre in its name was "Gay for Good," whose members proclaimed their everlasting gayness and who also contributed funds and volunteer time for charitable projects in the general community.

The exhibition features a chart helping people unfamiliar with the lexicon of the LGBTQ+ world to understand who is who.

Faderman said some of the labels have interesting histories. While "lesbian" derives from the Isle of Lesbos, where the ancient Greek poet Sappho wrote of love and attraction between women, the history of the word "gay" to describe homosexual men is murkier. "In the course of my research, I found a cartoon from about the 1880s or early 1890s of two prostitutes standing in front of a street lamp, looking exhausted, and calling themselves 'gay,' and the irony of it is very clear," Faderman said.

"My theory is that the term first came into the heterosexual prostitute community, and then gay hustlers in the late 19th Century took the term to describe themselves, and then the term was used to describe homosexual men, not necessarily hustlers, but all homosexual men in the early 20th Century. By 1912, it was used to describe lesbians as well, and I know that because there is a book by Gertrude Stein called A *Long Gay Book,* which talks about both men and women. Stein wrote an essay at that time called "Miss Furr and Miss Skeene" which was about two lesbian friends of hers and she keeps repeating in her inimitable style, "Miss Furr and Miss Skeene were gay; they were gay every day; every day they were gayer and gayer." The essay, or short story, was published not until 1922 in *Vanity Fair* and I'm sure most people had no idea except for lesbians and gay men who had an idea what that meant."

The historian said that when she came out in the 1950s, the term "gay" meant to be "out there, to be loose." At that time, she said, straight people generally didn't know the meaning of the word 'gay.' "In fact, a way that you could figure out if someone was gay or not was that you could say in a cheery voice, 'Are you gay?' and if the person said, 'I am a little depressed today,' you knew he wasn't."

The chart explains such terms as "bisexual," "transgender," "two spirit," "queer," "intersex," "asexual," "cisgender," "gender expansive," "pansexual," "straight" and "ally," affording a view into the diversity of sexuality within the community. Faderman said various terms came into vogue as different groups sought to assert their identity. Lesbians, for example, wanted to differentiate themselves from "gays," who were men.

The debate sometimes heard about whether homosexuality is a matter of "nature" or "nurture," in Faderman's view is an oversimplification, regardless of how one answers. She said, "It is a matter of who you meet at a particular time. Maybe nature has something to do with it. I think it is very complex; I'm just troubled by attempts to make a sweeping generalization. Some people say, 'I was born that way;' maybe they were, but not everyone would say that. Some people might say, 'I was born with the tendency, and my experiences confirmed my sexuality,' but it is the same for heterosexuals. I think sexuality is very complex. It bothers me when it is reduced to nature or nurture."

Survivor Ruth G. Sax Impresses Comic-Con Audience

San Diego Jewish World,
July 19, 2018

Although Ruth Goldschmiedova Sax of Chula Vista conceded that she didn't grow up with comics, or even know about Superman, whom she subsequently came to admire, she was clearly the hit of a panel on art and the Holocaust that was held Thursday, July 19, at the Comic-Con convention. The reason, as some attendees expressed out loud even before the program began: "How often will we get to meet a Holocaust survivor in person?"

Sax, 90, survived internment in three Holocaust camps—Theresienstadt, Oederan, and Auschwitz—and according to her daughter and fellow panelist, Sandra Scheller, she was forced to stand naked before the Auschwitz doctor Josef Mengele six times as he decided whether she should continue to live or be sent to the gas chambers. "I'm sitting next to a super-hero without a cape," Scheller declared to general applause from the audience. Scheller authored her mother's memoir, *Try to Remember, Never Forget.*

Sax won the hearts of her audience when she reflected humorously about her life, saying in some ways it had changed dramatically, from Holocaust camp to Comic-Con, but in others it hadn't changed at all. As a slide was projected of her as a one-year-old child, she quipped, "I was pushed in a baby carriage, and now I'm being pushed in a wheel chair."

She said she recalled how shocked and scandalized she was, even at the age of 11, by Nazi artworks that dehumanized Jews. As an example, a slide was projected of a cartoon that appeared in *Der Sturmer,* a Nazi publication, in which there was a vile caricature of a Jew begging a German whom he once used to bully to now give him help. She said that before she was sent to the Nazi camps she had thought that she might become an artist; perhaps even a fashion designer, but if she had drawn what she had seen in the camps and had been caught, she would have been put to death. In one of the camps where she was interned, Oederan, she was forced to make ammunition for the German war machine, a product she believes she helped sabotage by scratching the bullets with sand.

After the war, she married Kurt Sax, with whom she celebrated a 63rd wedding anniversary before his death. Kurt and Ruth moved to the United States, "the land of Superman," Ruth said. "Maybe if I had known about Superman, I might have had more faith that I would be free one day. It had taken longer than I thought."

Before turning the microphone over to other panelists, Ruth Sax dispatched Adolf Hitler and the Nazis in this fashion: "God created such a beautiful world, only some people make it so miserable." She also commented, "Some of the propaganda is difficult to see at times, but I am here now, in this country, and I can say, 'This is part of my past.'"

Author Igor Goldkind, whose latest book, which touches on the Holocaust, is titled *Is She Available,* reminded the audience in the well-attended panel session that the Superman character had been created before World War II by two Jews from Cleveland, Jerry Siegel and Joe Shuster. Other superheroes like Captain America, as well as most of the Marvel universe of super heroes also were created by Jews, Stan Lee being notable among them.

Sandra Scheller reviewed other artists of the Holocaust, starting with her cousin Kitty Brunerova, whose drawing of butterflies at the Theresienstadt ghetto and concentration camp has been placed on a commemorative stamp by Czechoslovakia. Her talent did not save her; she was sent from Theresienstadt (known as Terezin in the Czech language) to Auschwitz, where she was murdered.

Another artist, who had been a teacher to Ruth Sax, was Otto Ungar, whose representations of Theresienstadt were so graphic that the Nazis cut off his fingers as punishment, then transported him to Auschwitz to be murdered. Another artist of the era was Dina Babbitt, who drew Snow White and the Seven Dwarfs on a back wall of the children's barracks. Condemned with her mother to go to the gas chamber, she was saved when Mengele decided he needed someone to portray his work. Babbitt reportedly told Mengele that as long as her mother was in line for the gas chamber, they would die together. Instead, Mengele had both of them returned to their barracks.

Scheller completed her presentation by screening some drawings that Allied soldiers made at the end of the war, of the scenes they encountered in a cave where the Nazis had taken 336 prisoners and, in retaliation for the killing of some German policemen, shot each one of them in the back of the head.

Esther Finder, founder of the Nevada branch of Generations of the Shoah, an organization of children and grandchildren of Holocaust survivors, sketched the times in which Siegel and Shuster developed the Superman character. The Nazis believed in social Darwinism, in which the fittest human beings were destined to rule over those who were considered underhumans, among them Jews, Slavs, and Africans. This idea in large part was built upon American eugenics studies. Anti-Semitism was present not only in Germany but also in the United States, where "American Jews were discriminated against and were painfully aware that in order to get ahead they had to change their names and hide their ethnicity."

The American Superman character was the reverse of the Nazi superman, while the Nazi superman was immoral and a bully, who would trample others; the American Superman "represented strength, morality, justice, both legal and social, and the belief that everything would work out right," according to Finder. In the 1950s Superman television series, that motto became "truth, justice and the American way."

The Jewish origins of Superman can be seen by comparing his origin story to that of Moses in the Bible, Finder said. "Moses survived because his mother put him in a vessel and sent him down the river . . . set adrift in the hope that someone would find Moses and care for him." In the Superman mythology, added Finder, a former psychology professor at Montgomery University in Maryland, Kal-El was imperiled, put in a vessel, sent to Earth where it was hoped someone would find him and take care of him." She noted that the "El" in "Kal-El" is one of the Hebrew names for God. He did godly work: "America's Superman was moral, kind, sensitive . . . . He could easily destroy, but his powers were used for good. . . . He was mild-mannered except when he had to fight to save people."

The final panelist, Robert Scott, the Jewish owner of ComicKaze book store, said it was no coincidence that people from struggling Jewish families gave the world its super heroes. "Joe Shuster's parents couldn't afford paper. He would go from store to store to get paper" and even drew on unused wall paper. Scott said comic books are a democratic medium; all anyone needs is "the ability to tell your story, unedited, unaltered, and put it out there for anyone else."

I had an opportunity to pose a question to the panel, based on my interview the day before with comic book artist Miriam Libicki, whose Holocaust comic book, *Ruchie's Job*, contains enough humor that she was worried some readers might be offended. Some people believe there was nothing funny about the Holocaust. The panelists had reassuring words for Libicki. "Gallows humor is what people do, to try to make sense" of their situations, said Goldkind.

Scheller said in combatting the despair of the Holocaust, "We tried many medicines; the ones that worked the most were humor and hope."

And Sax said that on Friday nights in the concentration camp, she and other girls of her age (about 15) used to climb up onto the third bunk and pretend that they were back in their kitchens cooking. They'd laugh about their favorite meals, which in Sax's case was sauerkraut and dumplings!

Plaque Recalling First Roseville Hotel Unveiled

San Diego Jewish World,
October 9. 2018.

The new 16-unit Bellamar Point Loma condominium at the corner of Rosecrans and Byron Streets in the Roseville section of the Point Loma neighborhood gained some additional luster on Tuesday, October 9, when Mayor Kevin Faulconer, City Councilwoman Lorie Zapf, and members of the La Playa Trail Association and the Ocean Beach Historical Society unveiled a plaque that will be placed on the Rosecrans side of the property.

The plaque, sponsored by the La Playa Trails Association, declares the property at 3025 Byron Street/1180 Rosecrans Street to be the "Site of the 1869 Roseville Hotel." The plaque will be mounted above another, smaller plaque on the Rosecrans Street side of the property, which states: "Here Louis Rose Founded Roseville 1869."

The historical record is not clear whether the hotel actually was completed in 1869, but it is apparent that construction began that year, the very same year that Rose recorded the map for the Roseville subdivision, which was approximately 30 blocks long and about eight blocks wide.

Jen Schmidt, a realtor who chaired the public relations committee for the event, noted that the 1869 date indicated that the hotel, long since demolished, had its origins 149 years ago, and that 2019 will be its sesquicentennial. This proved a perfect segue for Mayor Faulconer, who noted that 2019 also will mark the 250th birthday, or sestercentennial of the City of San Diego. Other terms for 250th anniversaries are semiquincentennial and quarter-millennial. Whichever term becomes more popular next year, the occasion promises to be well marked as the 250th anniversary of Father Junipero Serra celebrating the first mass on what later became called the Presidio.

"Why this plaque is important is because it is always great to remind people of where we came from as a city, where we came from as Roseville," Faulconer said. "Our city constantly changes. . . . What makes Point Loma unique, as all of us who live here know, is that we treasure that history. Point Loma is the story of California," a story "not only for ourselves, but for our kids, and our kids' kids."

The mayor was followed to the microphone by City Councilwoman Zapf, who commented that she loves preserving history. She added that is why she constantly takes her daughter to Old Town San Diego State Historic Park and to the Presidio. Noting that the La Playa Trail Association has been marking various spots along the Point Loma Peninsula, Zapf suggested that La Playa Trail is "a modern-day Freedom Trail [of Revolutionary War-era Boston] where you can visit the sites." She thanked the organization "for keeping history alive."

Klonie Kunzel, the chair of the La Playa Trail Association, said that keeping history alive in fact was part of the mission of the organization, which was founded in 2005 and since has installed six markers and built two monuments along the trail that led from the San Diego Mission to Old Town San Diego to the tip of Point Loma.

Eric DuVall, president of the nearby Ocean Beach Historical Society, shared the honor of unveiling the plaque with Mayor Faulconer. Telling some of Louis Rose's biography, he noted that Rose was one of the earliest Jewish settlers in San Diego, having arrived in 1850. He went on to serve on the first Grand Jury, as a member of the City Board of Trustees, and the County Board of Supervisors. He purchased property in Old Town, Roseville, La Playa (another neighborhood on the Pt. Loma Peninsula), and in the area that became known as Rose Canyon, where he had cattle, horses, and operated the region's first tannery. In Roseville, he built both a hotel and a wharf.

In Old Town San Diego, Rose owned the house that became known as the Robinson-Rose House and which today serves as a visitor's center for Old Town San Diego State Historic Park, and also purchased the Pear Garden from landowner Lorenzo Soto, which later became known as Rose's Garden. Today the property, including the Casa de Carrillo, is the site of the Presidio Golf Course.

Rose was twice married. Divorced from his first wife, Caroline, in the 1850s, he married his second wife, Mathilde, in 1869, the same year that he started Roseville, when he was already 62 years of age. Louis and Mathilde had two daughters, one of whom died in infancy. The other, Henrietta, went on to be a longtime teacher, serving as the first schoolmarm at Roseville Elementary School, and later spending much of her tenure teaching Spanish at Roosevelt Junior High School adjacent to Balboa Park. She never married, and Rose has no descendants.

Rose died in 1888, the year prior to Congregation Beth Israel's first year in its own temple, a building that today has been relocated from Uptown to Heritage Park in the Old Town area. Rose was a member of a predecessor roving congregation, Adath Jeshurun, which held services in hotels and people's houses, including the Robinson-Rose House. He helped to found San Diego's Hebrew Benevolent Society and donated the first Jewish cemetery to the community. It was located near Roseville, on ground below the building now housing the Education First facility at 3455 Kenyon Street.

Crafts, Art, Books Featured at Temple Emanu-El Fair

San Diego Jewish World,
November 4, 2018.

O ften you will meet women who either are in their second careers, or have become very proficient at their hobbies, at the Artisan Festival sponsored annually by the Women of Temple Emanu-El.

On Sunday, I found that to be the case when I interviewed artist Enid Texler and cookbook author Linda Moskovics.

Texler, 77, recently retired as a pit boss at the Sycuan Casino, where she made guests welcome while supervising dealers in her area. In a 40-year casino career that took her to Nevada, New Jersey, New Mexico, and California, she had dealt all the card games, so she knew what dealers should and shouldn't be doing.

She was there as the women's movement made inroads into the gaming industry. When she started in 1965 in Las Vegas, she recalled, "Women weren't managers; they didn't even deal. In Reno and Lake Tahoe, they could deal, but they wouldn't put you in management. Then when Atlantic City, New Jersey, opened up, I think it was one of the best things for women in the business. They gave us the opportunity to go on the floor."

Texler first was attracted to the gaming industry at age 19 when she watched a dealer in Las Vegas and thought "he looked so awesome." But the restrictions on women's advancement in the industry discouraged her, so she moved to San Diego, and worked at restaurants, including the Butcher Shop in Kearny Mesa. Eventually, she decided to go to gaming school to learn roulette, and baccarat, and from there, went on to management school.

Art was her way of relaxing following a busy day at the casino. "I would come home about midnight, sleep, get up, have my coffee, and then I would draw and paint in the morning," she said. She doesn't follow any prescribed technique, she said. Instead, at her kitchen table, "I play—whatever comes out, that is what will come out. Sometimes I don't sketch, sometimes I just drop the paint, put some alcohol in there, and look at it, and I think, 'I should put a menorah in there, and perhaps some gelt.'"

Though she doesn't follow any "rules," Texler has had plenty of art training—having augmented her natural talent in drawing and sketching with classes emphasizing various media, including pastels and watercolors.

Although she was raised Catholic, Texler began studying Judaism after she married her Jewish husband. At first, she had no intention to convert, but simply wanted to know more about her husband's religion in order to teach it to their four daughters. But the more she studied, the more interested she became. Rabbi Morton Cohn of Congregation Beth Israel supervised her conversion in 1967-68. Over the years, she has gravitated more and more to painting Jewish subjects in watercolors. How might a painting begin? "I see the dreidel on my dresser, and then I will go and play with it, or I see the menorah by the coffee pot, and maybe I will throw a bagel in."

Texler is in the process of learning Hebrew, all the better to make her first trip to Israel—which she says is a big item on her bucket list.

Her drawings and paintings are reproduced on three sizes of greeting cards. She focused in this exhibit on those with Chanukah themes. A small card sells for $3.50, but five of them cost only $12. Similar volume discounts are given with the medium size cards ($4.50, five for $16) and the large size cards ($5.50, five for $20.)

Art, said the former casino pit boss, definitely "is a good deal."

Linda Moskovics retired six years ago as the librarian at the Benjamin branch of the San Diego Public Library. She told me that writing *The Fiber Rich Kitchen Cookbook* was the fulfillment of a lifelong dream. "I realized there was a need for recipes for people to get more fiber in their diets," she said. "You need your fiber to keep healthy. It helps with a lot of things like digestion, diabetes, heart health, keeping yourself regular."

She said she became an advocate of a fiber-rich diet after her cardiologist recommended a vegan diet, with lots of plant-based foods. While some people think vegetarian diets are bland, she said, "you can spice it up. A lot of my recipes say, 'Adjust seasonings to your taste.' I personally didn't grow up eating a lot of spices."

In creating the cookbook, "I tried to vary the recipes—one-pot meals, salads, breakfast foods, snacks, main dishes, desserts." She said she personally has cooked, tasted, and served every recipe in the book, using friends and her "significant other, Ray Bronco" as her official tasters. Most of the time her lunch or dinner guests liked the recipes as she prepared them, Moskovics said, but occasionally they suggested a little more of this or a little less of that.

She has many favorite recipes, such as Zucchini, Black Bean and Rick Quick Skillet, Dark Chocolate Nut Bark, Sweet Potato Pancakes, and the recipe from the $28 (on Amazon) cookbook which she gave me permission to republish below.

With Chanukah in mind, Moskovics told me that her book, available on Amazon, "makes a really nice gift, and the recipes are easy—with not-hard-to-find ingredients."

She hasn't lost her librarian skills. When I asked where in the library, her book would be shelved, she promptly replied under Dewey Decimal Number 641 in the Cookbook Section.

"Linda's Saucy Red Lentils and Corn" (from *The Fiber Rich Kitchen Cookbook*).

This is a quick, easy, one pot vegetarian meal. Serve it with a salad and a vegetable on the side for a delicious and nutritious meal.

Makes 4 servings, 1 cup lentil mixture and 1/2 cup grain each.

* 1 tablespoon grapeseed oil or oil of choice
* 1 medium yellow onion, chopped (approximately 1/2 cup)
* 4 garlic cloves, chopped
* 1 1/2 cups vegetable broth or stock (or use chicken broth or stock for a richer flavor)
* 1/2 cup dried red lentils, rinsed
* 1 tablespoon chili powder
* 1 1/2 teaspoons ground cumin
* 1 cup frozen corn, preferably organic or use fresh corn
* 1 cup tomato sauce
* 1/3 cup tomato paste
* 1 teaspoon dried oregano
* 1 teaspoon red wine vinegar
* 2 cups hot cooked brown rice, wild rice, barley, or farro
* 3/4 cup shredded cheddar cheese of choice

Coat a medium size saucepan with cooking spray. Add oil and sauté onion and garlic; approximately 5-10 minutes.

Add the broth or stock, red lentils, chili powder, and cumin. Slowly bring to a boil and reduce heat. Cover and simmer 30 minutes or until lentils are almost tender.

Stir in corn, tomato sauce, tomato paste, oregano, and vinegar. Slowly return to boil, and then reduce heat again. Cover and simmer 10 minutes more, or until the lentils are tender.

Serve over rice, barley, or farro. Sprinkle the cheese on top.

Variation: Substitute salsa for the tomato sauce for more zip.

Christina de Jesus Is a Jewish Song Leader

San Diego Jewish World,
November 5, 2018.

O n the third Friday evening of each month, the Shir Chadash (New Song) Band leads services celebrating Shabbat at Tifereth Israel Synagogue. The young mother whose alto voice provides the harmonies to the Shabbat melodies is an example of religious mobility. Just hearing that her name is "Christina de Jesus," informs you that she grew up in a Christian family. Just hearing her sing satisfies you that she is more than comfortable, she is at home, in her adopted faith: Judaism.

De Jesus, a native-born San Diegan, grew up in a Filipino family that came to San Diego via her grandparents' service in the United States Navy. Her father, Roland, continued in the Naval tradition, and until Christina was 8 years old, the family moved from one duty station to another, including Mississippi; Monterey, California; and Guam. Eventually, her mother, Miriam, put her foot down: Okay," she declared, "we are going to stay in San Diego where the rest of our family is. I am not traveling anymore." After that, Christina's father traveled from place to place, while the rest of the family settled into the San Diego County lifestyle. They lived first in Nestor, then moved to the Rancho Del Rey neighborhood of Chula

Vista, where she attended Chula Vista Junior High School and Chula Vista High School. She enrolled in the school's creative and performing arts program, where she sang soprano in the school choir.

"I had the same choir director throughout six years," de Jesus recalled. "He probably needed a strong soprano. In college, I found out that I am actually an alto. I can sing soprano parts, but my voice just isn't as suited for them. My voice's home register is in the alto range."

She's glad of that, she said. "In traditional choral music, it is the middle voices that make it sound interesting. The bass voice tells you what key you are in, the soprano tells you the melody, and the alto and the tenor can be the ones who make the difference between a boring song, and an amazing, interesting song to listen to."

There are two vocalists and four instrumentalists in the Shir Chadash band. Ted Stern plays bass guitar. David Ogul, who also is president of the Conservative congregation, plays lead guitar. Miriam Shoval sings soprano. Susan Levy, who was a co-founder of the band, plays piano. Bob Holloway, who like Christina is a Jew by choice, plays the clarinet. For the most part, the songs they play, with an upbeat tempo, are well-known Shabbat melodies. Members of the congregation sing along, sometimes clapping their hands, and occasionally dancing in the aisles. "When I sing a song, I try to inspire *rauch* (spirit)," says de Jesus. "I am trying to sing a song to help other people feel moved, feel some kind of connection to why we are there—to celebrate Shabbat, and to come together as a community."

"Christina brings far more than amazing vocals and a strong background in music composition to Shir Chadash," comments Ogul. "She brings *rauch,* energy, and inspiration to all she encounters, not to mention being a most loving and nurturing mom of two beautiful little cherubs. In all the years I've known her, I can't ever recall seeing her become angry at anyone, and I have rarely seen her without a smile. If the world were filled with more Christinas, it would be a much more beautiful place."

Holloway commented: "Christina learns her music very quickly; she is not only a talented linguist but a talented musician."

De Jesus is married to Paul Kalmar, who along with his parents, Dr. Frank Kalmar and Susan Stern, often sits in the front row so that his and Christina's children, Louis, 3 1/2 and Winifred, 7 months, can be close to their mother while she is performing. During the singing of the V'shamru prayer, Paul will toss Louis up in the air and catch him, to the rhythm, so often that the congregation has all but learned to expect it.

While growing up, de Jesus experienced the important rituals of Catholicism, explaining: "My mom and dad are pretty religious," she said. "They got us baptized when we were supposed to be baptized; they got us communion when we were supposed to have communion, and they got us confirmation when we were supposed to have confirmation. It was the whole gamut. . . . I definitely felt some sort of spiritual connection, wondering about man's place in the world and how our souls and spirits connect. But after going to college [at UC Berkeley], I was really starting to question, 'Is this really what I believe, or is this what I was raised to believe?'"

At the Newman Center on campus, she sometimes would debate theological questions with members of the Opus Dei, a lay Catholic organization, but as college wore on, "I thought this isn't jibing anymore, I can't agree with this. It didn't seem like the right fit spiritually. So, I stopped going, much to my parents' and grandparents' chagrin. For a while I was nothing, just agnostic, but I still was interested in religions and the philosophies behind them." So, she remained unaffiliated until after graduating from Berkeley with a degree in electrical engineering, and later meeting Paul Kalmar, a UC-Irvine graduate, through the OkCupid online dating website.

"That was in 2007 and he was my first close exposure to Judaism," she said. "There is a little joke in his family. My name is Christina de Jesus, and that is the most un-Jewish name you possibly could have. On caller ID, it shows up as 'de Jesus, Christ.' . . . and here is a Jewish boy dating a non-Jewish girl. Here is Paul, the grandson of Holocaust survivors, dating a non-Jew!"

Ever a student, de Jesus started Googling about Judaism, reading Wikipedia entries, which eventually led her to the Jewish Theological Seminary website. "Eventually, after we had been dating a little while, there was a Basic Judaism class that Rabbi [Leonard] Rosenthal was teaching at Tifereth Israel, and I thought, 'This is awesome, let's sign up.'" So, she enrolled, as did Paul, who took it as a refresher course. "I guess I am one of the few Jews who has ever read the entire Tanach [Jewish Bible] from cover to cover," said Christina. "One of the things that I thought was interesting is how different it can be, based on who is translating."

Recalling the Basic Judaism class, she said, "It was the first religious class where I had been encouraged to ask questions and there wasn't a predetermined answer that was right. In Judaism, you are supposed to ask questions. You are supposed to think critically. You are supposed to ask, 'Why would God say something like that,' like, 'Abraham, go bind your son Isaac'? There isn't one specific interpretation; whereas in [Catholic] catechism classes, they encouraged us to ask questions, but ultimately what the church said was right."

Another aspect of Judaism that appealed to de Jesus was the "emphasis on direct accountability—why should I go through some intermediary to get absolution?"—and on action in this world being important. "We live in this world, why shouldn't we take action to make this world better here and now?"

As part of the Basic Judaism class, de Jesus attended various services in the sanctuary, experiencing the cycle of Jewish holidays. "My first Jewish service was the Kol Nidre," she said. "Who does Kol Nidre first? But that was it. I thought it was beautiful. My connection there was the music, as you might imagine. The solemnity of Kol Nidre, the *rauch* in the sanctuary . . . the feeling there, the chills, and then I started reading through the *mahzor* [High Holy Day prayer book] and its commentaries."

There wasn't one "Aha" moment when she decided that she would convert; instead, the idea dawned upon her that Judaism was something to which she could commit herself. "You do a lot of study," she said. "You and your rabbi determine when you are at the point that you determine that you are ready. Rabbi Rosenthal was at that point that I was ready way before I was. He didn't say anything, but when I said I was ready, it was like, 'It's about time!' So, we went up to the American Jewish University in Los Angeles, and I went before the *beth din*. It was terrifying. Oh my gosh, there were these three guys [rabbis] who literally had the power to say. 'She's not ready yet, come back later,' and that would have been a bummer because I was supposed to go on Birthright (a free 10-day trip to Israel) that year, and if they had said, 'No,' I wouldn't have been able to go."

Most of the rabbis' questions dealt with her personal connection to Judaism, and why she felt it was right for her, but one rabbi asked a question that stumped her. How many times should one ask for forgiveness before letting the matter drop? "The correct answer is three, and that I didn't know," she said, but missing a question didn't disqualify her.

Following her appearance before the *beth din*, she went to the mikvah (ritual bath). "My parents will tell you that I am a water baby," she said. "I've loved water forever. The mikvah is this wonderful thing; there is all this stuff about it being a rebirth. It is a cliché, but it is totally true. It is just you in the warm water. You are totally immersed. Dunk, dunk, dunk, and you say a *baracha* (blessing), and you are a Jew. I felt warm and loved and new—brand new—coming out of there.

"Before you go on in you wash, comb your hair (for me that took forever), you scrub super well, clean your nails, and then you go into a room with [female] attendants. For the conversion ceremony, you dunk three times, and the mikvah attendant tells you if it is a good dunk, and I had three good dunks. After the third time,

299

you say the *shema* [a prayer proclaiming the oneness of God]—your first time as a Jew. I sang the *shema*. The chamber was small, the sound was echoing all over the room. Afterwards the rabbi [who was positioned behind a partition] congratulated me, and the attendant gave me some time to float and process and be there in that water. It was one of the highlights of my life, it was so beautiful."

Her conversion was in April 2011. She went on the Birthright trip to Israel in June, and she and Paul were married in the sanctuary of Tifereth Israel Synagogue that December.

At first, her parents "had a hard time" with her conversion. "Our child is becoming a Jew, what are we going to do?" she paraphrased. Then her aunt pointed out to her parents that they were really sad when Christina had stopped going to church, "so would you rather she had a connection now, even if not a Catholic connection, or would you rather her to continue to have no connection?" After that conversation, her parents became okay with it. "Their ideal? No. But they are happy the grandchildren will be raised in a fairly religious home."

Like Paul's mother, Christina keeps her birth name, aware that the name "de Jesus" is bound to occasion interesting conversation in Jewish circles.

Paul and Christina have numerous interests in common. Both are computer people. Christina works in the field of networking computers. Paul works in the field of translating human speech to computer algorithms, enabling the computer to find the answer to a spoken question. They both enjoy folk dancing, with Paul, an Israeli dancing enthusiast, having taught Christina some of the Israeli dances. They also have attended together Filipino folk dancing exhibitions. When their children are old enough, they would like them also to learn folk dances of the world.

Rosenthal, who today is Tifereth Israel's emeritus rabbi, recalled that de Jesus "was an enthusiastic, bubbly, and insightful student. She demonstrated not only a grasp of the details of Judaism, but more importantly, the overarching meaning of living a Jewish life. After her formal conversion she and her husband, Paul, continued to participate in synagogue life and especially educational programs. She continues to be a bright and inquisitive student. I was thrilled when she volunteered for Shir Chadash. I had no idea that she has such a beautiful voice and is so skilled at harmonizing. You can see the love in the sparkle of her eyes as she leads the service."

Variety of Form, Materials in SDMA Outdoor Sculptures

San Diego Jewish World,
November 10, 2018

I n some cases, sculptures are grouped to tell a story, but at other times their storytelling groupings are accidental. You'll find both sets of circumstances outside the San Diego Museum of Art.

For example, two Jewish artists who immigrated to the United States from the Czarist Russian Empire have sculptures located close together where the museum's outdoor café melds into the Sculpture Garden. *Night Presence II,* a large outdoor sculpture in welded, Corten steel by Louise Nevelson (1899-1988) is within a short distance of the copper relief *Sonata Primitive* by Saul L. Baizerman (1889-1957).

Nevelson moved as a child in 1905 from modern day Ukraine to Maine, where her father established a lumber business, and from which she later escaped to New York City as her artistic abilities blossomed. Baizerman had grown up in Vitebsk, Belarus, a city made famous by his fellow artist Marc Chagall. Opposing the czar's government resulted in Baizerman being sent to prison, and after he got out, he migrated in 1910 to New York. He was then 22.

If *Night Presence II* looks to some like it was carved from a dark wood, that may have been the influence of Nevelson growing up the daughter of a lumberman. Some critics said Nevelson's sculptures are too masculine, but Nevelson dismissed the criticism, saying that art transcends gender.

Baizerman, reacting to oppression by the Russian czars, dreamed of a worker's society in which class distinctions would be erased.

Leading me and my neighbor Bob Lauritzen on a tour of the outdoor sculptures, Anita Feldman, the museum's deputy director for curatorial affairs and education, commented about Baizerman's copper relief sculpture, featuring the torsos and heads of two figures. "Notice that it is all hammered by hand; it is very labor intensive. . . . For him, it is very important to show the physical, manual effort that goes into making a sculpture, and yet he creates something that is very poetic. He has these two figures together, sort of romantically entwined, especially as it's a relief, so there is air all around it."

As we stepped from the outdoor café to the Sculpture Garden, we saw a piece by Alexander Liberman (1912-1999), called *Aim I.* Like Baizerman and Nevelson, Liberman was born in the Russian Empire, but his Jewish family was given permission by the Leninist government in 1921 to move to London. As a school boy in England, Liberman developed an interest in photography, which eventually led to a career as editorial director with Condé Nast publications in New York. He turned to sculpting relatively late in his life.

"His works are at the Tate [in England], in other important collections, and here," Feldman told us. "He works with aluminum tubing and like Louise Nevelson he uses one color, but his colors are very bright." The sculpture before us was painted in a bright red.

"He really liked the idea of using modern materials for a modern age," Feldman added. His assemblage of tubes looked to me like a rocket about to be launched from a nest. "It has a vertical thrust to it, for sure," Feldman commented.

Perhaps the most impressive pairing in the Sculpture Garden—certainly from the standpoint of size—are the bronze sculptures by Henry Moore (1890-1986) and Barbara Hepworth (1903-1975). I was particularly curious to hear Feldman's commentary about these sculptures because she had worked at the Henry Moore Foundation in London for 18 years, first as a curator and later as head of their collections. She had traveled to 28 countries installing his sculptures. Feldman, daughter of a Jewish father and Christian mother, has been with the San Diego Museum of Art for approximately five years.

Feldman told us that Moore and Hepworth "were famously friends and rivals throughout their entire lives. For many years, they worked parallel to each other. They were exploring ways of opening out forms. Henry Moore started dividing his figures and you can see that in this two-piece figure (*Reclining Figure, Arch Leg*) a wonderful chasm coming between the forms, making them resemble shapes in landscapes. You can imagine it being a series of mountains." Moore's piece, suggesting a woman's torso and arched leg, is the largest sculpture in the garden, dominating the landscape. Next to it is Barbara Hepworth's *Figure for Landscape* in which Hepworth "has hollowed out this form so it becomes almost like a ghost. There is this idea of the relationship between man and nature in both of these sculptures."

Given the empty spaces that both artists purposely leave within their sculptures, "you can look through them; the landscape pervades the art; it comes right through," said Feldman. "The Henry Moore is a wonderful piece to walk around. The landscape changes. It changes from a distance and up close. You can see all the detail and the texture. Some parts are very smooth. You can see the green of the cast coming through, the patina, and the very dark brown as well."

I asked if, as the former head of collections of the Henry Moore Foundation, she would tell us more about the sculpture in the context of Moore's career.

"This was made in 1969 and at that time he was very interested in this idea of relating figures to landscape, but also his figures were in demand in these very urban settings," she replied. "He was thinking how can he make a figure work in a modern architectural setting, and so he started using bolder, more abstracted shapes in his figures so they could hold their own. He made them larger, so they would have more of a physical presence. Yet they still are recalling the landscape and still recalling the figure." The massive sculpture before us, she added, "is definitely a head, shoulders, and a torso coming through. . . . There are related pieces which are very interesting. For example, he has just this end-leg piece as a carving in black marble called *Arch* and he made this particular sculpture in three different sizes."

Could Feldman please tell us more about Moore's and Hepworth's rivalry and companionship?

"They both came from the north of England from towns— Henry Moore from Castleford, which is a coal mining town, very industrial, and Barbara Hepworth came from Wakefield, which was six miles away! They both went to study at the Leeds School of Art, which was in the nearest big town, and then they both went to the Royal College of Art in London, within a year of each other. Henry Moore started first and then he went to London, and she followed him there. He was creating carvings first of all, these opening out forms. He said that making a hole in a sculpture was a revelation because you have a space coming through, and she did the same thing at the same time. They both experimented with strings, putting strings in their sculptures at the same time. In the 1930s they lived almost next door to each other in a neighborhood in Hampstead in North London. Another neighbor of theirs was [avantgarde artist] Naum Gabo, and [painter Piet] Mondrian came over.

A lot of the artists and architects and intellectuals were fleeing Europe in the 1930s and a lot of them came to this suburb of Hampstead. So, there was this huge dialogue and exchange of ideas and it was a really exciting moment in England for the arts. [Architect Walter] Gropius came over and a lot of the artists from Germany came over. . . .

"When England entered the war, and London was being bombed in the blitz, Moore lost his studio/home in London. It was damaged in the bombing. He also had a cottage in the south of England, in Kent, which he had to evacuate because the British were convinced that was where the Germans would invade England, from that coastline, so he lost both places at the same time. That was when he moved to Hertfordshire [to 70 acres of sheep fields] and Barbara Hepworth moved to Cornwall in the south of England, so they weren't neighbors anymore, but they still were very close. She married [abstract painter] Ben Nicholson, and had triplets, so it was an interesting time."

Their rivalry, while friendly, developed as "Henry Moore became increasingly famous and Barbara Hepworth tended to take a second seat," Feldman said. "Part of that was due to the fact that she was a woman. Female artists were not given the same opportunities that male artists were, but also Henry Moore was involved in all kinds of projects all over the world, so his reputation began building on itself as cities got Henry Moore sculptures. He made over 1,000 sculptural ideas and many of them were cast in editions, so you can multiply those out. There would be six or nine of each one. And he made many thousands of drawings and graphics. There is a seven-volume resume just for the sculpture, another six for the drawings, and four for the graphics."

I asked about the manner in which Moore went about his work.

"He had a very routine way of working," Feldman said. "He didn't like to vary it too much because if he kept to a routine, he could get more done. He had three assistants who helped him keep it going. He would get up very early and would work into the night. After it got too dark to sculpt, he would go into the house and draw."

He drew his ideas from nature, Feldman said. "Say, he would find a piece of stone or something in the garden that he liked the shape of, he then would make a plaster cast of that, maybe add a head, maybe other elements, and then he would make a plaster cast of that [overall] shape. He would use that to make a small sculpture that he could hold in the palm of his hand. He worked on a very small scale. People always think of Henry Moore with these very big sculptures, outdoors, but 90 percent of everything he made was small enough to hold in the palm of his hand. Then his assistants would help him enlarge on those. He would have a middle size that he would call a working model, and that would be about three feet long, table top size, and then after that maybe only 10 percent would be enlarged to life size or bigger."

Feldman came to work for the Henry Moore Foundation after the artist's death, and never had the opportunity to meet him prior to that. As a San Diegan, she said, she would have liked to have escorted him along the rocks of Sunset Cliffs, as "he would have loved that." He used to draw inspiration from the famous white cliffs of Dover, England.

Also in the Sculpture Garden are stainless steel sculptures by David Smith (1906-1965) and George Warren Rickey (1907-2002); a painted iron sculpture, *Spinal Column* by Alexander Calder (1898-1976), and a pedestal awaiting a new sculpture, *Rain Mountain* by Isamu Noguchi (1904-1988). Feldman expected it to be installed some time during the month of November.

The unintended pairing that caught my eye, just outside the café, were a fiberglass sculpture, *Border Crossing* by Luis Jimenez (1940-2006), which depicts a man carrying his family on his back, crossing a river into the United States, and on a wall nearby *The Watchers,* depicting three faceless guards, by Lynn Chadwick, (1914-2003). Given today's political context, in which a caravan of families from Central America is making its way to the United States border, where Border Patrol officers, backed by the United States military are preparing to prevent the caravan from crossing into the United States, the two sculptures appear to be related.

Actually, they are not, said Feldman. It is just happenstance. Chadwick's piece "was made during the Cold War," she said. "You have these very stark, hard geometric lines. These three figures watching; it has that definite chill of the Cold War." She noted that whereas the *Border Crossing* is facing north—the very direction that migrants head in their journeys to the United States—*The Watchers* are looking to the east. "They are not meant to be watching them," she said. "The reason for this site is that this is the west wing of the museum [where] we have this huge empty wall and it was just crying out for a piece of art." She said the west wing of the museum was constructed during the same time period as when Chadwick created her art.

In front of the main building of the San Diego Museum of Art, moving from west to east, are *The Prodigal Son,* a 1905 work by Auguste Rodin (1840-1917); *Mother and Daughter Seated,* a 1971 sculpture by Francisco Zúñiga (1912-1998) *Solar Bird,* sculpted in 1966 by Juan Miró (1893-1983); *Odyssey III* by Tony Rosenthal (1914-2009), the fourth Jewish artist represented in the collection of outdoor sculptures, and *Big Open Skull* by Jack Zajac (1929-), the only sculptor in the collection who is still living.

I asked Feldman what she hopes that visitors to the outdoor collection will remember about their encounter with these sculptures.

"The joy of sculpture, of art, in a public place and in the open air, that art is not just something to hang on the walls of museums, that it can be enjoyed out in nature, with light and weather affecting it, and it comes in many different sizes, forms, and materials, and it is a pleasure," she answered.

Also, she noted, considerable construction work is planned in Balboa Park near the end of next year, to create a direct access route to a planned parking structure that is intended to eliminate some of the traffic congestion within the park. That construction will necessitate some of the outdoor sculptures to be removed temporarily, Feldman said, "but be assured we will be bringing them back!"

I'd recommend seeing them sooner rather than later.

Jews of the U.S. Military Honored at Veterans Museum

San Diego Jewish World,
November 13, 2018

A famous U.S. Navy admiral, two U.S. Air Force officers, and a U.S. Army major currently are being saluted in a display sponsored by the Jewish War Veterans of San Diego at the Veterans Museum and Memorial Center in Balboa Park.

Honored are Admiral Hyman J. Rickover, Colonel Clark J. Kholos, Lieutenant Colonel Allen R. Miliefsky, and Major Abraham J. Baum.

Perhaps the most dramatic description of heroism under fire was accorded to Baum, who headed a controversial World War II task force that General George S. Patton had ordered to charge through enemy German lines to liberate a prisoner-of-war camp where Patton's son-in-law, John L. Knight, had been imprisoned.

Patton presented Baum with the Distinguished Service Cross for extraordinary heroism in 1945. The citation read: "On March 26, 1945, Captain Baum led an armored force in daring action into enemy territory to liberate Allied prisoners held by the Germans near Hammelburg, Germany. Enroute, as the column entered the town of Germunden, Captain Baum was wounded by enemy rocket fire. Despite his wound, he continued to lead the force throughout the day and the following night until he was again wounded during action on the outskirts of Hammelburg. Captain Baum's fearless determination and his inspiring leadership and loyal courageous devotion to duty are in keeping with the highest traditions of the military service." Baum subsequently was promoted to major.

Admiral Rickover (1900-1986), who is considered to be the father of America's nuclear Navy, is remembered at the museum with a copy of the citation that had accompanied a commemorative medal that Congress approved in his honor in 1982. It described Rickover as an educator, patriot, and engineer, who made "distinguished contributions to the defense of our nation," was responsible for the "peaceful development of nuclear reactor technology," and gave "sixty-three years of service to our country and world-renowned contributions in development of safe nuclear energy."

Air Force Col. Clark J. Kholos was stationed during the Vietnam War at Udon Royal Thai Air Force Base, where he "served as a fire control officer on AC-130A and AC-130H gunship aircraft, coordinating and directing combat aircrew missions in Cambodia, Laos, and Vietnam," according to the display.

Kholos had flown 269 combat missions, compiling 560 combat flying hours as part of his overall total of 8,600 flying hours. "His military decorations include the Legion of Merit, Distinguished Flying Cross, Meritorious Service Medal with two Oak Leaf Clusters, Air Medal with eight Oak Leaf Clusters, Air Force Commendation Medal, Armed Forces Expeditionary Medal, Combat Readiness Medal, Vietnam Medal with four devices, the Republic of Vietnam Gallantry Cross with Palm, and the Republic of Vietnam Campaign Medal," according to a printed resume at the museum.

Lt. Col. Allen R. Miliefsky, USAF Retired, had been trained as a fighter pilot, but because of illness retrained as a navigator. He flew 258 combat missions during the 1968 "Tet" offensive in Vietnam, logging over 860 hours of combat flying and a total of 5,500 flying hours.

"While flying these missions not a single American outpost or fire support base in his area of responsibility, though under heavy attack, was ever overrun by the enemy," according to the Museum's display. Among numerous awards and decorations was "The Distinguished Flying Cross for preventing the enemy from overrunning a Special Forces Camp near Da Nang Air Base." In 1977, "Allen received an assignment as the Air Adviser to the Shah of Iran," according to the printed legend. "Upon his retirement on October 1, 1978 as a lieutenant colonel, Allen began working as Director of Veteran Services for the Commonwealth of Massachusetts. He worked in this position until he moved to San Diego where he assumed the position of Transition Service officer for the Disabled American Veterans."

A 2005 resolution from the California State Assembly noted that the Jewish War Veterans organization was founded in 1896 by Jewish veterans of the Civil War, and that "thousands of Jews have died in combat for their country and thousands more have been wounded, and thousands of Jews have been awarded combat medals for performing their duty in time of war."

The resolution went on to state that "a study of Jewish participation in the military during World War II clearly indicates Jews served in the Armed Forces beyond their numerical proportion to the general population, and they received more than 52,000 awards, including the coveted Congressional Medal of Honor."

Besides honoring Jewish veterans, the JWV also "combats anti-Semitism and bigotry . . . assists the Office of Special Investigation in pursuing Nazi war criminals, supports American youth through scouting, scholarships, and anti-drug programs, and assists oppressed Jews worldwide," according to the Assembly resolution.

It added that "JWVUSA (Jewish War Veterans of the United States of America) is dedicated to America's veterans through its hospital, rehabilitation and veterans service programs [and] assists the Veterans' Service Office in major cities throughout the country, and supports the underprivileged, homeless, and handicapped of the nation through a variety of civic projects including low-cost, federally subsidized senior citizen housing."

The Veterans Museum and Memorial Center in Balboa Park is housed in the former, multi-religious Navy Chapel that had been part of Balboa Naval Hospital before city-owned Balboa Park and the Naval Hospital participated in a swap of land at Inspiration Point and Florida Canyon. The chapel has numerous stained-glass windows relevant to each of the many religions it served. The JWV display case is located immediately below a stained-glass window depicting the Tablets of the Law (10 Commandments) inscribed within a Magen David.

"Escape the Nat" Diversifies the Museum Experience

San Diego Jewish World,
November 27, 2018

The San Diego Museum of Natural History, familiarly known as "The Nat," began attracting new visitors last July when it installed an Escape Room on its bottom floor, with the idea of inducing gamers to come to the museum. Escape Rooms grew out of video games, only instead of being virtual experiences; they are real experiences.

In the case of The Nat, the Escape Room occupies two rooms, and in solving the puzzle, one deals with botanical specimens, insect specimens, and maps. All these are instrumental in the museum's mission of studying the ecosystems of the three Californias—the U.S. state, Baja California, and Baja California Sur.

For accomplished gamers, Escape the Nat may not be very hard, but for neophytes such as my 11-year-old grandson, Sky, and myself, it was indeed a puzzle that we were unable to solve within the 60 allotted minutes, not withstanding that the attendant, James, kindly gave us hints—as he is allowed to do. Escape The Nat is a modified experience, in that one really doesn't have to "escape" at all. Players who might be claustrophobic, ill, or bored, may leave any time. Some other Escape Rooms require that you solve the puzzle to get out before the time elapses.

Notwithstanding our first-time inability to solve the puzzle— which has to do with counteracting a toxin that terrorists might be planning to use—Sky pronounced the challenge very enjoyable. "It was a very well-thought out Escape Room," he told me afterwards over Mac n' Cheese in The Nat's café. "There were some things that I just didn't notice, and I was annoyed at myself for missing them; they were things that I should have realized. It's kind of confusing, but I did find it fun, entertaining, and harder than I expected it would be."

Since July, there have been more than 600 people who have tested their skill at Escape the Nat, many of whom—it is assumed— might not otherwise have been exposed to the Museum of Natural History.

Beth Redmond-Jones, The Nat's vice president of engagement and education, told me that her museum is the first in the United States to create its own Escape Room, and possibly is the first in the world. She expressed the hope, during an interview, that other museums, especially those in Balboa Park, might design similar rooms to thereby create a tradition of gamers making museums regular stopping places.

The expectation is that after the gamers complete Escape the Nat, they will tour the museum's other exhibits, and thus be exposed to The Nat's core area of study. Touring the museum was exactly what Sky did while I interviewed Redmond-Jones, and it was clear later that he had enjoyed discovering various exhibits throughout the multi-story museum building.

"Escape rooms are unique and challenging in their own right," Redmond-Jones told me. "What we really are hoping is that this presents an opportunity to do something that our scientists at The Nat do every day, which is to ask questions and solve problems, and to take clues and put things together. What I love about science is that questions lead to more questions, which lead us to new answers and new findings. So, part of this was to 'gamify' that process and get people thinking about what scientists do."

She said that the game involves not only plants, but insects, and maps as well, because in real life, "they are really interconnected, or work together, in specific geographic regions. . . . We want visitors to understand that we are—besides a place where you can come and experience exhibits and go to movies—a place where we have active research going on. We are studying the biodiversity of Southern California and the Baja Peninsula and that is really critical to us because our ecosystems are changing with urban development and pressures from climate change."

Redmond-Jones told me that museums across the country have experienced declining attendance, prompting them to think of new ways to attract visitors. Escape the Nat is only one example. Creating interactive exhibits rather than those that require visitors to stand-and-stare is another strategy, which is strongly in evidence at the Fleet Science Center, located in Balboa Park on the other side of the Bea Evenson Fountain from The Nat. Visitors can push buttons to activate displays; run their hands through vapor; whisper into a device on one side of the room and be heard whispering on the other side; watch balls revolve clockwise around a metal basin, and generally enjoy a large variety of kinetic and tactile experiences.

At the San Diego History Center, yet another strategy has been to develop exhibitions about the history in San Diego of various population groups. There was an extensive exhibition last year about how Jews impacted and were impacted by San Diego. Currently another exhibition traces the history of San Diego County's LGBTQ+ community.

For The Nat, "our 21+ Secret Society of Adultologists is another one," Redmond-Jones said. We had an event based on our exhibition, 'Hidden Gems,' and it was called 'Pretty Shiny Things.' It was everything from a DJ on the rooftop with a bar, to a drag queen doing a show, to a costume party with dazzling outfits, to scientists on the floor talking about color and shiny things in nature and animals that might live in mines where gems would come from. We had our paleo lab open. We had arts and crafts, and a lot of crown-making with shiny glittery things. So, it was really fun to see a whole new audience come in who hadn't been here before and have an opportunity to experience the museum without school kids around and in a way that is engaging to them."

I asked what was the process that led to the creation of Escape The Nat. "We were very fortunate to receive funding from the Sefton Foundation for something called the Evolutionary Venture Fund," Redmond-Jones responded. "Then, what we did was put out a request for proposals from the staff to present ideas about things . . .that would put our science first and engage our visitors, and one of our Visitor Services Associates, Zack Stevens, who worked at the front desk as one the leads, is a big gamer, an Escape Room guy, and he put forward the idea of a botany escape room.

"Everyone who made a proposal put together what the costs would be and how their idea would benefit the museum, how it would align with our strategic plan, and then it was reviewed by a committee. A short list of proposals was selected, and then each of the individuals had to do a pitch to executive management and to other key staff as well as to the committee. They had to explain in 5 to 10 minutes what they wanted to do and why. All the projects were ranked and prioritized, and then we had to see how much money we had in our evolutionary venture fund to allocate."

Stevens refined the Escape the Nat concept with Dr. Michael Wall, who is the museum's vice president for conservation and science.

Some other recent innovations at The Nat have included an "Artist in Residence" program, which saw Larry and Debbie Kline draw James Audobon-style portraits of endangered birds, and a "Make and Take" Art Cart program, in which volunteers invited museum visitors to sketch items from the collection.

Rather than considering each other as rivals, the museums of Balboa Park often work together, occasionally developing companion exhibits. Redmond-Jones said the real competitors for visitors in San Diego are such premier attractions as the Zoo, SeaWorld, and the beaches. "We consider ourselves as Day Four on a San Diego visit, but we are moving our way up," she said.

Immigrant Stories Told at New Americans Museum

San Diego Jewish World,
December 18, 2018

Immigrants Tammuz Dubnov and Gad Shanaan from Israel and Michel Cohen of Mexico are among 76 New Americans who are featured in an innovative exhibition that was created by the staff of the *San Diego Union-Tribune* in cooperation with the New Americans Museum at Liberty Station.

Each life-size portrait of an immigrant to San Diego County is accompanied by a Quick Response (QR) Code which enables viewers to view on their smart phones a video in which the New American tells of his or her life in a statement that lasts approximately a minute.

We learn, for example, that Dubnov was born in Jerusalem and came to California when he was eight years old. Accelerating through high school, he began at age 15 studying theoretical mathematics at UC Berkeley, graduating when he was 18 in 2014. In the four years since, he has founded a technology company that creates "interactive environments for any sort of industry or brand."

Currently he is preoccupied with managing, fundraising, and marketing his business, in which "everything is sensor driven."

Although born in Israel, Shaanan arrived in the United States via Canada. He explained that his father was an Israeli diplomat who had been posted in different countries in Europe before being stationed in Canada, where Shaanan spent his formative years going to high school. "I felt very much more Canadian than Israeli because I never really lived there although I did identify with the country," Shanaan said.

Shanaan is the chief executive officer of Gadlight, a design consulting firm which "designed the new trolley in San Diego for Siemens years ago" and also "designed the air train in JFK (Kennedy Airport in New York)."

Married and the father of two daughters, Shanaan concluded his video statement saying, "Obviously I am proud to be an American. I think it is a terrific country. There is a tremendous amount of opportunity here."

Cohen came to the United States from Mexico City in 2010. "I'm a financial advisor and I also own a real estate company," he said. When he and his wife decided to move to the United States with their children, "we wanted more security; we wanted less pollution; we wanted less traffic," he stated.

"I think I have made a fantastic decision because my kids are happy, my wife is happy, and I am very happy."

The video testimonials are part of the "New American Voices: Our Immigrant Stories" exhibit that will continue on through February 3 at the museum, which is located at Liberty Station (the former Naval Training Center) at 2825 Dewey Road, #102. It is open Wednesday through Friday from 10 a.m. to 4 p.m., and on weekends from 11 a.m. to 4 p.m.

The portraits, in much smaller size, were originally published in the September 16, 2018 edition of the *San Diego Union-Tribune*, accompanied with articles based on research detailing the impact of immigrants on San Diego County, where 799,357 people—or 24.1 percent of the region's population—were born in countries other than the United States.

The article and exhibit reported that 44 percent of San Diego County's immigrant population is from Mexico, 12 percent from the Philippines, 5 percent from China, and 5 percent from Vietnam. Some of the many other countries represented in the sample include Canada, England, Germany, Iran, Iraq, Ireland, Italy, Japan, and Russia.

According to the museum's instructional legend, immigrants in San Diego County "are restaurant owners and doctors, university professors and musicians, writers, and farmers, beauticians and lawyers, engineers and cashiers, architects and nurses—almost every kind of pursuit imaginable."

The research found that 28.4 percent of the San Diego region's immigrants over age 25 have a bachelor's degree, 35 percent of them are entrepreneurs, and 1 in 5 is the "estimated number of immigrants who are unauthorized."

Collectively, immigrants in San Diego have $16.3 billion in spending power, pay $7.5 billion in federal taxes, and $2.1 billion in state and local taxes, according to researchers.

Although many people were involved in designing, photographing, and printing the special project, special mention was given to *San Diego Union-Tribune* writers John Wilkens, Kate Morrissey, Luis Cruz, and George Varga.

"Reflecting on the notion that we all have a story to tell and in the case of immigrants it often involves a journey, family, seeking opportunity, freedom, and safety, the stories begin to take shape, some at times harrowing, perhaps sad; many hopeful and highly personal accounts speaking to the universal human condition of seeking a safe refuge, a place and a space to call home," according to the museum exhibit.

"America historically has been that home to many for generations."

Sightseeing Review: Seal Tours

San Diego Jewish World,
January 4, 2019

"Seal Tours" is the name that Old Town Trolley Tours of San Diego gives its sightseeing excursions in an amphibious vehicle on the waters of San Diego Bay and on land along the Embarcadero and Point Loma. That name might cause a bit of confusion because a mainstay of the tour is the sea lions—not seals—that have taken up occupancy on a large bait barge from which anchovies and sardines are sold by the bucket to anglers heading out to the Pacific Ocean.

Tom, the guide aboard our vehicle, explained that SEAL is an acronym for "Sea and Land." He contrasted California Sea Lions with seals. "Sea Lions are bigger than seals, the males get up to 750 pounds," he said over the loudspeaker. "Sea lions have ear flaps, seals don't. Sea lions are smarter than seals; the Navy actually trains sea lions to help recover dummy torpedoes that Navy submarines have shot off. The sea lions have the mental capacity of a four-year-old [human] child; seals are just not smart. Sea lions have four large flippers; they can walk, run, and swim incredibly fast. Seals have four small flippers; they can't walk or run at all, they just flop."

The sea lions on the barge live in family groups, with each of the male sea lions having a "harem of about 5 to 6 females," according to Tom. "These females stay pregnant almost their entire adult lives. The gestation period of each pregnancy is 11 months, and three weeks after a female delivers, she gets pregnant again. Her entire adult life ranges from 10 to 20 years, and during that, she is pregnant every 11 months with a three-week break."

Our amphibious boat motored past the barge one way, then turned around and motored past it in the opposite direction so that passengers on both sides could get a clear, unobstructed view.

"The sea lions are sleeping; they are like American teenagers," Tom quipped. "They sleep 16-18 hours a day. They eat about 10 percent of their body weight, then go back and sleep." The sea lions form themselves into a circle with adults around the perimeter and babies within "so it keeps them warm and safe."

Sharing space on the barge with the sea lions are various sea birds, including black cormorants. Tom describes the cormorants admiringly. "Their feathers actually absorb water," he said. "They can dive down to 100 feet to fish and when they come back up they are so waterlogged they have to stand out and dry in the sun before they can fly away."

One reason that the bait barge, which looks like a floating dock, is so popular with the sea lions, cormorants, and other sea birds, is that "these animals will stick their heads and bills down the slats and steal the fish," according to Tom.

One might quibble whether the bait company has any greater right than the sea birds and marine mammals have to the formerly free-swimming anchovies and sardines, but however many snacks the birds and sea lions purloin, there are plenty more. Many thousands of the little bait fish fill up a pair of 14-foot deep underwater cages.

We didn't see any dolphins on this trip, but we certainly heard quite a bit about them. Just as the U.S. Navy trains sea lions to recover dummy torpedoes, so too does it employ dolphins to patrol San Diego Bay "looking for bad people." Tom didn't specify exactly what bad people might be doing that would attract the attention of a military-trained dolphin, but perhaps in matters of national defense, a bit of ambiguity goes a long way.

What Tom did tell us was that the "Navy has been training dolphins for 60 years; they have trained 120 dolphins." These are not the dolphins you might see romping around in the Pacific Ocean; in fact, they are "Atlantic Dolphins which are smarter than Pacific Dolphins," according to our guide. "There is nothing in the Pacific Ocean that [Atlantic] dolphins can eat, so the Navy flies out food for them from the East Coast . . . ."

Besides having catered food, the dolphins have comprehensive medical care. "Even though this is a program run by the Navy," says Tom, "the dolphins are cared for by Army veterinarians."

The dolphins also have a dental plan, according to Tom. "Every couple of days they get their teeth brushed."

Such VIP treatment for the dolphins has paid off. Tom says dolphins typically live between 7 and 9 years in the wild, whereas the life span of the Navy dolphins is between 20 and 25 years.

The Space and Naval Warfare Systems Command (SPAWAR) has jurisdiction over the training programs for the dolphins and sea lions. That Navy command also has cameras and radar stationed over the 14 1/2 miles of San Diego Bay as part of its defenses against any possible intruder. San Diego Bay is home to two nuclear powered aircraft carriers and more than 50 other U.S. naval ships, most of which are berthed south of the San Diego-Coronado Bay Bridge. Along the north shore where the Seal boat goes is a submarine base at Ballast Point, home to six submarines and a drydock built especially for their repair. Nearby, there is the Navy's gas station, which fills up outbound Naval vessels using pumps that Tom says can output 6,000 gallons per minute. Eight tanks on the shore store a combined total of 42 million gallons of fuel, according to Tom.

Among the defenders of San Diego Bay and the Pacific Ocean is a "little gray boat with pontoons on the side" that Tom describes as a "submarine hunting boat."

"When it goes out, it is totally autonomous; there are no humans aboard," our guide informed. "It is run by somebody at a computer in one of these many buildings over here. The pontoons and the hull are made of carbon fiber invisible to radar."

Old Town Trolley's own fleet includes seven of the amphibious vehicles, three of which were on duty the winter day we took ours on a narrated tour from Seaport Village to Shelter Island, where it drove down a ramp and into the bay, later reversing course to return to Seaport Village, taking a total of 90 minutes. In the summer, all seven amphibious vehicles are utilized to help tell the story of San Diego's sea life and Naval installations. Cost of the tour is $32 for adults; $25 for children between the ages of 3 and 12; and $10 for children under age 3.

Sightseeing Review: "Living with Animals" Exhibit

San Diego Jewish World,
January 9, 2019

Now through the end of 2020, visitors to the Museum of Man may see the "Living with Animals" exhibit, which offers new perspectives on animals that we consider pets, those that we consider pests, and those that we serve on our plates.

The idea for the exhibit originated at one of the periodic brainstorming sessions held among staff, volunteers, and board members, according to Erika Katayama, the museum's senior director for audience engagement. At first, the idea was very general, no more than something like "let's do something about animals," but over time, the idea was refined. The exhibit covers an upstairs wing of the museum, yet it couldn't include every kind of interaction between humans and animals, so some possibilities were winnowed. For example, the exhibit does not address microscopic animal life, nor does it deal with animals as carriers of diseases such as the avian flu. What it does consider are those interactions that might occur in or near someone's home.

Katayama's 17-year museum career has included responsibilities for education, curatorial, retail shops, visitor services, exhibitions, and cultural resources management. She arrived at the Museum of Man after this exhibit was developed by Sarah Crawford, who since has moved on to Los Angeles. Once here, Katayama's responsibility included coordinating the work of developers, designers, and fabricators and making certain that deadlines were met, and that the budget was observed.

Unlike other museums, the Museum of Man does not typically contract with outside curators. It prefers instead to do everything in house, from creating the story boards to fabricating the exhibit. The museum has its own woodshop and workshop on the site.

Some of the information that you encounter in the "Living with Animals" exhibit may surprise you. For example, said Katayama, "if a beetle ran through my house, I might stomp on it, but across the globe, a lot of people keep them as beloved pets. If you stomped on it, they would be heart-broken."

Here in the United States, we keep dogs as pets, but in some other cultures, they are raised as food. If someone ate our pet dog, we would be heart-broken.

The museum staff intends for people to gain a different perspective about what is a pet. "Around the world, we often have different ideas," so the purpose of the exhibit is "expanding our thinking a little bit."

One activity within the "pets" section of the exhibit is a game involving matching owners with their dogs. In a display case, there is a collection of dog collars; elsewhere there is a small collection of crickets.

In the "pests" section are individual exhibits about pigeons, rats, and cockroaches—all of which thrive because humanity has been so good to them. Cockroaches would perish in cold weather, if they didn't have human dwellings where they could keep warm.

Pigeons would find very little to satisfy their inherent need to perch on cliffs if humans didn't build cities where there are rooftops, fences, telephone wires, walls, and other places for perching. And rats might have remained in central Asia, where they originated, had not travelers had suitcases, saddle bags, and other places where they could "hitchhike" rides to new destinations.

We know, of course, that pigeons and rats can play beneficial roles in human society. Rats are used in the medical research that lead to the development of life-saving pharmaceuticals. Homing pigeons can carry messages for long distances back to their home base. So even as concepts of "pets" are fluid, so too are concepts of "pests."

In the "Animals on our Plates" section, there is a caution sign warning parents that they may not wish their children to see photographs of a sow being unable to move in a tight pen as she is suckled by piglets. Images of live chickens being vacuumed into a processing machine are disturbing. So is a photograph of a giant, round table with slots for several scores of dairy cows, in which the cows are confined for mechanized milking.

I wondered if the intent behind this display was to promote vegetarianism.

"We leave that up to our visitors," responded Katayama. "The idea is to encourage conversation among folks. They might talk about the way animals are being kept, about animal treatment, or possibly where they are having lunch."

She said that children today don't know where their food comes from. "When we go to Ralph's or Vons, we see meat on a tray. We don't see the animal that it came from." Our modern era is different from previous times when many families raised their own food and did their own butchering, Katayama said. "We wanted to show people where their food comes from. For some visitors this is new information."

329

Before an exhibit is undertaken, the Museum of Man questions paid visitors whether they would like to attend such an exhibit, and perhaps even pay a fee in addition to the museum's admission charge. Ideas that receive the most positive responses then go into the development phase. Now that the exhibit is underway, visitor reaction has been positive, with some visitors returning on multiple occasions, according to Katayama.

The "Living with Animals" exhibit is included in the price of admission to the Museum of Man, which is $13 for adults; $10 for students, seniors, military, and children between the ages of 6; and free for children aged 5 and under. Information may be found on the museum's website at https://www.museumofman.org/exhibits/living-with-animals.

Intermarried Couple Honors Each Other's Beliefs

San Diego Jewish World,
January 13, 2019

B efore David Ogul and Sharon Wilson were married, they learned about each other's faiths. David attended Mass at Sharon's Catholic church. Sharon attended Friday night Shabbat services at David's Reform temple in Riverside, the city where the two had met and worked for the daily *Press-Enterprise*. David was a reporter there, and Sharon worked in the finance department.

They had known each other casually for four years, and only started dating September 22, 1994, after realizing that in the period since they had first met, both had become divorced from their previous spouses. Their dating, and learning about each other's religions, was approximately a 2 1/2-year long process, finally culminating in their civil marriage on a racquetball court April 5, 1997, officiated by a Protestant minister who agreed not to invoke the name of Jesus during the ceremony. David shared custody of his two sons, Justin and Jeremy, then 5 and 3, with his former wife. Sharon had no children by her first marriage.

Today, Sharon continues to attend and actively volunteer at a Catholic church in San Diego, where they moved after David accepted a job as an editor with *The San Diego Union-Tribune* and she found work as an accountant for a property management company. David, who subsequently opened his own public relations firm, continues to be active in his Jewish congregation, Tifereth Israel Synagogue. So active, in fact, that David recently was elected as the Conservative congregation's president—a reflection of the fact that Jewish congregations throughout the nation are reaching out more and more to intermarried couples. There was once a time that David, or any other Jew who had married "out of the faith," could not even serve as a member of a synagogue board, much less become the congregation's president.

The couple had one child together, Allison, whom they had agreed to expose to both faiths and let her decide for herself which one she would choose. Ultimately, Allison opted for Judaism. Recently she was elected president of her Jewish sorority, Sigma Alpha Epsilon Pi, at Colorado State University, where she is an undergraduate.

A Pew study released in 2013 suggests that intermarriages involving a Jew and a non-Jew have become increasingly common. At that time 64 percent of all the nation's Jews were married to other Jews while 36 percent had non-Jewish spouses. However, if one looked only at marriages entered into between 2008 and 2013, 45 percent of the Jews married during that period had Jewish spouses, while a majority—55 percent—had non-Jewish spouses.

Sixty-nine percent of the Jews who did not affiliate with any denomination were married to non-Jews; 50 percent of those affiliated with the Reform movement had non-Jewish partners as did 27 percent in the Conservative movement (like David Ogul) and just 2 percent in the Orthodox movement, according to that Pew study. At Tifereth Israel Synagogue, slightly less than 11 percent of the Jews in the congregation have non-Jewish spouses.

The Oguls were asked during an interview to relate the process by which they learned about each other's religions and what customs they followed after they were married.

Sharon said she remembered thinking at her first Erev Shabbat service how lively was the music, played by a cantor on his guitar. She contrasted the upbeat melodies favorably with the organ music of a Mass. On the other hand, David remembered being "definitely uncomfortable" attending a Mass. "I wasn't going to kneel, I just sat there," he recalled.

In discussions between them that followed, David insisted "don't try to convert me," and Sharon said, "Don't make me give up my religion." They agreed they would honor each other's beliefs.

Before Allison was born, David added, "We ultimately resolved that I would be free and uninhibited to take the child to services, and adhere to Judaism, and that Sharon would be free to take the child to church, but there would be no baptism and no bar/bat mitzvah or confirmation unless the child was old enough to make an informed decision, with no influence from one parent or the other."

If Allison had been born a boy, would he have had a brit milah? "My mom is a nurse, and from the medical standpoint, circumcision is standard," Sharon responded. "But as far as having a religious ceremony associated with it, I don't know if we would have done that."

Allison went to a pre-school run by San Diego State University, and later on attended a public elementary school. But after attending services at church and at synagogue, she decided that she wanted ed also to attend Torah school, and not go to Mass anymore.

Asked why she made such a choice back then, Allison, who studies political science and sociology, responded: "Here is a weird analogy. Sometimes certain areas of academia don't make sense to me. I don't like physics because I don't understand why it is, but I understand social sciences really well . . . it is something that I can wrap my head around . . . Judaism, the whole philosophy, is something I can wrap my head around. I think *tikkun olam* (repair of the world) was a really big deal for me; also there were discussions about trying to be good, about being cognizant of what it actually means to be a good person, and to do good things, rather than thinking that I have to be a good person because there is something in it for me. That was pretty valuable for me when I was a kid."

When Allison made her decision for Judaism, David was worried for Sharon. If Allison didn't go to Mass, then Sharon would be all alone when she went to church. But Sharon accepted the decision, as did her mother Doreen. Later, when Allison started studying to become a *bat mitzvah*, Doreen was the one who patiently would listen to her repeat the prayers that had been recorded for her by Rabbi Leonard Rosenthal of Tifereth Israel Synagogue. Before Allison's *bat mitzvah*, she needed to formally convert, which she did before a *beth din* at the University of Judaism (today called American Jewish University.) The rabbis permitted Sharon to accompany Allison into the *mikvah*, even though Sharon was not herself converting.

Household observances were agreed upon by David and Sharon early in their marriage. David would have a Chanukah celebration, and after it was over, Sharon would put up a Christmas tree, one which grew smaller and smaller year by year because of Sharon's concern for the ecology. Now the couple purchases a boxed tree. If Chanukah and Christmas shared the same date, then Sharon would wait until December 23 to put up her tree.

When they were first married, David was less observant than he is today. But after a time, David started wearing a kippah and tzitzit and became increasingly *shomer* Shabbos. With Sharon's agreement, a mezuzah went up on the door.

David's sons, meanwhile, spent some time with him, and even more time with their mother. Jeremy is today a legislative advocate with Madaffer Enterprises, and like Allison, he would go to Friday night services and also attend services at different churches while growing up. This was the time before David became so observant, Jeremy said, so "there was never any strong religion either way."

Asked how he identifies religiously today, Jeremy answered, "Probably, I would say agnostic, although I identify culturally more with Judaism than Christianity."

Sharon said her advice for anyone considering an intermarriage is that "you have to totally respect the other person's beliefs and you have to make sure that you are okay with them."

David said if religion is an important part of one's life, then one must seriously consider the potential problems. "When the relationship is new and there is a lot of excitement, couples have the tendency to think everything will be all right. But there are complications and we would be lying to you if we were to say that this has been a tension-free marriage, that religion has not created conversations and disagreements, because it has. We are both devout in our faith and even when I was not practicing as closely as I am now, I was always devout in my faith."

Further, said David, "You have to be aware that you are going to get criticism, if not from your family, then from other people. What I tell those people in my community who say things that I don't necessarily appreciate is, 'Read about Moses: His wife was a Midianite, she was not Jewish,' and, 'Read about Ruth, who is the great-grandmother of King David, who by some accounts is in the line of the *moshiach* (messiah) . . . .'"

Allison commented that while she still is single, she is aware that "there are some things you have to bring up with your partner if you are going to have a life together." For example, she said, some sects of Christianity oppose a woman's right to choose, and "that really needs to be talked about. It has a lot to do with family planning . . . ."

Having parents of two different faiths can provide a child with the "advantage of seeing things from a different perspective," Jeremy said. "I think that made me a better person because I became used to and learned how to see the world from different people's perspectives."

Those Jews who oppose intermarriage contend that it will lead to complete assimilation, if not in this generation, then in subsequent ones. Those most vehemently opposed to intermarriage call it finishing the job that Hitler started of eradicating the Jewish people. The Ogul family rejects this notion, saying that just as Allison and Jeremy felt closer to Judaism than to Christianity, so too may other children of intermarriages—provided that the Jews with whom they associate either in synagogue or elsewhere, are welcoming.

The Oguls credited two leaders in Tifereth Israel Men's Club's "Keruv" ("Bring Close") program—Phil Snyder and Norman Katz—for helping to establish the tone at the Conservative synagogue where intermarried families feel welcome. Sharon recalled that Rabbi Rosenthal, now retired, enabled her side of the family to participate on the *bima* in Allison's *bat mitzvah*.

"I think that our community has this thing going that because we think the religion is dying, we try to police the Jewish identity and that does more harm than good," Allison said. "If someone tells me that because I haven't gone to shul for a while, I am less Jewish, I would probably deck them, because it is not in their right."

Sharon said while some people at her church are not thrilled about her intermarriage, "others say, 'Oh my gosh, I love the Jewish people; they are guardians of the faith.'"

David plays guitar in the Shir Chadash (New Song) band that leads musical Erev Shabbat services the third Friday of every month at Tifereth Israel Synagogue. That is just one way that the synagogue is evolving, says the congregational president. "This is a congregation open to tradition as well as to new ideas. We are not afraid of accepting the LGBTQIA community, nor interfaith marriages, nor people who have never been to synagogue before in their lives."

Sharon attends Jewish services and events periodically and has surprised David with the amount of Hebrew she has picked up. One night at a family Thanksgiving celebration, Sharon asked if she could say a prayer. She then proceeded to surprise the family by reeling off an English translation of the *Shehekiyanu* prayer, in which supplicants thank God for allowing them to arrive at this special moment.

Sightseeing:
Adventure Hornblower
Whale Watching

San Diego Jewish World,
January 14, 2019

E ven before one comes aboard the *Adventure Hornblower* for a 3 1/2-hour whale-watching tour, one begins learning about the California Gray Whale, which is the sightseeing vessel's quarry. Yellow-shirted volunteer "whalers" from the San Diego Museum of Natural History—known familiarly as "The Nat"—tell visitors as they queue to board that the whales we are soon to see are in the midst of their southbound migration, having come all the way from the Arctic Circle and still having a long way to go to reach their calving grounds in the lagoons along Mexico's Baja California Sur peninsula.

The first part of our journey is at the required slow speed of 5 knots per hour through San Diego Bay, where a guide over the loud-speaker points out familiar sights and ships. Over there, on our port (left) side is the aircraft carrier USS *Theodore Roosevelt*, named for the 26th U.S. President. Next, we see the state tall ship *Californian* enjoying the balmy day. Farther along is the *Stars & Stripes,* the

America's Cup-winning racing boat made famous by San Diegan Dennis Conner. And if we squint our eyes, we can see FA-18 jets parked in a row at the North Island Naval Air Station, one of the last landmarks before we pass the Zuniga Jetty, taking us out into the Pacific Ocean, where the swells remind us of a gentle roller coaster.

Because of the way the lone entrance and exit to San Diego Bay is angled, our boat's direction as we enter the Pacific Ocean is southbound, just a few miles above the U.S.-Mexican border. Ahead of us, we can clearly see Los Coronados (The Crowns) the four islands in Mexican waters that were named by Spanish explorer Sebastian Vizcaino in 1602. However, our motor yacht makes a turn to the starboard (right), heading us out on a westbound course, to a point between three and four miles from the San Diego coast. Here, announces our captain, is the area where we are most likely to see some whales in the midst of their journey.

Gray Whales have two side-by-side blow holes, so when they expel air from their lungs through these orifices, the vapor caused by their warm breath hitting the cold ocean air forms a characteristic V-shaped spout. Passengers were told to watch for these spouts, and also to scan the ocean surface for flat whale-sized depressions, which are indicators of the large mammals swimming nearby under the water.

Some passengers hugged the rails of our three-deck, 151-foot long, 32-foot wide motor yacht, while others stayed seated indoors and outdoors as the 94-gross-registered-ton ship slowly maneuvered to the whale route. At last, a whale was spotted off the port bow, and nearly everyone moved to that side of the 24-year-old steel motor yacht to get a better look. Our captain said that the whale we were seeing appeared to be either a calf (new born) or a juvenile.

Amid the clicking of many cameras, we watched as the young whale's back came out of the water—much as a human swimmer's back does in the "butterfly" stroke—and then disappeared to be replaced moments later by its tail—or fluke—that propelled the California Gray in a downward direction. Seeing the whale's tail is interesting, but not nearly so exciting as seeing a relatively rare instance of the whale jumping out of the water—or breaching—so that you can see its face and upper body. The two whales we spotted on our journey were not so inclined; they seemed intent on immigrating from United States waters to Mexico waters without further ado.

Our captain decided to abandon these two whales and turn in a northbound direction towards La Jolla in an unsuccessful attempt to spot more playful California Gray Whales. While the boat thus was headed to a new position, I had the opportunity to chat with Natural History Museum volunteer Yvonne Tempel, who was taking a break from her job as an elementary school teacher to work as a "whaler." In true Passover night fashion, I asked what makes this whale different from all other whales, and she replied that before its migration, when it is up in the Arctic, the California Gray Whale swims on its side along the ocean bottom and scoops into its mouth all the goodies it can find in the silt. You can imagine the underwater furrows created by such feeding habits. The whale's baleen strains the huge amount of material, keeping out rocks and sand. The whale uses its tongue to convey massive amounts of yummy arthropods, measuring about 2 centimeters each, off the baleen and down its gullet.

Tempel told me that there are approximately 7,000 California Gray Whales in the Pacific Ocean, and that "they stay pretty close to North American shores, about three to six miles when they migrate south and within nine miles when they migrate north."

The whales stay in the Mexican lagoons approximately six to eight weeks, although it may be longer for mothers with newborns. Neither on the roundtrip between the Arctic and Mexico, nor in the lagoons where they concentrate on mating and birthing is it typical for the California Gray Whale to eat. It continues to fast until it returns to the Arctic in the summer.

During the summer feeding season, the California Gray Whale gorges itself, Tempel said. "A 35-ton whale can consume 4,200 pounds of food per day—which is about 6 percent of its body weight."

Climate change has its impact on the California Gray Whale, Tempel told me. Sometimes because of weather conditions, to find food, "they have to go farther north. As they are coming south, sometimes they have their babies sooner, before they get to Mexico, because they have farther to travel. Also, sometimes they don't leave as early because the ice doesn't form as early."

The journey for the whales and calves is very dangerous around California's Monterey Peninsula because that is where Orcas like to congregate and "they like to eat the baby Gray Whales."

Because our January 13 cruise started at 1:30 p.m., it didn't end until 5 p.m., plenty of time to see a beautiful sunset as we rounded Point Loma to enter San Diego Bay.

Towards the end of the cruise, when we were safely back inside San Diego Bay, Tempel and four other volunteers from "The Nat," showed our group some vertebrae and a baleen of a Gray Whale. They also showed a barnacle and the lice that make their homes on the whale's back—the barnacle simply to hitchhike a ride, while the lice feed off the whale's skin.

The general admission price is $43 for this 3 1/2 hour cruise that leaves at either 9:30 a.m. or 1:30 p.m. from Pier 2 at 970 North Harbor Drive, San Diego. Tickets may be reserved by phoning (619) 686-8715. The *Adventure Hornblower*, one of seven ships in Hornblower's San Diego fleet, is also used for dinner cruises, and has a seating capacity of 550 over its three decks. In addition to San Diego, Hornblower has its boats homeported in San Francisco, Berkeley, Sacramento, Marina del Rey, Long Beach, and Newport Beach, California, as well as in New York City.

The Fleet and "The Nat" Teach about Water

San Diego Jewish World,
January 17, 2019

Quite a bit of information overlaps in the exhibits on San Diego's water supply, conservation, and runoff at the Reuben H. Fleet Science Center and the San Diego Museum of Natural History, two museums that face each other in Balboa Park. The "Fleet" and "The Nat" are "separated"—or perhaps, given their mutual interest in water—"joined" by the landmark Bea Evenson Fountain, one of Balboa Park's most photographed venues.

The fountain recycles 55,000 gallons daily. It was named in 1981 for Bea Evenson, one of San Diego's far-seeing civic leaders, who led the Committee of 100's efforts to maintain and improve upon the Spanish colonial buildings in Balboa Park. It was designed by the late architect Homer Delawie, a member of the Jewish community.

The thrust of the two museums' exhibits is to encourage San Diegans to be far-seeing about this area's water and ecological needs and to improve upon the status quo.

Both museums explain that most of San Diego's fresh water is transported by pump stations and aqueducts from Northern California and from the Colorado River. Both exhibits urge water conservation. The Reuben Fleet Science Center dwells a bit more on the technology of moving water to San Diego, whereas the Natural History Museum focuses more on what effects that water has on the ecology after it is used by San Diego County residents.

The Nat makes the point that 97 percent of the water on earth is too salty for natural consumption, while another 2 percent is either tied up in ice or is buried deep underground. "Water that we can get to and use is a rare and precious resource, amounting to only 1 percent of Earth's water."

The Fleet's exhibit includes a 10-step explanation of the water cycle, along with an illustrated flow chart showing such steps as condensation, evaporation, groundwater flow, infiltration, plant uptake, precipitation, run off, sublimation, transpiration, transportation. The Fleet's glossary of these terms may be found at the end of this article.

While these natural processes provide approximately 10 percent of San Diego County's water supply, far more is delivered via the California Water Project and via the Colorado River. Both sources of water are mixed together, then sent via pipeline to the San Diego County Water Authority, which disseminates it to local water districts. Those districts, in turn, pipe the water to San Diego County homes, businesses, and agricultural lands.

Pumping water from Northern California and the Colorado River takes lots of energy. To illustrate the concept, the Fleet has a sink with a crank that one must turn to make water flow from the faucet.

According to The Nat, "San Diego County imports up to 90 percent of its water supply from the Colorado River and northern California. . . . A vast infrastructure, pumping stations, canals, aqueducts and treatment plants—delivers water to millions of users every day."

The Fleet explains that the California Water Project was built in the 1960s to connect Northern California to Southern California. "The Project includes 34 storage facilities, reservoirs and lakes; 20 pumping plants; 4 pumping-generating plants; 5 hydroelectric power plants (and) 700 miles of canals and pipelines."

Faucets juxtaposed against a map at The Nat illustrates the competition for imported water from the Colorado River.

It adds: "The 243-mile long Colorado River Aqueduct built by the Metropolitan Water District of Southern California is another critical piece of water infrastructure because it provides Southern California communities with water from the Colorado River."

Because other cities, counties, and states compete for this imported water, San Diego County has attempted to diversify its water sources. Desalination has been an important breakthrough. The Fleet reports: "It became a reality when the Claude 'Bud' Lewis Carlsbad Desalination Plant opened in 2015. It now provides a new core water supply for San Diego County. Seawater desalination protects the San Diego region from the impacts of drought and unplanned interruptions of imported water deliveries due to an earthquake or another emergency. The Carlsbad plant uses reverse osmosis technology to separate salts from seawater producing about 10 percent of the region's water supply."

The storyboard adds: "Did you know? The Carlsbad facility is the largest seawater desalination plant in the U.S. The San Diego Water Authority buys all its water." As a point of Jewish pride, I'd like to add that the technology used by the Carlsbad facility was developed in Israel.

Even with desalination, there is a need to better conserve the water we already have.

Both museums have suggestions for how we can do that.

The Nat suggests the following steps:

* Pay attention to how much water you use.
* Don't waste water, turn it on, turn it off.
* Fix plumbing and irrigation leaks.
* Take shorter showers.
* Compost kitchen scraps instead of using the garbage disposal.
* Garden with plants that don't need a lot of water—or grow food, not lawns.
* Mulch your garden and don't overwater.

"You can eat to save water—eat less meat and eat more unprocessed plant-based foods."

The Fleet offers ways to conserve water both outside and inside your house.

Outside:

* Don't overwater plants.
* Irrigate early in the morning or late in the evening.
* Adjust sprinklers so they don't hit pavement.
* Don't irrigate on rainy or windy days.
* Plant drought-tolerant or low-water-use plants and grasses.
* Use shrubs and groundcover to reduce turf grass.
* Place mulch around plants to reduce evaporation and discourage weeds.
* Consider upgrading to efficient irrigation equipment and controllers.

Inside, there also are ways to conserve, according to the Fleet.

Average household toilets use about 33 gallons per day. Low flush toilets could reduce that to 7 gallons per day.

In the average household, faucets use about 28 gallons per day. Upgraded faucets can reduce that to 15 gallons per day.

Similarly upgraded clothes washers can reduce water usage from 23 gallons per day to 11 gallons.

More so than the Fleet Museum, The Nat draws attention to the possibility of turning wastewater into drinking water. The Nat reports: "The North City Water Reclamation Plant purifies 30 million gallons of wastewater every day, powered by methane from the Miramar Landfill. Purple pipes distribute reclaimed water for irrigation and industry. What if we refilled reservoirs and aquifers with reclaimed water, like they do in Orange County? We already use reclaimed water from the Colorado River. What do you think?

"When we shower, flush, and turn on the tap, our wastewater flows into the sewer system then to a water treatment plant. The plant on Point Loma treats 175 million gallons per day, then discharges that water into the ocean through a 4.5-mile-long pipe. With freshwater so scarce, should we expand our water recycling program?"

The Fleet addresses the issue this way: "Water is too valuable to use just once. It can be recycled by treating wastewater from homes and business. Recycled water extends dwindling water supplies, reduces dependence on distant sources, and reduces wastewater discharges to the environment. Most water agencies in San Diego County recycle water, and most recycled water is delivered through specially marked purple pipes for landscape irrigation. Other uses include industrial processing, dust suppression at construction sites, crop irrigation, recreational lakes, and ornamental fountains. The next frontier is using reverse osmosis and other advanced technologies to purify wastewater for drinking. The process is called potable water reuse."

The issue of storm water runoff is briefly addressed by the Fleet, and more extensively by The Nat. The Fleet says that "storm water is a valuable resource. It can be captured in rain barrels and in specially designed landscapes, reducing runoff and helping to sustain plants."

When we fail to capture storm water, the Fleet says, "runoff collects pollutants from yards and streets and carries them to the nearest storm drain. Unfortunately, this delivers automotive fluids, brake dust, leaves, grass clippings, pet waste, cigarette butts, dirt, and trash directly to rivers, bays, beaches and the ocean." To reduce the amount of pollutants carried in runoff, the Fleet recommends the following steps: "Instead of using a hose, sweep driveways, sidewalks, curbs, and gutters. Pick up trash near roads, parks, and other public places. Collect pet waste immediately. Prevent sewer overflows by having sewer pipes professionally inspected for cracks or blockages."

The Nat emphasizes that "when we water the yard or wash the car, our wastewater flows into the storm drain system and directly to the ocean, carrying cigarette butts, plastic bags, pet poop, and pesticides—without any treatments. Urban runoff is the number one cause of ocean pollution."

We have learned from our mistakes, according to The Nat: "During the 1960s, scientists saw a decline in many fish-eating birds—especially Brown Pelicans. At that time the pesticide DDT flowed from farmland into waterways and entered the marine food chain. Among other bad effects, DDT weakened the shells of pelicans' eggs so they cracked easily. After the ban on DDT in 1973, pelican populations rebounded. In 2009, they were removed from the Endangered Species list."

Concerning pet poop, The Nat reports: "Sea otters—furry and curious—lived all along the California coast until fur hunters decimated their population. They still live from central California north, yet today they face other challenges. Besides chemical pol-

347

lution, parasites found in cat feces enter the ocean carried by rainfall runoff and treated toilet water. Sea otters get infected with the parasite and die. Surfers may be suffering too. A simple solution to promote ocean health: Pick up cat poop and put it in the trash, not the toilet."

The Nat also inveighs against the unnecessary use of plastic: "Over 5.5 million tons of trash—mostly plastic and covering an area twice the size of Texas—floats in the center of the North Pacific between San Francisco and Hawaii. At least 80 percent of that trash—plastic bags, balloons, water bottles—originated on land. Plastic doesn't biodegrade. Sunlight makes plastic brittle and it breaks into tiny pieces that attract and concentrate toxic pollutants. Marine life mistakes the floating trash for food. They eat plastic and die. In some places, trash outweighs marine plankton by a ratio of 6:1. Take action—limit your use of plastic; use reusable shopping bags; don't litter."

Glossary

Condensation is the process where water vapor (a gas) changes back into water droplets (a liquid.) This is when we begin to see clouds.

Evaporation is the change of state of water (a liquid) to a vapor (gas). On average about 47 inches is evaporated into the atmosphere from the ocean each year.

Groundwater flow is the flow of water underground in aquifers. The water may return to the surface in springs or eventually seep into the oceans.

Infiltration is the movement of water into the ground from the surface.

Plant uptake is water taken from the groundwater flow and soil moisture.

Precipitation is water that falls to the earth. Most precipitation falls as rain but includes snow, sleet, drizzle, and hail.

Runoff is the variety of ways in which water moves over the earth's surface. This comes from melting snow or rain.

Sublimation is the process where ice and snow (a solid) changes into water vapor (a gas) without moving through the liquid phase.

Transpiration is evaporation of liquid water from plants and trees into the atmosphere. About 50 percent of all water that enters the roots transpires into the atmosphere.

Transportation is the movement of solid, liquid and gaseous water through the atmosphere. Without this movement, the water evaporated over the ocean would not precipitate over land.

Sightseeing Review: Birch Aquarium

San Diego Jewish World,
February 6, 2019

If you want to know if a fish you see at the Birch Aquarium is kosher, look carefully. Does it have fins? Does it have scales? If the answer to both these questions is "yes," then probably it is a kosher fish.

That doesn't mean, however, that you should eat one like it, should you happen to pull one out of the sea. It could be dangerous to your health.

One of the current exhibits at the Birch Aquarium deals with fish and sea creatures that are "oddities." Among them are two fish that indeed have fins and scales, but their descriptions ought to warn you away.

"Fugu Pufferfish *(Takifugu alboplumbeus)*—It may look appetizing but don't try to eat me! Beyond being able to inflate my stomach to massive proportions, my tissues house bacteria that generate a toxin called Tetrodotoxin that is 1200x more lethal than cyanide."

"Stonefish *(Synanceia verrucosa)*—My coloration, shape and stoic presence make me look like an algae-covered rock, but don't let me fool you! The 13 hypodermic, venom-delivering spines on my back make me the most venomous fish in the sea."

Speaking of non-kosher fish, people at Birch Aquarium can take silly photos of themselves pretending to be inside the mouth of a great white shark, which has no scales. There also is an installation about leopard sharks *(Triakis semifasciata)*, in which we learn that they can grow to a length of six feet, and that "hundreds of leopard sharks appear at La Jolla Shores every summer, where they play an important role in the local ecology and support ecotourism."

The reason they like La Jolla is neither the proximity of UC San Diego and its Scripps Institution of Oceanography (of which the Birch Aquarium is a part), nor the trendy stores of La Jolla Village. The real reason is that "leopard sharks typically stay on or near the bottom and favor warm shallow water near shore. At La Jolla Shores, they spend much of their day in water 6.5 feet deep or less."

Lest this concern you about visiting the La Jolla Shores, the Birch Aquarium's storyboard adds that leopard sharks "will flee from disturbances and are harmless to humans if not provoked."

Luckily, other fish in the permanent collection are not only edible but also are beautiful or fascinating (or both) to look at. I was particularly taken with such species in the collection as the Flag Rockfish, Garibaldi, California Halibut, Blue Throated Fairywrasse, Koran Angelfish, Diamond Fish, Azure Damselfish, Powder Blue Tang, Yellow Tang, Palette Surgeonfish, King Angelfish, and the Broomtail Grouper.

I did a double-take when I read about the "Koran Angelfish," wondering if there were also a "Torah Angelfish," and a "Christian Bible Angelfish." Subsequently, I found on the *Saltwater Aquarist* website this explanation: "The white stripes on its body become stretched, curved and elongated resembling something similar to Arabic script, thus leading to its name 'Koran'. They are also commonly referred to as 'Half-circle Angelfish' and 'Semicircle Angelfish.'"

A current exhibit deals extensively with seahorses, which are fish that adapted their shape to feed off vertically-growing vegetation. Turns out that in mating, the female seahorse passes her eggs to a pouch of the male's body, where the roe grow to become baby seahorses, and then, in a process similar to labor, the male seahorse expels them from his pouch. I'm willing to bet that there are many women out there who wish that human reproduction was a similar process!

Two species of sea life that I found rather fascinating were the Atlantic Flashlightfish *(Kryptophanaron alfredi)* and the Fried Egg Jelly *(Phacellophora camtschatica).*

A storyboard, written as if the Flashlightfish were talking to us, said: "Under my eyes, I have specialized light organs (like headlights) that help me find prey at night. I can also use them to distract predators and communicate with members of my species."

Wouldn't such a feature be handy for humans, especially if they ran out of batteries?

The Fried Egg Jellyfish has a central mass "which resembles the cooked yolk of an egg in appearance." This mass contains the jellyfish's reproductive organs. This particular species of jellyfish, according to the aquarium's printed explanation, "spends much of its time motionless. When searching for food, it pulses slowly through the water with its string tentacles trolling 10-20 feet below. Capable of growing up to 2 feet in diameter, the bell is frequently inhabited by symbiotic amphipods and juvenile crabs."

I wondered if any sea creature occasionally jostled the Fried Egg Jellyfish, gently flipping it over so that it became the "Over Easy Jellyfish"? Oh well, probably not.

Following the tour of the aquarium, in which I was joined by cousins Harry and Sherry Jacobson-Beyer of Louisville, Kentucky, I stopped by the Splash! Café, which is on the grounds. I wondered what tasty denizens of the sea would be on the menu, and whether any of them would be kosher.

To my surprise, neither fish nor crustaceans were offered on the menu. Instead, there were land-based foods including various vegetarian options and turkey hot dogs, bratwurst, ham sandwiches, chicken panini, roast beef panini, and steak caesar wraps.

I asked one of the countermen why there were no fish on the menu. He said it might be an affront to the fish swimming so happily nearby in their tanks. Who knew fish might consider us humans to be *chutzpahdik*?

Weinberger v. Taft in Arizona Statehood Battle

San Diego Jewish World,
February 14, 2019

One hundred seven years ago today, on February 14, 1912, President William Howard Taft signed a proclamation making Arizona the 48th State of the Union. The Republican president may have thought that his signature culminated a long fight with Progressive Democrats in Arizona over the question of the independence of the judiciary. He was wrong.

One of Taft's key adversaries in the fight was Jacob Weinberger, who later would become a moving force in San Diego's Jewish community as well as the first resident U.S. District Court judge in San Diego.

At the time of Arizona's 1910 state constitutional convention, Weinberger was a young lawyer living in the mining town of Globe, Arizona. Because of his legal background and because of his friendship with George W. P. Hunt, who had been a territorial legislator and would later become Arizona's first governor, Weinberger was nominated and elected as a convention delegate. Furthermore, to draft the state's constitution, he was made chairman of the committee on the judiciary—quite an honor for a young man who had immigrated to the U.S. at the age of 7 with his family from the Hungarian town of Hedrei, which today is known as Hendrichovce of the Slovak Republic.

Weinberger was a Democrat, and very much a believer in Progressive reforms that were sweeping the nation. Among these was the idea that if citizens were dissatisfied with an elected official, they could initiate a petition, and if a sufficient percentage of voters signed that petition, the elected official could be subjected to a recall election, in which a majority of voters could then decide the fate of the elected official one way or the other. We take such elections for granted today, but the idea was controversial back then—especially as it applied to the judiciary.

Taft was a great believer in the independence of the judiciary—foreshadowing the role he would play following his presidency as the Chief Justice of the U.S. Supreme Court, appointed by President Warren G. Harding. When President Taft saw that the proposed Arizona constitution enabled judges to be recalled, he cried "foul," worrying that if judges had to worry about how their decisions would be received by the popular electorate, concerns about reelection might take precedence over administering justice.

So, after the proposed Arizona state constitution was submitted to Taft, he refused to approve it, demanding that the provision enabling the recall of judges be taken out of the constitution.

Arizonans complied with his demand, and he then signed the proclamation.

Once Arizona became a state, it had sovereignty. That meant that it was able to enact its own laws with or without the President's approval. Very quickly, Governor Hunt and the Arizona Legislature, then controlled by Democrats, reenacted the provision enabling judicial recall.

355

The controversy was much ado about nothing. Notwithstanding President Taft's fears, the procedure has been very rarely used.

Between the time of the state convention and the signing of the proclamation by President Taft, Weinberger and his wife, Blanche, moved to San Diego. He initially went into private law practice, during which time he served as a member of the San Diego Unified School District board for 21 years, and also was the founding president of the United Jewish Fund, which today is known as the Jewish Federation of San Diego County.

He served as a city attorney for the City of San Diego, later was appointed as a Superior Court Judge, and following his defeat for reelection, was appointed by President Harry S. Truman as a federal court judge.

The federal bankruptcy court downtown is named for the judge, as was the Benchley-Weinberger Elementary School in the San Carlos area, in which his name was paired with that of longtime San Diego Zookeeper Belle Benchley.

Weinberger, who lived to be a nonagenarian, stayed active as a senior judge almost to the end of his life, which came in 1974. One of the judicial duties he most welcomed was conducting naturalization ceremonies for immigrants to the United States, telling the new Americans that even as he had been able to advance in his field, so too could they live the American dream.

Community Mourns Rabbi Leonard Rosenthal

San Diego Jewish World,
February 15, 2019

A parade of rabbinical colleagues and family members mourning Rabbi Leonard Rosenthal, praised him, which they acknowledged he would have hated, and told jokes about him, which they said he would have loved. The rabbi's funeral service was attended by hundreds of congregants and friends Friday afternoon in the congregation he had served for nearly 30 years, Tifereth Israel Synagogue.

Rosenthal, 66, died suddenly Thursday of what was described by one speaker as a probable cardiac event. He had been hospitalized weeks before with a blood clot, and later had a stroke. After being released to the home he shared with his wife Judy, he complained of not feeling well, and died suddenly, according to a family member who added that the rabbi did not suffer.

Rosenthal grew up in the Sepulveda area of the San Fernando Valley, attended public school, loved musical instruments, particularly the accordion and violin, studied computer science at

UC San Diego, and served as a counselor at Camp Ramah and also as a youth group adviser at Tifereth Israel Synagogue, where he met his future wife, Judy Feigelson. He enrolled at the University of Judaism (today called American Jewish University), at the time a program of the Jewish Theological Seminary in New York, to begin his rabbinic studies before completing them in Manhattan. He occupied a student pulpit in New Jersey, where daughter Adina, and son Adam were born, and next moved to Tampa, Florida, to serve as the first rabbi of a brand new congregation, Kol Ami. He moved to Orange County, California, to take a rabbinical position at Temple Sharon (which later merged with B'nai Israel in Tustin) and the Jewish Studies Institute Day School (now Tarbut v' Torah). Rosenthal's daughter Margalit was born during these years.

In 1988, he accepted a position as associate rabbi at Tifereth Israel Synagogue, serving with then senior Rabbi Aaron Gold, z"l, who retired in 1990. Rosenthal, in turn retired in 2017, but continued as Rabbi Emeritus until the day he passed.

Rabbi Joshua Dorsch, who had succeeded Rosenthal as Tifereth Israel's spiritual leader two years ago, set the tone for the hour-long service in the synagogue's sanctuary by recalling the time he first spoke to Rosenthal by telephone about the position he planned to vacate. "So, you're the jerk who is trying to take my job," Rosenthal joked, stunning Dorsch into silence until Rosenthal explained he was just kidding.

Dorsch suggested that Rosenthal had a "unique and somewhat snarky sense of humor."

Relations between a new rabbi and an emeritus rabbi can be dicey, Dorsch related. However, he said "Len and Judy" went out of their way to make him comfortable. Standing on the *bima*, with Rosenthal's plain wooden casket on the floor near him, Dorsch said he felt awe at being, on such an occasion, in the sanctuary for which

Rosenthal had raised funds over the years and had so faithfully served the congregation. He added that he would miss him as a mentor, confidante, and friend.

To officiate the service, the Rosenthal family called upon the San Diego Community Chaplain, Rabbi Ralph Dalin, who was not only a classmate of Rosenthal's at the UJ and the Jewish Theological Seminary in New York but also was his Torah study partner. Dalin recalled that when he and his wife Hedy arrived in San Diego about 20 years ago, they were greeted warmly by Rosenthal, who urged him to please not call him by the name everyone used at JTS, "Lenny." So thereafter, it was "Len."

Dalin said Rosenthal either was a "serious funny person" or a "funny serious person." He was fond of wisecracking, no more so than when he was standing next to Dalin during a reading of the *megillah* at a Purim celebration. Rosenthal, who technically was serving as a *gabbai*—the person who is supposed to make sure no word of Scripture is misspoken—often would whisper jokes and twirl a large wooden *grogger* while Dalin was trying to read aloud from the *Book of Esther*.

Rosenthal was serious in his "dedication to the Jewish people" and was "deeply caring of his congregants individually and collectively," Dalin said. There were occasions when Rosenthal would visit family members out of town, and then would hear that a member of his congregation had died. He would compose a eulogy, even though he was on vacation, and send it to Dalin, so the words spoken by a substitute at a funeral could be from someone who personally knew the deceased.

At a recent tribute dinner for Rabbi Rosenthal, Dalin said he asked Rosenthal's sister-in-law Beth Klareich, the program director at Tifereth Israel Synagogue, what kind of gift would the rabbi welcome. She responded that if he really wanted to honor Rosenthal, he could contribute to the fund to redo the synagogue's bathrooms. Dalin explained that "from a fundraising perspective," renovation of restrooms is a hard sell.

Rabbi Michael Gotlieb, spiritual leader of Congregation Kehillat Ma'arav in Santa Monica, told the mourners at Tifereth Israel that in 1974 when Rosenthal had not yet decided to become a rabbi, he had served as Gotlieb's confirmation teacher at Congregation Beth Tefilah, a Conservative congregation that later merged with Adat Ami Synagogue to become Ohr Shalom Synagogue.

He remembered that Rosenthal cared that his students learn the material and added that "genuine goodness was his hallmark." He said by chance he spoke to Rosenthal on Wednesday, just the day before he died, and that Rosenthal told him that having survived a stroke, his appreciation of life had intensified.

Rabbi Adam Rosenthal, who followed in his father's footsteps and currently serves as the Ritual Director of Sinai Temple in Los Angeles, related that there is a Talmudic passage in which rabbis ponder whether one should save one's father or one's teacher, in the event that only one could be saved from drowning. The Talmudic rabbis decided that it was more important to save the teacher. When Adam spoke to his father about it, Rabbi Leonard Rosenthal quipped that passage "no doubt was written by a teacher." Adam said he always thought he would be safe from that Talmudic predicament because in saving his father, he would be saving his teacher, and vice versa. But now, he said, he has lost both.

Margalit Rosenthal, who is The Jewish Federation of Greater Los Angeles's senior vice president of Nu-Roots, which fosters adult engagement in Jewish life, described her father as her role model and as one who was optimistic, selfless, and honest. "He never wanted to be the center of attention," she said. She added that he loved Arnold Schwarzenegger movies, a great beer, bad TV, and good books.

Rabbi Rosenthal's other daughter, Adina Rosenthal, was represented by her husband Jeremy Gerstle, who described the rabbi as both a wonderful father-in-law and a model grandfather. "I'll have to tell them about their *saba*, by exemplifying his moral compass," he said.

The final speaker was Rabbi Devorah Marcus of Temple Emanu-El, a Reform congregation which routinely partners with Tifereth Israel Synagogue for Tashlich services at Lake Murray. Marcus, the current president of the San Diego Rabbinical Association, reeled off a number of adjectives to describe Rosenthal, among them "beloved . . . cantankerous . . . ornery . . . sarcastic, loving . . . devoted."

She added that he would hate to be the subject of such a commentary.

She met him after she started as the new rabbi at Temple Emanu-El, which previously had been served for many years by Rabbi Martin S. Lawson, who retired and was himself a very close friend to Rosenthal. Rosenthal came to Temple Emanu-El and, after introducing himself, "offered to beat up Marty, if I ever needed it." Marcus and Rosenthal became fast friends.

Marcus added that Rosenthal took the time to make meaningful contact with others. He also had his zany side. The first time she saw him at Tashlich services (on the first day of Rosh Hashanah, when Jews symbolically cast their sins onto the water), he was wearing a chili pepper shirt, a hat, and an accordion. She said she decided there and then "that rabbi was definitely going to be my friend."

Marcus said Rosenthal spoke "truth to power," and recalled when the Orthodox Rabbinate in Israel created a "blacklist" of rabbis in the Diaspora, whose conversions they would not accept, Rosenthal wrote to them an indignant letter, signed by multiple other San Diego rabbis, demanding that they too be put on the list.

She added that Rosenthal had a "signature cheekiness" along with a deep "belief in Jewish pluralism."

Following the chanting of *El Moleh Rachamim,* Rabbi Rosenthal's coffin was wheeled from the sanctuary to a waiting hearse, which transported him to the Home of Peace Cemetery for a private burial.

Shiva services will be held 7 p.m. Saturday, February 16, through Wednesday, February 20, in the Tifereth Israel sanctuary at 6660 Cowles Mountain Boulevard, San Diego. Those wishing to honor Rabbi Rosenthal's memory may donate to the Rabbi Rosenthal Memorial Fund at the Jewish Community Foundation via www.jcfsandiego.org.

The Charity We Need Now: The Bus Station Project Serves Migrant Families at the Border

L'Chaim San Diego Magazine,
March 2019

While the political situation for asylum seekers who come to the United States' southern border seemingly changes day by day, Mimi Pollack, 65, and Paula Sassi, 71, are among the few constants.

Twice a week since last July, the two women have driven from Mimi's storeroom/garage in the suburb of La Mesa to the Greyhound Bus Station in downtown San Diego to bring food, water, blankets, toiletries, U.S. maps, and children's toys to weary migrants who are en route to the homes across the nation of their temporary sponsors.

Pollack is a retired ESL teacher of American birth who grew up in Mexico City before returning to the United States. Sassi also taught English-as-a-Second-Language, but is better known as a graphologist who examines people's handwriting for prospective employers and other clients.

Using their own money and that of donors, Sassi and Pollack assemble in Pollack's garage numerous sets of two bags packed with such supplies as water, juices, and various trail snacks, including peanut butter and crackers, cheese and crackers, nutritional bars, cookies, and potato chips filling one bag; and toiletries, including soap, shampoo, conditioner, tissue packets, toothbrush, and toothpaste stuffing the other. In addition, the two women put into the trunk of Pollack's car some blankets and stuffed animals—in short, everything that will make a long bus ride to an unknown destination more tolerable for the migrants, most of whom speak little or no English.

When they greet the migrants at the bus station and explain in Spanish what they have brought for them, huge smiles brighten the faces of both parents and children. Their kindness is unexpected, and as a result all that more appreciated.

The Bus Station Project—as Pollack's and Sassi's endeavor has been called—is one of the last steps in a process that saw the migrants travel to San Diego's border with Tijuana, Mexico, and there ask Immigration and Customs Enforcement (ICE) officials for asylum in the United States.

Once they have made such a request, at least up until recently, the would-be asylees went through identification processing, and, if they had people living in the United States willing to sponsor them, they were sent on their way—wearing electronic ankle bracelets—to the homes of the sponsors. Once at their destinations, they were instructed to contact immigration officials immediately to begin their court proceedings.

When a large flow of asylum seekers started arriving at the Mexican border last July, ICE first processed them, and then dropped them off without further ado at the Greyhound Bus Station, often with no more than a bus ticket and $10 for expenses. Not speaking English, the migrants often were quite confused about what they were supposed to do next.

Learning of this situation, Pollack and Sassi decided to help in any way that they could. Realizing that in some cases the migrants hadn't eaten for several days, Sassi and Pollack made sandwiches or bought food for them at a nearby convenience store.

As luck would have it, the store closest to the Greyhound Bus Station is operated by Iraqi Christians (Chaldeans), who themselves were refugees not so very long ago. Pollack taught many Chaldeans in her ESL classes at Grossmont College in El Cajon, a city that boasts the nation's second-largest concentration of Chaldeans. When the store managers learned of the asylees' situation, they donated corn dogs and other food stuffs to help feed the hungry families.

After a few months, social service agencies in San Diego, including Jewish Family Service and Catholic Charities, combined to create the San Diego Rapid Response Network. Rapid Response opened temporary shelters for the migrants so that they could shower, eat, sleep, and get a change of clothing before embarking on their bus or plane trips to their sponsors' homes. Sassi and Pollack told me that they have noted a big difference in the moods of the traveling families ever since. Whereas before they seemed sad, depressed, and scared, now they seem happier, aware that big-hearted people in America welcome them—no matter what might be said on the news about immigrants.

Laurie Hall, a therapist with a master's degree in social work, volunteers at the Rapid Response shelter on a *pro bono* basis, filling in wherever she can. A Spanish-speaker, Hall, who like Pollack, is Jewish, says she particularly enjoys being in the playroom at the shelter, where the children can enjoy simply being kids. On a recent night, she was assigned as an escort, driving three migrant families from Guatemala in a van to the Greyhound Bus Station where, with money provided by the Rapid Response Network, she purchased tickets for each of the families. One was headed for Corpus Christi, Texas; another to Houston, Texas; and the third, to Sacramento.

The Greyhound tickets are difficult to decipher, particularly so for people who have no real working knowledge of English. Hall patiently explained the bus routine to the families, telling them about transfers and the rest stops along the way. She confided, "I have a master's degree and I find the tickets hard to understand; imagine what it's like for people who don't read English or are completely illiterate."

After Hall purchased the tickets and briefed her temporary wards, Sassi and Pollack opened their bags of goodies. "Fruta!" exclaimed one of the four children as he espied the small tangerines in the bag. Pollack said, whereas American children seem to gravitate toward baked goods like cookies, the Guatemalan children seem to prefer the fruit. Causing an even bigger stir, and the broadest of smiles, were the stuffed animals that the American twosome bestowed upon the children. As for the parents, they gratefully accepted blankets, knowing that riding in a bus at night sometimes can be quite cold.

In addition to the three families transported by the Rapid Response Network, on that evening there was another family from Cuba and two families from Haiti who were awaiting Greyhound transportation to sponsors' homes. Pollack went to the trunk of her car and delivered bags of goodies to them as well.

The Cuban father, Dennis, told Pollack in Spanish that he and his wife Jaisi and daughter Mia left Cuba because of their opposition to Communism and because "there is lots of poverty and no jobs." He had saved money to fly from Cuba to Mexico, and from there made it to the U.S. border by bus and by foot. His hope is to "resolve our immigration status, find jobs, and go to school." He said that all along his journey, in Mexico and thus far in the United States, he had found people to be friendly and welcoming.

Iliana, a Guatemalan who was travelling with her daughter, said that it took her 20 days to travel by bus, car, and foot to get to the American border. In Houston, she has a friend who has agreed to be her sponsor. How has she been treated by U.S. authorities? she was asked. In reply, she gave a big, enthusiastic thumb's up.

The Greyhound Bus Station at 1313 National Avenue in San Diego is surrounded by a homeless encampment. Men and women in sleeping bags line the sidewalks adjacent to the outdoor seating area where people wait for the buses. On occasion, homeless people will ask Sassi and Pollack if they too can have some food, or a blanket—requests with which the generous-hearted ladies always comply.

The two benefactors over the months also have made friends with the Greyhound Bus Station employees, bringing for their families boxes of candy and other presents. On a recent night, one of the security guards was suffering with a cough, and Sassi immediately retrieved for him a package of cough drops from her car.

Late in January, the U.S. Department of Homeland Security announced that henceforth people seeking asylum would be required to wait on the Mexican side of the border until their cases are ready for adjudication. On appointed dates, the applicants for asylum are expected to present themselves to U.S. officials at the border, and from there be driven to the federal courthouse in downtown San Diego, where a judge will hear their case.

There was immediate talk of a court challenge to this procedure, and HIAS (which was founded in 1881 as the Hebrew Immigrant Aid Society) initiated a letter-writing campaign to Congress to repeal of the Remain in Mexico policy. HIAS said the policy "violates the rights of those seeking safety in our country by making it nearly impossible for asylum seekers to access the legal protections available to them under both U.S. and international law."

Whether the change in procedure will end the need for programs by the Rapid Response Network and the Bus Station Project on the American side of the border is, at this date, still an open question.

Pollack said in February that there were numerous families still "in the pipeline" who needed assistance as they traveled to their sponsors' homes.

"As long as people keep coming, we will be there!" Pollack vowed.

Index

-A-

AIDS 6, 32, 278
Abraham 298
Abrams, Chanah 37, 38
Acapulco, Mexico 40
"Acharai" (Follow Me)
    111
Acheatal, Larry 112
Ackerman, Diane 156
Adam 123
Adamcik, Jo 117
Adat Ami Synagogue 59,
    360
Adath Jeshurun 289
Adkins, Ina 190
Adler, John 110
Adventure Hornblower
    338, 341
Afghanistan 245
Africa, African 68, 164,
    223, 284
"Ahmed" from Somalia
    162
Aim I 303
Ajzenberg-Selove, Fay 172

Akiva, Rabbi 254-255
Albertson's Market 128,
    131
Allen, Marcus 134
Allied Contractors 129
Allied Gardens 125, 129,
    130
Allied Powers 223
Allison, William 181-182
Alto 296
Alvarado, Juan Bautista
    137
Alzheimer's Disease 24
America's Cup 339
American Ex-Prisoners of
    War 196-197
American Jewish
    Committee 55-56
American Jewish
    University 299, 334,
    358
American Library
    Association 154
Amos, David 218-220
Amsterdam, Holland 261
Anaheim 231

Andrusier, Rafi, Rabbi
    254-25
Angel's Trumpet 128-129
Angola 62
"Ani Ma'amin" 2, 3
Anschluss 152
Antarctica 247, 250-251
Anti-Defamation League
    41, 89
Anti-Semitism 31,
    233-234, 285
Antler, Joyce 156
Arabic 47, 161, 200, 270
Archer, Jonathan *(Star
    Trek* character) 193
Arctic Circle 338
Arctic Ocean 340
Arias, Oscar 69
Arizona 10, 12, 217, 225,
    354-356
Arizona, State of flag 8
    State Constitutional
    Convention 8, 9, 12,
    354-
Arnost of Parbudice,
    Archbishop 56

Aron Kodesh (Holy Ark) 74

Arts and Antiques 28

Asia 124

Ascension Lutheran Church 129

Ascent of Man, The 20

Asian Pacific Thematic District 162

Aspen Mine Company 97

Assemblies of God 257

Associated Press vii

Atkins, Toni 226, 272

Atlanta, Georgia 61, 132, 172

Atlantic City, New Jersey 290

Atlantic Ocean 325

Attia, Alberto 58, 59

Audubon, James 318

Auschwitz 2, 3, 282, 284

Auslander, Shalom 156

Austin, Jim 108

Australia 257

Austria 152, 158, 224

Austria-Hungary 161

Avenida de Judios 138

Axis powers 129

-B-

BDS (boycott, divestment, sanctions) 257

Bagel 291

Baharan, Avraham, Rabbi 96

Baird, Carol Davidson 51-55

Baird, Daniel 51, 53

Baird, Geoffrey 51, 53

Baird, Stephen 51

Babitt, Dina 284

Baizerman, Saul L. 302-303

Baja California 314

Baja California Sur 314, 338

Baja Peninsula 316

Bakula, Scott 193-195

Balboa Park 138, 144, 164, 186, 260, 289, 309, 315

Casa de Balboa 191

Committee of 100 341

Cottage of Israel 9, 200-202

Evenson, Bea, Fountain 217, 316, 342

Fleet, Reuben H., Science Center 214-217, 316, 342-349

Golf Course 146

Hall of Champions 134

House of Charm 186

House of Pacific Relations 9

Mingei International Museum 185-188

Model Railroad Museum 142, 189-192

Museum of Art 302-309

Museum of Man 327-330

Natural History Museum 314-318, 338, 340, 342-349

Organ Pavilion 202

Panama-California Exhibition 186

San Diego Historical Society/ History Center 191-192, 240, 317

San Diego Zoo 10, 318, 356

Veterans Museum and Memorial Center 165, 310-313

Ball, Lucille 152

Ballast Point 325

Baltazar, Fausto 248

Bandini, Arcadia 137

Bandini, Don Juan 136-138, 141

Bandini, Josefa 137

Bandini, Ysidora 137

bar/ bat mitzvah 1, 3, 13, 51, 54, 84, 91, 276

baracha 299

Barker, Scott 153

Barnes, M. Virginia "Ginny" 109

Barragan, Luis 26

Bashir, Omar Al- 71

Battle of the Wilderness 167

Baum, Abraham J. 310-311

Bavaria 167

Baylor College of
Medicine 172

"Beautiful Dreamer" 130

Becker, Richard 196

Begin, Menachem 80, 81

Beirne, Barbara 160

Beiser, Kevin 219, 273

Bel Air Country Club
146

Belarus 302

Belgium, Belgians 66, 234

Bell, Diane 153

Bell, William F. 146

Bell, William P. 146

Bellamar Point Loma 287

Ben Gurion Airport 182

Benami, Amir 126-127

Benchley, Belle 10, 356

Benchley-Weinberger
Elementary School
10, 356

Bening, Annette 220

Benjamin, Edwin. A.,
Branch, San Diego
Public Library 130,
292

Benson, Ezra Taft 230

Bergen-Belsen 234

Berkeley, California 146,
341

Berkson, Marsha 110,
239

Berman, David 218

Berman, Sharlene 218

Berman, Shelly 59

Bernstein, Arlene,
Cantor/ Rabbi 78, 84

Bernstein, Nicole 259

Bersin, Alan 41, 118, 119

Beth Din 299, 334

Beth Israel Day School
79, 83, 99s

Beth Jacob Congregation
37, 38, 98, 222, 245

Bethesda, Jerusalem 267

Bibel, Barbara 154

Bible, King James version
87, 90

Big Bang 121

Big Open Skull 308

Bima 5, 54, 74

Birch Aquarium 350-351

Bird of Paradise 128-129

Birthright/ Taglit 222,
299-300

Black Madonna 233

Blockbuster Video 131

Blois de Forge, France
167

Blood Sisters 279

Blue Ribbon School 102

B'nai B'rith 10, 244

Boateng, Boatema 164

Boeing 747 47

Bogomilsky, Moshe,
Rabbi 36

Bogopulsky, Avram,
Rabbi 38

Bohemia, Czech Republic
49, 56, 58

Bollenbacher, Walter 129

Bondurovska, Dasha 164

Boniecka, Eileen 18

Boosters of Old Town 140

Border Crossing 307

Bosnia 61, 62, 64, 69, 70,
81

Boston, Massachusetts
174, 288

Boston Latin School 174

Boulder, Colorado 172

Bowers, Wendy 13

Brandeis, Louis 5, 6

Brandeis University 182,
240

Brandenburg, Rian 164

Brazil 118, 164

Breitbard, Robert 134

Bren, Donald 78

Brenner, Sy 197

Breslin, Patrick 204

Brewster, Rudi 14

Briggs, John 278

Brin, Herb viii

Brno, Czech Republic 48

Broad Art Foundation
154

Brodsky, Nina 259

Brody, Arthur 154

Brody, Barbara 115

Brody, Sophie 154

Bronco, Ray 292

Bronowski, Jacob 20, 27,
34

Brooklyn, New York 159,
241

Brooklyn Child
Development Center,
San Diego 115

Brooks, Avery 193-195

Broudy, Abraham, Dr. 95

Brown, Edmund G. "Pat" 18

Brown, Leroy 142

Brown, Stuart 114

Brown Pelicans 347

Brunerova, Kitty 284

Brussels, Belgium 66

Bry, Barbara 224

Bryant, Sydney 263

Bunton, Nechama 200

Burma 9, 245

Burman, Shirley 189

Burnham Institute 177

Burning Bush 229

Bus Station Project 363

Bush, George W. 80, 105, 171, 196

Butcher Shop 291

butterfly, caterpillar 3, 93, 112, 187, 229, 284

Buttino, Frank 275

-C-

C-Span 11

Caballero, Fabian 116

Cabrillo Yard 192

Cal Tech 174

Caco bandits 167

Calder, Alexander 307

Caliente, California 190

California 61, 112, 148. 189, 273, 276, 290, 314, 319

California, State of Assembly 106, 147,

148, 162, 224, 272, 312

Attorney General 148

Business and Transportation Agency 13

Cultural and Historic Endowment

Flag 8

Governor 13, 44, 46, 153

Industrial Act 190

Legislature 225

Municipal Courts (County administered) 17, 18, 273, 356

Proposition 8 (anti-gay marriage-2008) 276

Proposition 13 (tax limitation – 1978) 220

Proposition 40 (clean water, air, parks, coast-2002) 137

Proposition 187 (benefits-undocumented aliens) 44

Senate 137-138, 226, 272, 278

State Library 136

Superior Court (County administered) 12, 18, 273, 356

California Gray Whale 338-341

California Sea Lions 323-324

California State University – Fresno 274

California Water Project 343

Californian, Tall Ship 338

Californios 140

Cambodia 62, 159, 311

Camp Pendleton 245

Canada 320-321

Captain America (comic book character) 283

Carlebach, Zalman 222

Carlsbad, California 46

ComicKaze 285

Camp David, Maryland 80, 182

Camp Ramah 358

Campbell, Mark A., Msgr. 139

Captains (Star Trek documentary) 193

Carlsbad, California 344

Carmel Valley 46, 111, 112

Caribbean 159

Carrillo, Josefa 145

Carson, Kit, Park 186

Carter, Charles 219

Carter, Jimmy 61, 68-71, 80-82

Carter, Rosalynn 69

Carter Center, The 68-72, 81

Casa de Bandini / Cosmopolitan Hotel 136-142

Casa de Carrillo 145, 289

Casper, Billy 134

Castano, Carolyn 203

Castleford, England 305

Casuto, Morris 41

Catholic (Roman), Catholics 53, 56, 61, 82, 39, 242, 291, 297, 331-337

Catholic Charities 242, 365

Catholic Church of the Immaculate Conception 139

Cats 348

Cedars of Lebanon 229

Cell phone technology 174-175

Cellint 176

Central California viii

Chabad Hebrew Academy 99

Chabad Lubavitch 35-37

Chabad of East County 253

Chabad of La Costa 222

Chadwick, Florence 134

Chadwick, Lynn 307-308

Chagall, Marc 302

Chai (Life, 18) 47

Chaldean 365

Chambers, Erin 10

Chambers, Richard 10

Chanukah 292-293, 334

Charles IV (Emperor, Holy Roman Empire) 56

Chiang Kai-Shek 188

Chicago 116

Chicken Nest 127

Chile 145

China, Chinese 124, 166, 175, 181, 188, 200, 321

Chinese-American 162

Chofetz Chaim Yeshiva 84, 97, 99

Christensen, Lynne Newell 141

Christian, Christianity 25, 41, 71, 107, 257-258, 295, 365

Christmas 249, 334

Chula Vista 231, 286, 295-296

Chula Vista High School 296

Chula Vista Junior High School 296

Chumash 100

Chuppah (ceremonial canopy) 49

Church of the Immaculata 230

Cincinnati, Ohio 248

City Farmers Nursery 91

Civil Rights Act of 1964 190

Civil Rights Movement 195

Civil War, U.S. 125, 167, 190, 312

Clairemont 91

Cleator, Bill vii

Cleveland, Ohio 161, 241

Cleveland Elementary School 98

Climate change 223

Clinton, Bill 69, 103

Code Division Multiple Access (CDMA) 170

Coffey, Daniel 109

Cohen, Hal 237

Cohen, Helen 237

Cohen, Michel 319

Cohen, Peter 188

Cohn, Abraham 167

Cohn, Morton, Rabbi 25, 291

Cohn, Sally 25

Colburn, Tom 266

Cold War 308

College Area 98

Cologne, Germany 2

Colombia, Colombian 203

Colorado 11

Colorado River 343-244

Colorado River Aqueduct 344

Colorado State University 332

Columbus, Christopher, Award for Science 172

Comic-Con ii, 193-195, 282-286

Coming Together 186

Communism,
Communist 49, 51,
58, 59, 188, 366
Conde Naste 303
Coney Island 159
Congo, Democratic
Republic of 245
Congregation Adat
Yeshurun (La Jolla)
73-76, 155, 222
Congregation Beth Am
(San Diego) ii, 45-60,
163
Congregation Beth Emet
(Anaheim) 231
Congregation Beth El (La
Jolla) 85, 91
Congregation Beth Israel
(San Diego) 9, 18,
77-79, 83, 97, 138,
144, 242, 275, 289, 291
Congregation Beth
Tefilah (San Diego)
59, 98, 360
Congregation Beth
Sholom (Chula Vista)
231
Congregation B'nai Israel
(Tustin) 358
Congregation Dor
Hadash (San Diego)
207
Congregation Kol Ami
(Tampa, Florida) 358
Congregation Kehillat
Ma'arav (Santa
Monica) 360
Conner, Dennis 339
Connolly, Maureen 134

Coons, Bruce 141
Copernicus 20, 34
Cormorant 324
Cornwall, England 306
Coronado, California 278
Coronado Historical
Association 142
Coronado Island 123
Corpus Christi, Texas
365
Cory, Alec 17
Cory and Schwartz 17
Coskey, Laurie, Rabbi
275
Costa Rica 81
Cowles Mountain 231
Cowles Mountain
Community
Foundation 219
Cramer's Bakery & Deli
135
Crawford, Sarah 328
Crawford High School 91
Crenshaw, Booker, Jr. 248
Crick, Francis 22
Crosby, Nancy 198
Crosby, Thomas 198
Crosby, Thomas, Jr.
197-198
Crosby, Tommy 198
Crowell, Frederick "Pat"
18
Cruz, Luis 321
Cuba 366
Cudal, Aurora 109
Cultural Revolution,
Chinese Communist
188

Cummins, Eilene 102
Cunin, Shlomo, Rabbi 35,
36
Cushman, Steve 209
Cuyamaca Mountains
126
Czech, Czechs 4, 5, 45,
51, 58, 60
Czech Republic,
Czechoslovakia ii,
4, 46-51, 55, 56, 57,
58, 284
Czestochowa, Poland 233

-D-

DDT 347
DNA (building blocks of
life) 22, 173, 252
Da Nang Air Base,
Vietnam 312
Da Vinci, Leonardo 20,
34
Dakar, Senegal 67
Dalin, Hedy 359
Dalin, Ralph, Rabbi 359
DalMonte, Carolyne 231
Daniel, Jenny 239
Danzig, Micah "Mitch"
259-261
Dartmouth College 225
Darwinism, Social 284
David, King 335
Davidson, Ernest 51
Davidson, Eva 51
Davies, Darlene Gould
109
Davis, Gray 46, 103

Davis, Sam and Freda, Library 27

Davis, Susan 148

Davis, Terrell 134

Dayton Peace Agreement, Dayton Conference 62, 70

De Jesus, Christina 295

De Jesus, Miriam 295

De Jesus, Roland 295

De Maio, Carl 272

Deadly Nightshade 128-129

Del Rio, Patricia ii

Delaware North Corp. 137

Delaware River 186

Delawie, Ettie 25

Delawie, Homer 342

Delta Airlines 132

Democrat, Democratic 15, 46, 80, 137, 355

Denmark, Danish 66, 214

Dennis, Ed 181

Depression, Great 159

Der Sturmer 283

Descendants of Old Town 140

Devers, Gail 134

Diaspora, Jewish 361

Diegueno Indians 122

Dillon, Mike 141

Disabled American Veterans 312

Ditler, Joseph 141

Diversionary Theatre 279

Dixon, T.J. 9

Dnepropetrovsk, Ukraine 263

Dobias, Milos 60

Dolphin 324

Dorsch, Joshua, Rabbi 222, 232, 237, 358

Dosick, Wayne, Rabbi 45-52, 54

Dover, England 307

Dream Big: Engineering Our World 216

Dreidel 291

Dubnov, Tammuz 319-320

Ducheny, Denise Moreno 138

Duke University 172

Dulbecco, Renato 19

Dumanis, Bonnie 273

Durban, South Africa 266

Durham, North Carolina 172

DuVall, Ed 288

-E-

Earth 20, 22, 122, 343

Easter 202

Echeandia, Jose Maria 145

Eckhart, Walter 22-25

Eden Memorial Park 152

Education First 289

Egypt 80, 182

1850 (Eighteen-Fifty) New Roots 163

Ehrenfried, Agathe 238

Ehringer, Martha 186-187

Einhorn, Estee 239

Einstein, Albert 5, 6, 27, 174, 214-216, 224

Einstein, Albert, School of Medicine 163

Einstein Brothers bagels 127-128

Einstein: His Life and Universe 155

El Cajon, California 103, 122, 198, 365

El Camino Memorial Park 233

El Fandango Restaurant 142

El Moleh Rachamim 362

El-Sayed, Mostafa A. 172

Elbe River, Germany 47, 107

elephant 92

Elias, Jacob 138

Elijah Minyan 46

Ellis, Richard 90

Ellis Island Museum 204

Ellison, Larry 262

Emancipation Proclamation 186

Embarcadero 323

Emory University 68, 81

Encinitas 18, 144, 236, 245

Encinitas Historical Society 141

Encinitas School District Farm Laboratory 211

Encyclopaedia Judaica 48

England , English 45, 234, 265, 303, 306, 321
Englander, Nathan 156
English language 66, 68, 101, 159-160, 235, 363
Enriquez, Maria Elena 116
Entrance to the Garden of Eden 163
Epix (premium channel) 193
Escondido 186
Esther 111, 112
Estline, Einat 112
Estline, Levana 110, 112
Estline, Ofer 112
Estline, Tsvi 112
Estline, Yael 112
Ethiopia 68
Europe 4, 5, 41, 45, 55, 95, 124, 146
European and American Car Center 128
Evangel University 265-266
Eve 121, 123
Evenson, Bea 342

–F–

FA-18s 339
Faderman, Avrom 276
Faderman, Lillian 271-281
Fagan, Candice 54
Far Rockaway Beach, Brooklyn 159
Farsi 200

Faulconer, Kevin 108, 287-288
Faulk, Marshall 134
Feder, Richard, Rabbi 48-50, 58
Federated Jewish Charities 240, 244
Feinstein, Dianne 226
Feinswog, Inge 239
Feldman, Anita 303-309
Ferrell, Jeanne L. 140
Fiber Rich Kitchen Cookbook, The 292
Figure for Landscape 304
Finci Building, Joseph and Lenka 177
Finder, Esther 284
Finkenberg, Kira 239
Finland 172
Finley, John ix
Fiser, Tana 60
Fitch, Henry Delano 145
Flashlightfish 352
Fleming, Guy, Trail 148
Ford, Patrick 115
Ford, Sharie 115
Foreskin's Lament 156
Forman, Gail Feinstein 156
Forman, Jack 154-157, 222
Fort Guijarros Museum Foundation 142
Fort Riviere, Haiti 167
Fossen, Linda 127
Foster, Lisa 118

Foster, Pauline 117
Foster, Stan 117
Foster, Stephen, Elementary School 130
Four Seasons Hotel 262
Four Tops, The 153
Fouts, Dan 134
Foxman, Abraham 40-44
Fradkin, Yonah, Rabbi 35, 36
France, French 66, 187, 197
Franciscan Padres 107, 122
Franco, Leticia Gomez 205
Frank, Anne, House 261
Franklin, Benjamin 210, 212
Franklin, Benjamin, STEAM Magnet Elementary School 210-213
Frazer, Leland 129
Fredman, Mickey 13
Freedom Trail 288
Freud, Sigmund 5
Freund, Berta 58
Freund, Gisela 58
Friars Road 126
Fried Egg Jellyfish 352
Friedkin, Morris 181
Friedman, Hugh 46
Friedmann, Pavel 3, 229
Friestedt, Suzanne 18

Froehbrodt, Rick 211-213
Fugu Pufferfish (Takifugu alboplumbeus) 350

-G-

Gabbai 359
Gabo, Naum 305
Gadlight 321
Gallagher, Bruce G. 139
Gallup Poll 272
Garden of Eden 149, 163
Gardner, Charles 167
Garlow, Jim, Pastor 260
Gaslamp Quarter Historical Foundation 141
gatesphotography.com ii
Gay/Lesbian 258
Gay for Good 279
Gay Liberation Front 279
Gay Men's Chorus 279
Gay Pride 278
Gay Revolution, The 277
Gaza 260, 269
Geller, Sara 111
General Electric 197
Generations of the Shoah 284
Genesis 122, 123
Genesis, A New Beginning 129
Genoa, Italy 172
Gentile (non-Jew) vii, 38, 77, 298
Georgia, USA 61

Georgia Institute of Technology 172
German, Germany 2, 45, 52, 107, 159, 167, 172, 197, 224, 283, 285, 306, 311, 321
Gerstle, Jeremy 361
Gethsemane, Garden of 268
Ghana 164
Gillingham, Listy 219
Gillman, Sid 134
Gilot, Francoise 26, 28, 34
Glick, Caroline 260
Globe, Arizona 12
Gloria, Todd 224, 226, 272
God (Hashem, "the Name") 2, 32, 50, 86, 87
Gold, Aaron S., Rabbi ii, 5, 227-231, 237, 358
Gold, Jeanne Weissbuch 227-231
Goldberg, Jerry 39, 78
Goldberger, Eugene, Cantor 230
Golden, Sandy 201
Golden Door Spa 158, 203
Golding, Susan 38, 106
Goldkind, Igor 283, 286
Goldstein, Meg 209
Goldstein, Shlomo, Rabbi 94, 95, 95
Golem 4

Goloboy, Sheila, Rabbi 78, 84
Goodman, Murray 182-184
Goodman, Zelda 183-184
Google 277, 298
Gomez, Georgette 273
Gospel 263
Gotlieb, Michael, Rabbi 360
Grace Assembly Church 129
Grand Colonial Hotel 151
Grand Street Settlement 161
Granet, David 115
Granlund, Paul T. 132
Grant, Ulysses S. 125, 126, 1219
Grant, Ulysses S., Jr. 126
Grantville 125, 126, 129
Grapes of Wrath 44
Great White Shark 90
Greater San Diego Business Association 279
Greece, Greek 26, 200
Greene, Norman viii, 106, 138
Greenwich Village 274
Greyhound Bus 366
Greyhound Bus Station, San Diego 363, 367
Gropius, Walter 306
Gross, Samuel 167

Grossmont College 200, 365

Guam 295

Guatemala 365-366

Gubler, Dale 140

Gumpertz, Sydney 167

Guterman, Harry 79

Gutknecht, Heidi 253

Gwynn, Tony 134, 222

-H-

HIAS (Hebrew Immigrant Aid Society) 367

Hafter, Jeri 13

Haganah 182-183

Haiti 62, 145, 167, 366

Halacha 50, 76

Hall, Jim 13, 14

Hall, Laurie 365-266

Hallel 50

Hallenbeck, Harry C. 10

Hallenbeck, Chamorro & Associates 10

Hamas 260

Hammelburg, Germany 311

Hammer Center for Cancer Research 22

Hampstead, North London 305-306

Haole 262

Harbor Drive 132

Harding, Warren G. 355

Hardistry, Kari 198

Harrison, Brian 214

Harrison, David 128, 152, 214

Harrison, Donald H. i, ii, vii, 22, 23, 24, 55, 91, 106, 163-164, 173, 214, 247, 292, 305, 314, 317, 340

Harrison, Hui-Wen Chang 152, 163, 214

Harrison, Jessica 222

Harrison, Martin B. 152

Harrison, Nancy ix, 91, 214

Harrison, Sara 214

Harvard University 101, 174

Harvey, Fred 190

Harvey Girls 190

Hasson, Rachel 163

Havel, Vaclav 60

Hawaii, Hawaiian 226, 257, 262, 267, 348

Hawk, Tony 134

Hazan, Marcia 116

Hazan, Shana 116

Hebrew 47, 48, 100, 200, 221, 270, 292

Hebrew Academy of Washington D.C. 94

Hebrew Benevolent Society 289

Hebrew Home for the Aged 245

Hebrew Immigrant Aid Society 245

Hebrew Sisterhood 240

Hebrew University, Jerusalem 259, 261, 268

Hedrei, Hungary 355

Henderson, Brian 19

Hendrichovce, Slovak Republic 355

Henri Christophe, "King" 145

Henry, Patrick, High School 218

Hepworth, Barbara 304-306

Heritage Park 144, 289

Hermann, Myra 143

Hertfordshire, England 306

Herzl, Theodor 260

Hier, Marvin, Rabbi 98

Higgs, Fletcher & Mack 12

High Holidays (also see Yom Kippur, Rosh Hashanah) 75, 138, 144, 171

Hildreth, Susan 136

Hillcrest 272

Hillel at UCSD 155

Himalaya Mountains 199

Hispanic 140-141

Historic Tours of America 142

Hitler, Adolf 9, 232, 283, 336

Hiyashi, Colonel (Japanese prison commander) 198

"H'nai Matov" 78

Hoffman, Trevor 134

Holiday Inn 56

Hollander, Chaim, Rabbi 99-100

Holloway, Bob 296

Holmes, Sherlock (fictional detective) 217

Holocaust ii, 1, 3, 5, 41, 45-46, 49, 51, 58-59, 95, 103, 166, 172, 175, 229, 232, 233-238, 244, 282, 285-286, 297

Holon, Israel 126

Holy Roman Empire 56

Hom, Dorothy 162

Hom, Gayle 162-163

Hom, Tom 162-163

Home of Peace Cemetery 362

Honi 111

Hooper, Selden 278

Hoover, Edgar J. 275

Hopkins, Michael 206, 208, 239, 243

Horace Mann Junior High School 91

Hot P'Strom'i 201

Hotel del Coronado 74

Houston, Texas 173, 365

Hungary 8, 51, 166

Hunt, George W.P. 354

Hunter, Duncan 103

Hustana, Laa 116

-I-

"I Never Saw Another Butterfly" 229

Idaho 187

Illinois 51

Imperial County, California 15

Impham, Scott 211

In Search of Wilderness 133

Independence War, Israel (1948) 182

India 175, 187, 257

Indian Detour Couriers 191

Innis, Jack Scheffler 122

Institute for Peace and Justice, Joan B. Kroc 61-72, 80-82

Institute for International Peace Studies, Joan B. Kroc 72

Institute for Scientific Information 20

Inter-American Foundation 159, 204

International Negotiation Network 69

Interstate Highway 5 41

Ipai 123

Iran 184, 257, 260, 321

Iraq 245, 321, 365

Ireland 321

Irvine Company 78

Irving, Joan 133

Irwin, Phyllis 273, 275, 277

Is She Available? 283

Isaac 298

Isaacson, Walter 155

Islamic Studies 259

Israel 42, 55, 63, 80, 112, 126, 135, 162, 172, 175, 180-184, 186, 200, 210-212, 221, 241, 254. 256-261, 267-270, 300, 344

Israel Defense Forces (IDF) 260

Israel Philharmonic 220

Israel Venture Network 176

Israelites, Hebrews 48

Italy 26, 170, 172, 321

Izetbegovic, Alija 70

-J-

Jacobs, Jacqueline 3, 229

Jacobs, Karl, Dr. 95

Jacobs, Irwin 153, 174, 206, 208

Jacobs, Joan 153, 206, 208

Jacobs & Cushman San Diego Food Bank 209

Jacobson-Beyer, Harry 148, 352

Jacobson-Beyer, Sherry 148, 352

Jaffa 86

Jaffe, Jules 178-179

Japan, Japanese 163, 168, 172, 187, 197, 321

Japanese-American 187

Japanese Red Army 182

Jarvis, Howard 220

Jaws 89

Jay, Allen 110

"Jeanie With the Light Brown Hair" 130

Jerusalem 77, 96, 184, 267-269, 319

Jerusalem Cherry 128-129

Jerusalem Post 183

Jerusalem Zoo 186

Jesus 139, 267-268, 331

Jet Propulsion Laboratory 174

jewfish (giant grouper) 89

Jewish, Jews vii, ix, 4, 6-7, 9, 32, 38, 45, 48, 53, 60, 61, 73, 79, 125, 128, 134, 136-138, 155, 162, 165, 175, 184, 189, 197, 200, 204, 206, 218, 224, 233, 244, 256, 258, 277, 291, 295, 297-298, 312, 316, 331-337, 344, 365

Jewish Big Pal/ Little Pal 222

Jewish Community Center (54th Street) 97, 220, 245

Jewish Community Foundation of San Diego 176, 362

Jewish Family Service of San Diego 176, 206-209, 239-246, 365

Jewish Federation of Greater Los Angeles 360

Jewish Historical Society of San Diego 58, 278

Jewish Museum, Prague 4, 55, 59

Jewish National Fund 221-222

Jewish Social Service Agency 240

Jewish Star (Magen David) 49, 112, 143, 145

Jewish Student Union 156

Jewish Studies Institute Day School 358

Jewish Tales (Richard Feder) 49

Jewish Theological Seminary, New York 58, 298, 358-359

Jewish Tragedy (Richard Feder) 49

Jewish War Veterans 165, 310, 312

Jewish Welfare Agency 240

jewishsightseeing.com viii

Jews and Christians (Richard Feder) 48

Jiminez, Luis 307

Johnson, Lyndon B. 12, 190

Jolly 16 240, 242

Jonah 86-90, 121, 124

Jordan-Connor, Stacey C. 143

Josephson, Jenny 259

Journal of San Diego History ix

Judaism, Judaic 2, 100, 101

  Chasidic 5, 35, 39

  Conservative 1, 5, 85, 91, 229, 237, 240, 242, 332, 336

  Lubavitcher 35-38

  Mitnagdic 38

  Orthodox 38, 73, 83-85, 98, 152, 229, 240, 242, 331-332, 361

  Reconstructionist 206

  Reform 77, 83-85, 138, 242, 332

  Satmar 38

Junior Charity 240

-K-

Ka'ahumanu Hou 262

Kaddish 50

Kafka, Franz 5, 6

Kahn, Louis I. 19, 26-29, 155

Kaiser-Permanente Hospital and Medical Center 127-129

Kal-El (Superman's name on Krypton) 285

Kalal, Matthew 219

Kalmar, Frank 297

Kalmar, Louis 297

Kalmar, Paul 297, 298, 300
Kalmar, Winifred 297
Kamin, Ben, Rabbi 77-78, 84
Kansas 140
Kaplan, Nathan 181-182
Karadzik, Radovan 70
Kassar, Barry 74
Katayama, Erika 327-329
Katsell, Nellie 49
Katz, Norman 336
Katzir, Aharon 182
Katzir, Ephraim (ne Katchalsky) 180-184
Katzir, Irit 180
Katzir, Nina 180, 183
Kay, Veronica 153
Kaye, Marianne 239, 245
Kearny Mesa 99, 127, 245, 291
Keep, Judith 11, 14
Kehoe, Christine 272
Kellogg Park 223
Kelton, Louis L. 129
Kennedy, John F., Airport, New York 320
Kent, England 306
Kentucky 148
Kentucky Fried Chicken 126
Keruv 336
Kholos, Clark J. 310
Khosla, Pradeep K. 224
Kiddush 74, 75
Kiev, Ukraine 263

King, Stephen 248
King's Cathedral 261, 267
Kippah 334
Kirk, James T. (*Star Trek* character) 193
Klareich, Beth 228, 359
Kleinpastor, Ben 211
Kleinrock, Leonard 172
Kline, Debbie 317
Kline, Larry 317
Klitofsky, Wayne 104
Knight, John L. 310
Knotbusch, Frank 17
Kobey, Kara 79
Koew 168
Kojetin, Czech Republic 48
Kol Nidre 298
Kolbuk, Poland 233
Kolin, Czech Republic 48
Koran 351
Koran Angelfish 351
Korean War 165
kosher, kashrut 1, 75, 201, 206, 221, 350
Kosovo 63, 161
Krakow, Poland 234
Krasnoff, Nancy Seiman 37
Krav Maga 261
Krichevsky, Marina 162
Kristiansen/ Christiansen Family 214
Kroc, Joan B. 61, 65
Kulefsky, Yaacov 94, 96
Kulp, Don 267

Kumeyaay Indians 120, 121, 138-139, 146, 253-254
Kumeyaay Lake 253
Kunzel, Klonie 288
Kupahulehua, Kimoteo 226
Kurd, Kurdish 63
Kurtz, Lori 228
Kvaas Construction Company 74
Kwaaypay Peak 253

-L-

L'Chaim San Diego Magazine 363
LGBTQ+ 271-281, 316, 337
La Jolla 19, 31, 33, 35, 73, 111, 151, 155, 170, 173, 180, 183, 185, 208, 224, 340, 351
La Jolla Country Club 146
La Jolla Cove 152, 238
La Jolla Gateway 78
La Jolla Grand Canyons 224
La Jolla High School 151
La Jolla Playhouse 151, 153
La Jolla Shores 183, 223, 351
La Mesa, California 35, 231, 363
La Mirage Hair Salon 128
La Pastorela 139

La Playa 289

La Playa Trails
Association 287

La Valencia Hotel
151-153

Labem River, Czech
Republic 47

Ladies Hebrew Aid
Society 240

Lag B'Omer 253

Lagos, Nigeria 263

Laguna Woods, California
163

Lake Miramar 14

Lake Murray 178, 361

Lake Tahoe 290

Lambda Archives 278

Lamed Vavnik 233

Lanai, Hawaii 262

Laos 311

Lapidus, Susan 211

Las Vegas 290

Latin America 159

Latino 42

Lauritzen, Bob 303

Lawrence Family Jewish
Community Center
183

Lawson, Martin S., Rabbi
232, 275, 361

Le, Ethan 211

Leberman, Hanan, Cantor
227, 230-231

Lee, Christopher 135

Lee, Stan 284

Leeds School of Art 305

Lefkowitz, Robert J. 172

LEGOs 214

Leinen, Margaret 224

Lenin, Vladimir 303

Lepow, Elaine 101

Lesbos, Isle of 280

Levens, Monroe, Rabbi
237

Levitow, John 169

Lewis, Claude "Bud"
Carlsbad Desalination
Plant 344

Levy, Susan 296

Lew, Shana 111

Liberation Moment, The
196

Liberia 68

Liberman, Alexander
303-304

Liberty Station 106, 158,
164, 203, 319-320

Libicki, Miriam 285

Lincoln, Abraham 186

Linda's Saucy Red Lentils
and Corn 293-294

Lindbergh, Charles A.
132-133

Lindbergh Field 47,
132-135

Ling-Yaiin Lious, Joyce 9

Lion's Gate, Jerusalem
267

Lithuania 41, 161

Lively Arts History
Association 142

Lizerbram, Lauren 221

Lizerbram, Sol 221

Lo Buglio, Redecinda 142

Lobkovic, Count 59

Lod, Israel 182

Lodge at Torrey Pines
164

Loew, Judah, ben Bezalel
4

London, England 5, 265,
303, 305-306

London Symphony 220

Long, Elgen M. 261

Long Gay Book, A 280

Longenecker, Martha 186

Lopes, Fernanda 153

Los Angeles vii, viii, 12,
61, 96, 98, 141, 146,
172, 203, 237, 244,
299, 328, 360

Los Angeles County 189

Los Angeles Herald-
Examiner vii

Los Angeles Times vii

Los Californianos
Publications 142

Los Coronados Islands
339

Louis Rose: San Diego's
First Jewish
Settler and Entrepreneur
viii

Louis Rose Society for the
Preservation
of Jewish History 138

Louisville, Kentucky 148

Louny, Czech Republic
48

Lozano, Mimi 140
lungfish 90
Lupsha, Amy 91, 92
Lvov, Poland 163

-M-

Ma'ale Adumim, Israel 260
Maccabees 6
Madaffer, Jim 130
Madaffer Enterprises 335
Madonna (singer) 164
Maftir 54
Magen David 313
Maharal 4, 5
Maher, Leo, Bishop 230
Mahzor 298
Maimonides 2
Maine 257, 263, 302
Man Unfolding (Metaphor Biologique) 21, 32
Manchester, Betsy 153
Manchester, Doug 153
Mandeville Auditorium 112
Manhattan, New York city 358
Manhattan Pizza 128
Mannasse, Heyman 138, 144
Mannasse, Joseph S. 138, 144
Mannasse, Moses 144
Mannasse & Schiller Addition 144
Mantell, Michael 102

Maranatha Chapel, Rancho Bernardo 88
Marburger, John 171
Marcus, Devorah, Rabbi 275, 361
Margulies, Samuel 167
Marianas Islands 168
Marina del Rey, Los Angeles 341
Markov, Andrey 173
Marriott Hotel 267
Marston, George 145
Marvel Comics 284
Marx, Julius "Groucho" 151
Marx Brothers 152
Masori, Sandi ix, 132
Masori, Shahar 132, 133
Masori, Shor M. ix, 91, 92, 128, 132-135, 247
Masori, Sky 214, 314-315
Mass, Catholic 331, 333
Massachusetts, Commonwealth of 312
Massachusetts Institute of Technology (MIT) 174, 187, 217
"Material Girl" 164
"Material Men" 164
Maui 226, 262, 266-267
Mauritania 81
May, Ronald V. 142
May Company 274
Mazzella, Daniel 108
McCosker, John 90

McIlworth, Colleen W. 190
McInnis, Scott 16
McNeil, George 36
Mead, Benjamin 238
Medal of Honor 165-169, 312
Mediterranean Sea 87, 89
Megillah 359
Mehitza 74
Meltzer, Scott, Rabbi 106, 275-107, 110, 275
Melville, Herman 88
Mengele, Josef 282, 284
Mennell, Bill 137
Menorah 35
Meron, Israel 256
Messiah 2, 335
Metropolitan Water District of Southern California 345
Mevasseret Zion, Israel 200
Mexicali 200
Mexican-American 42
Mexican-American War 140
Mexico, Mexican 40, 42, 43, 123, 137, 139, 145, 158-159, 243, 321, 338, 340-341, 366
Mexico City 320, 363
Meyers, James 11, 12
Meza, Amalia L. 41
Mezuzah 201, 207, 334
Michelangelo 204

Michigan 277
Mickelson, Phil 134
Middle East, global region 43
Middle West, USA region 41
Midianite 335
Midrash 20
Mikvah 75, 299, 334
Milch, Jim 144
Miliefsky, Allen R. 310-312
Milk, Harvey 271
Miller, Mark 257, 268-269
Miller, Sara Schoonmaker 257-270
Mills, James R. 137
Mines, Zechariah, Rabbi 96
Ministry of Special Cases 156
Mintz and Levin 261
Mira Mesa 273
Miramar National Cemetery 196-199
Miro, Juan 308
"Miss Furr and Miss Skeene" 280
Mission Bay 238
Mission Gorge Road 126
Mission San Diego 122, 125, 126, 140, 221, 288
Mission Trails Regional Park 120, 121, 124, 126, 253
Mission Valley 56

Mississippi 295
Mississippi River 107
Missouri 133, 257, 263, 267
Mix, Ron 134
Mobula munkiana 225
Moby Dick (Herman Melville) 88
Mogilner, Geoffrey 141
Mondrian, Piet 305
Monterey, California 295
Monterey Peninsula 341
Montgomery University 285
Moon, The 122
Mooney, Jones & Stokes 143
Moore, Archie 134
Moore, Henry 304-307
Moore, Henry, Foundation 304, 307
Moores, Becky 153
Moores, John 153
Moravia, Czech Republic 48, 58
Morgenstern, Abe 235
Morgenstern, Jack 233, 237
Mormon Battalion 140
Mormon Battalion Historic Site 140
Mormons (Latter Day Saints) 10, 138, 230
Morocco, James, Rev. 261
Morrissey, Kate 321
Moses 48, 121, 135, 285, 335

Moskovics, Linda 130, 290, 292
Mother and Daughter Seated 308
"Mother Nature" 93
Mound, Ann 79
Mount Helix 35
Mount Herzl 184
Mount Rabbi Schneerson 35
Mount Soledad 35
Mr. Chick 126
Muir, John, School 98
Munk, Mary 224
Munk, Walter 223-226
Munk, Walter, Way 223-226
Muro, Steve 199
Murphy, Dick 105,
Museum of Tolerance 237
Musevini, Yoweri 71
Muslim, Muslims 70, 161
My Darling, My Hamburger 155

-N-

Nakamura, Katherine 219
Nakashima, George 186-187
Nakashima, Mira 186
Nakashima Woodshop 186
Nate's Deli 92
National City 98

National Institute of Standards and Technology 172
National Medal of Science 170
National Museum of American Jewish History 205
Native Americans (also Indians) 167
Naval Training Center (Liberty Station) 106, 163, 203
Nazis 2, 3, 4, 6, 45, 54, 56-57, 59, 133, 197, 224, 229, 238, 283-284, 312
Nelson, James 9
Nelson, Walter 142
Neptune 226
Ner Israel Rabbinical College, Baltimore 94
Ner Tamid Synagogue 231
Nestor, California 295
Neu, Joyce 61-72, 81
Neuhaus-an-der-Oste, Germany 107, 163
Neumann, Al 241
Neumann, Rose 239-246
Nevada 290
Nevelson, Louise 302-303
New Americans Museum 158-164, 203-205, 319-322
New Hope, Pennsylvania 186-187
New Jersey 290, 358

New Life Club 2, 235
New Mexico 290
New Orleans, Louisiana 99, 107
New York (city) vii, 36, 59, 65, 97, 98, 108, 132, 161, 163, 204, 274, 302, 341
New York Times, The 225, 277
Newby-Fraser, Paula 134
Newman Center 297
Newport Beach, California 341
Nicholson, Ben 306
Nietzche, Frederic 47
Niger River 263
Nigeria 164, 257, 263-265
Night I Got Killed, The 197
Night Presence II 302-303
Nikigator 185
Nisman, Yevgenia 162
Noah 135
Nobel Prize 19, 21, 31
Noguchi, Isamu 307
Nore, Nicole 165
Normandy 223
North America 257, 340
North City Water Reclamation Plant 346
North County (San Diego) 245
North Island Naval Air Station 339
North Korea 166

North Park 243, 245
Northern California 343-344
Norway 224
Notre Dame University 72
Nu-Roots 360

–O–

O'Malley, Bert W. 172
ORT (Organization for Rehabilitation and Training) 230
Obama, Barack 199, 266, 276
Ocean Beach Historical Society 288
Oceanography 224
Odd Girls and Twilight Lovers 274
Odessa 162
Odio, Rodrigo Carazo 81
Odyssey III 308
Oederan 282-283
Ogul, Allison 332-336
Ogul, David 296, 331-338
Ogul, Jeremy 331, 334-336
Ogul, Justin 331
"Oh, Susannah" 130
OkCupid 297
Ohr Shalom Synagogue 59, 106, 110, 201, 275, 360
Oklahoma 266
Okmin, Linda 238
"Old Folks at Home" 130

Old Town San Diego 106
Old Town San Diego State
    Historic Park 136,
    143, 288
Old Town Trolley Tours
    of San Diego vii, 323,
    327
Olshansky, Igor 134
Olson, Arthur J. 215
On the Go service 245
Operation Gatekeeper 42
Oppenheim, Ellie 105
Opus Dei 297
Oracle 262
Orange County viii, 16,
    346, 358
Orange Julius 152
Orcas 87, 341
Orvis, Bill 116
Otay Mountain 42
Otter, Sea 348
Ottilie, Robert 109
Ould-Abdallah,
    Ahmedou 81

-P-

PHAME Performing Arts
    Center (Patrick Henry
    Arts,
    Media and
    Entertainment) 219
POW/ MIA 199
Pacific Beach Middle
    School 211
Pacific Desert Lines 192

Pacific Ocean 26, 42, 126,
    152, 323, 325,
    339-340, 348
Padre Dam 126
Palestine, Palestinian 9,
    63, 162-163, 260
Palestine Liberation
    Organization (PLO)
    161
Palm, Elephant-Foot 93
Parberry, Rise 163
Parham, Donna 86
Paris, France 132
Parry, Charles C. 146
Parry Grove Trail 148
Passover, Pesach 202,
    238, 340
Patton, George S. 310
Peace Corps 265
Pear Garden 145, 289
Pearl Harbor 187
Peck, Gregory 151, 153
Pennsylvania State
    University (Penn
    State) 68
Perez de Cuellar, Javier
    69
Perhacs, Les 133
Perlis, Leslie 229
Penguin Encounter
    247-252
Penguins 247-252
    Adelies 252
    Chinstraps 252
    Emperor 248, 251-252
    Gentoo 251

King 248, 251
    Macaroni 248, 251
Peru 137
Petco Park 221
Peters, Scott 226
Petrarca 56
Pew Research study 332
Philadelphia,
    Pennsylvania 172,
    205
Philadelphia Phillies 222
Philippines, Filipino,
    Filipina 118, 197, 295,
    300, 321
Phoenix (mythical bird)
    145
Picasso, Pablo 25
Pico, Pio 145
Pierce, Hilda 152
Pieta 204
Pig Man 155
Poekes, Michoel 84
Poet and Muse 185
Point Loma 106, 163,
    288, 323, 341, 346
Point Loma Nazarene
    College 269
Pojar, Milos 55-56, 59, 60
Poland, Polish 5, 51, 204,
    233
Pollack, Mimi 363-368
Pollak, Bernard 2
Pollak, Brigitte 2
Pollak, Gary 1
Pollak, Jeffrey 2

Pollak, Tanya 1

Polyxena of Lobkovic 57

Pope Francis II 225

Popperova, Berta 58

Popular Front for the Liberation of Palestine 182

Poway, California 196, 245

Poynor, Mike 18

Prague, Czechoslovakia 3, 4, 45, 47, 51, 57, 59

Precious Legacy Exhibition 5

Presenting Paul Zindel 155

Presidio Golf Course 143, 145, 289

Presidio Hill 107, 143, 145, 146, 288

Presley, Priscilla 153

Price, Sol 17

Price and Knotbusch 17

Prim, Janie 231

Principi, Anthony 196

Prisoner of War (POW) 166

Procopio, Cory, Hargreaves & Savitch 17

Prodigal Son, The 308

Protestant 331

Provigent 176

Prussia 167

Public Broadcasting System (PBS) 20

Puente, Consuelo 142

Puente-Reynolds, Oliva 108

Punta de Los Arboles 148

Purim 359

Pusan, Korea 165

-Q-

Qing Dynasty 188

Qualcomm 153, 170, 174, 209

Queen Califa's Magic Circle 186

Queen Elizabeth II vii

Quick Response (QR) Code 319

-R-

Racine & Laramie 141

Radio Frequency Identification (RFID) 176

Rady, Ernest 134

Rady, Evelyn 239

Rady Children's Hospital 177

Rady School of Business / Management 134

Rain Mountain 307

Ralph's Market 208, 329

Ramallah, Palestine Authority 161

Ramirez, Marco 41-43

Rancho Bernardo 38-39, 88, 273

Rancho Del Rey, Chula Vista 295

Rancho La Puerta 158, 203

Rancho San Diego 257

Rancho Santa Fe 153

Rapid Response Network 365

Rashi 95, 100

Ratner, Abraham 114

Ratner, Abraham, Torah School 114

Ratner, Abraham & Anne, Scholarship in Residence 227

Ratner, Anne 114

Ratner, Anne & Abraham, Children's Eye Center 115, 117

Ratner, Anne F., Endowed Chair of Pediatric Ophthalmology 115

Ratner, Isaac 114, 119

Reagan, Ronald 13, 16

Reclining Figure, Arch Leg 304

Recht, Pearl 237

Recht, Ruben 238

Redmond-Jones, Beth 315-

Redondo Beach, California 66

Rehovot, Israel 180, 182

Religious Practices of the Diegueno Indians 122

Reno, Janet 43

Reno, Nevada 290
Republican 15, 103, 354
Revel, Henrietta 2
Revolutionary War 288
Rhoades, John 8- 11, 15, 16
Richmond, Lois 239
Rickey, George Warren 307
Rickover, Hyman 69, 310-311
Ridberg, Yael, Rabbi 207
Rights Watch 71
Rigoli, Jill 13
Riverside, California 331
Riverside *Press-Enterprise* 331
Robbins, Shira 117
Roberts, Ron 224, 226
Robinson, Keith 86, 88
Robinson, Robert L. 109
Robinson-Rose House 289
Rodin, Auguste 308
Romania 248
Room Service 153
Roos, Rachel 164
Roosevelt, Franklin D., Jr. 190
Roosevelt, Theodore 12
Roosevelt Junior High School 289
Root, Sherry 25-28
Rooty Hill, Australia 265
Rome, Roman 26
Rose, Caroline Marks 289

Rose, Henrietta 289
Rose, Louis viii, 105, 106, 107, 138, 144, 163, 287, 289
Rose, Louis, Point 105
Rose, Mathilde 289
Rose Canyon 289
Rosenberg, Marcia Morgenstern 232, 235-237
Rosenfeld, Leah 189
Rosenthal, Adam, Rabbi 358, 360
Rosenthal, Adina 358, 361
Rosenthal, Judy Feigelson 228, 357-358
Rosenthal, Leonard, Rabbi 221, 228, 232-238, 298, 300, 334, 336, 357-362
Rosenthal, Margalit 358, 360
Rosenthal, Tony 308
Roseville 106, 108, 144, 163, 287-289
Roseville Elementary School 289
Rosh Hashanah 171, 178, 238, 247, 361
Ross, Betsy 137
Rothstein, Roz 259
Rotsart, John 142
Roudnice, Czech Republic ii, 45, 47-48, 51, 54-57, 59
Royal College of Art,

London 305
Rubenstein, Henrietta 239, 244
Rubin, Tibor 165
Rubio's 127
Ruchie's Job 285
Rund, Karen 110
Russia, Russian 159, 173, 204, 302-303, 321
Ruth 335
Ryan Air Lines Inc. 132
Ryan Aircraft 229
Rzesow, Poland 161

-S-

SEAL Tours 323-326
Sabat, Eleanora 58
Sacramento vii, 241, 341, 365
Sadat, Anwar 80, 81, 182
Safdie-Rabines Architects 206
Saint (St.) Louis, Missouri 194
Saint (St.) Louis, Senegal 66
Saint Phalle, Niki de 185-186
Saigon 245
Saipan 168
Salah, Tahani 161
Salk, Jonas 6, 19-29, 30-34, 155, 214, 216
Salk Institute for Biological Studies ii, 19-29, 30, 155, 183

Salomon, Ben 168

San Carlos 111, 130, 356

San Diego, City of vii, 146

Board of Trustees 138, 144, 289

City Attorney 356

City Council 38, 105, 106, 130, 152, 224, 226, 272

Historical Resources Board 139

Library 130

Mayor 38, 105, 106

Mayor, Acting vii

Parks and Recreation Board 105

Parks and Recreation Department 105

San Diego Agency for Jewish Education 176

San Diego & Arizona Eastern Railway 192

San Diego Archaeological Center 139, 144, 146

San Diego Bay 105, 108, 123, 323, 338

San Diego Chargers 134

San Diego Convention Center ii. 186, 193

San Diego-Coronado Bay Bridge 325

San Diego County vii, 2, 152, 221

San Diego County, government

Board of Supervisors 224, 226, 289

Parks and Recreation Department 141

San Diego County Log Cabin Club 279

San Diego County Place Names A to Z 129

San Diego County Science Fair 102

San Diego County Water Authority 343-344

San Diego Cruise Industry Consortium vii

San Diego Democratic Club 279

San Diego Grand Jury 289

San Diego Hebrew Home for the Aged 236

San Diego History Center 274-275

San Diego House of Coffees and Tea 142

San Diego International Airport (also Lindbergh Field) 229

San Diego Jewish Academy 99, 110, 176

San Diego Jewish Book Fair 183

San Diego Jewish Press-Heritage viii, 9, 13-14, 30, 41, 44, 62, 74, 79, 91, 95

San Diego Jewish Times viii

San Diego Jewish World viii, 156, 170, 181, 201, 213, 218, 240

San Diego Legends 122

San Diego Masonic Lodge 144

San Diego Mesa College 154-157. 186

San Diego Model Railroad Club 192

San Diego Padres 126, 153, 221

San Diego Rabbinical Association 107, 361

San Diego River 120, 126, 253

San Diego State University (SDSU) 91, 129, 201, 245, 261, 273, 333

San Diego Transit 129

San Diego Trolley 129

San Diego Trust and Savings Building 17

San Diego Unified Port District 13, 46

San Diego Unified School District 10, 138, 218, 219, 273, 356

San Diego Union, The vii

San Diego Union-Tribune 153, 319, 321, 332

San Diego Watercolor Society 163

San Diego Women's Chorus 279

Sandlinks 176

San Fernando Valley, Los Angeles 152, 357

San Francisco 271, 273, 341, 348

San Francisco Bay Area 216

San Pasqual Battlefield 140

San Rafael, California 167

Sanborn maps 192

Santa Barbara, California 148

Santa Clarita 189

Santa Fe Railroad 191

Santa Monica, California 360

Santa Rosa Island 148

Sarajevo 70

Sassi, Paula 363-368

Saugus, California 189

Save Our Heritage Organization (SOHO) 141, 144

Sax, Kurt 283

Sax, Ruth Goldshiedova ii, 282-286

Saxons 48

Sha'ar Hanegev, Israel 176

Shabbat 231

Schaffer, Dan 158, 161, 163, 164

Schaffer, Maurice 161

Schaffer, Norma Diamond 161

Scheller, Sandra ii, 282

Schenk, Elsa 46

Schenk, Fred 46

Schenk, Lynn 7, 11, 14-16, 18, 46-47, 49, 60, 103

Schenk, Sidney 46

Schiller, Marcus 138, 144

Schindler, Rose 238

Schlepping Through the American West: There Is a Jewish Story Everywhere ix

Schmidt, Jen 288

Schneerson, Menachem Mendel, Rabbi; "Rebbe" 35-37

School and Society 274

Schoonmaker, Harriet Williams 263

Schoonmaker, Jenny 262

Schoonmaker, Jonathan , Pastor 257

Schoonmaker, Julie 262

Schoonmaker, Kathleen 262

Schoonmaker, Paul, Pastor 263

Schoonmaker, Rebecca 262, 266, 268

Schraer, Miriam 38

Schreiber, Salomon 58

Schwartz, Edward J 7, 11, 12, 14, 16, 17

Schwartz, Edward J., Courthouse and Federal Building 7

Schwartz, Gertrude 14

Schwartz, Lloyd 139

Schwartz, Stan 58

Schwartz, Stephen 18

Schwartz Judaica 58

Schwarz, Yael 95, 102

Schwarzenegger, Arnold 153, 360

Science Watch 20

Scott, Robert 285

Scripps Clinic 183

Scripps Institution of Oceanography 178, 224

Scripps Ranch 35, 37, 38, 39

Scripps Research Institute 177, 215

Sea of Cortez 225

Sea Rhythms 133-134

Sea World 86-90, 247-252, 318

Seacrest Village Retirement Communities 176-177, 232, 236, 245

seahorses 351-352

seal 323

seal, elephant 89

Seaport Village 326

Seattle, Washington 187

Seau, Junior 134

Seeley, Alfred 136, 141

Sefton Foundation 317

Senegal 66

Sepulveda 357

Serbia, Serbs 69, 70

Serpent, Snake 121, 123, 149

Serra, Junipero, Father 288

Serra, Junipero, Father Trail 120

Serra Museum 145

77 (Seventy-Seven) Miles of Jewish Stories: History, Anecdotes & Tales of Travel Along I-8 ix

Shabbat, Shabbos 2, 54, 295, 331, 333

Shacharit 84

Shah of Iran 257, 312

Shainman, Harry (also Szainman) 158

Shakespeare, William 102

"Shamu" 88

Shanaan, Gad 319-321

Shark, Great White 89, 351

Shark, Leopard 351

Shatner, William 193-195

Shavuot 95

Shefer, Yigal 200

Shefer-Vanson, Dorothea 200

Shehekiyanu prayer 337

Shelter Island 326

Shiley Eye Clinic 114

Shiminski, Karla 138

Shir Chadash Band 295-296, 301, 336

Shonbrun, Anita 236

Shoval, Miriam 296

Showel, Morris 9

Shuster, Joe 284-285

Siegel, Jerry 284

Siemens 321

Sigma Alpha Epsilon Pi 332

Silesia 58, 167|

Silva, Paige 248

Silverman, Charles 227

Silverman, Ethel 227

Simchat Torah 38

Simmons, Stuart 79, 83

Sinai (Richard Feder) 49

Sinai Temple, Los Angeles 360

Sisko, Benjamin (*Star Trek* character) 193

Skyline Church 257, 260

Skype 259

Slavs 284

Slicher, Charles P. 172

Slutsky, Herman 152-153

Smalheer, Doug 186-187

Smith, David 307

Smithsonian Institution 160

Smolin, Max 153

Smolin, Noah 153

Smolin, Rocky 153

Snelling, Marsha 140

Snow, C.P. 22

Snow White and the Seven Dwarfs 284

Snyder, Faye 102

Snyder, Phil 336

Society of Hispanic Historical and Ancestral Research 140

SodaStream 260

Sofer (Torah scribe) 50, 58

Soille, Esther 99

Soille, Henry, Rabbi 99

Soille San Diego Hebrew Day School 83, 94-102

Solana Beach 45, 54

Solar Bird 308

Solomon, King 77

Somalia 162

"Sonata for Winds" by Charles Carter 219

Sonata Primitive 302-303

Soprano 296

Soto, Lorenzo 299

South Africa 159, 257, 265-266

Southern California 120, 316, 343-344

Southern California Yeshiva (SCY) High School 261

Southern Hemisphere 250

Southern Pacific Railroad 189-190

Southwest United States 189

Soviet Union 245

Spain, Spaniards 120, 122

Spanish language 43, 160, 364

Sperm Whale 88

Spielberg, Steven 89

Spinal Column 307

Spirit of St. Louis 132-133

Spitzer, Jill 239, 241, 246

Springfield, Missouri 263, 265

Springville, California 12

StandWithUs 257-270

Star-Spangled Banner, The 197

Star Trek franchise 193-195

Star Trek original series 193

Star Trek: Deep Space Nine 193

Star Trek: Enterprise 193

Starbucks 267

Stars & Stripes (sailboat) 338

Statue of Liberty 128

STEAM (Science, Technology, Engineering, Art, Math) 210

Stearns, Abel 137-138

Steele, Mark I. 75, 155

Steiman, Barbara 37

Steiman, Maury 37-38

Stein, Gertrude 280

Steinberg, Yael 261

Stern, Susan 297

Stern, Ted 296

Stevens, Zack 317

Stewart, Lorin 142

Stockton, Robert, Commodore 137, 140

Stonefish (Synanceia verrucose) 350

Stonewall Bar 274

Strom, Yale 201

Strubel, Abbey 190

Stuttgart, Germany 197

Sucov, Joel 230

Sudan 61, 68, 71, 81

Sudman, Rebecca 158

Sufi Mediterranean Restaurant 260

Suhler, Simon 167

Sun, The 20, 122, 135

Sun God 186

Sun Yat-Sen 188

Sunbelt Publications 122

Sunlight Juxtaposed 133

Sunset Cliffs, San Diego 307

Superman (comic book character) 282-284

Sutton, Marsha 153

Sweden 234

Sycuan Casino 290

Sydney, Australia 265

Szekely, Deborah 158-164, 203-205

-T-

Tablets of the Law 313

Taegu, Korea 165

Taft, William Howard 354-356

Tahiti 159

Tall, Bill 91-93

Tall, Nate 92

Tall, Rebecca 91

Tall, Samuel 91

Tall, Sarah 91

Talmud 100, 147, 360

Tampa, Florida 358

Tanach (Hebrew Bible) 87, 90, 121, 285, 298

Tanapag Village 168

Tarbut v'Torah 358

Tarbuton 201

Target 260

Tarshish 86

Tashlich 178-179, 361

Tate Gallery 303

Taussig, Oskar 58

Tecate, Mexico 158, 203

Technion 176

tefillin 222

Tehachapi Pass 192

Tel Aviv 132

Tel Aviv University 30

Tempel, Yvonne 340-341

Temple (in Jerusalem) 6, 77

Temple Emanu-El, San Diego 275, 290-294, 361

Temple Sharon, Orange County 358

Temple Menorah, Redondo Beach 66

Tender Greens 164

Terezin, Theresienstadt 3, 4, 48, 51, 52, 58, 60, 229, 282, 284

Terezin Foundation 59

Tetrodotoxin 350

Texas 348

Texler, Enid 290

Thailand, Thai 127

Thaler, Gert 106, 108
Thanksgiving 225
The Effect of Gamma Rays on Man-in-the-Moon Marigolds 155
The Zookeeper's Wife 156
Thomas, Paul 106-108
Thornsley, Terry 133
Tifereth Israel Community Orchestra (TICO) 218
Tifereth Israel Synagogue ii, 1, 4, 97, 114, 221-222, 227-231, 232-238, 240, 242-243, 295, 298, 300, 332, 334, 357-361
Tijuana 98, 243, 364
Tijuana Jewish Relief Association 244
Tikkun Olam 26, 32, 334
Tilden Park 146
Tobias, Jeanette 239, 244
Toler, Dennis 142
Toler, Heidi 142
Toler's Leather Depot 142
Tolson, Clyde 275
Tom Ham's Restaurant 237
Torah ii, 1-6, 38, 45-47, 49-51, 54-56, 58-59, 73, 75, 95, 99, 102, 201, 229. 255, 359
Torah High School 83, 84
Torrey, John 147

Torrey Pines 74, 146-149
Torrey Pines High School 261
Torrey Pines State Reserve 147, 150
Tower of Babel 124
Treblinka, Poland 58, 234
Trinity Lutheran Church 106
Truman, Harry S. 9, 12
Trump, Donald 260
Try to Remember, Never Forget 282
Tu B'Shevat 91, 110
Tutu, Desmond 69
213 (Two-Thirteen) *Magazine* 153
Tzedakah 112, 222
Tzitzit 334

-U-

UCLA *Daily Bruin* vii
U.S. Grant Hotel 126
U.S. Israel Center on Innovation and Economic Sustainability 210
U.S.S. *Connecticut* 167
U.S.S. *Theodore Roosevelt* 338
U.S.S. *Uhlmann* 278
Udon Royal Thai Air Force Base 311
Uganda 61, 71, 81
Ukraine 164, 257, 263, 302

Umeham, Gail 91
Umeham, Okoronkwo 91
Ungar, Otto 284
United Jewish Fund/ Federation 9, 18, 39, 99, 117, 176-177, 356
United Nations 70, 224
International Children's Emergency Fund (UNICEF) 71
United States of America, country 52, 53, 60, 67, 159, 161, 163, 165, 187, 205, 235, 260, 264, 285, 315, 356, 364-366
United States of America, government vii
Air Force 169, 310
Army 125, 140, 165-169, 198, 310
Attorney 41
Attorney-General 43
Bankruptcy Court 11
Base Realignment and Closure (BRAC) 106
Border Patrol 41-44, 308
Circuit Court of Appeals 10
Commerce Department 171
Congress 16, 46, 80, 103, 148, 189, 243, 266, 311
Customs 47
Defense Department 100

District Court (Southern District of California) 11, 14, 354

Education Department 102

Equal Employment Opportunities Commission 190

Federal Bureau of Investigation (FBI) 40, 171, 275

Flag 7, 10, 125

Foreign Aid 67

Homeland Security Department 367

House of Representatives 7, 16, 226

Immigration and Customs Enforcement (ICE) 364

Immigration and Naturalization Service 40

Inspector General, Office of 43

Joint Chiefs of Staff 167

Library of Congress 103

Marine Corps 8, 167

Mexico border 40-44, 62, 200, 307-308, 339, 364, 367

Naturalization 356

Navy 137, 271, 278, 295, 310-311, 313, 323-326, 338-339

Office of Special Investigation 312

Peace Corps 66

President 9, 12, 61, 68, 69, 80, 103, 105, 126, 171, 186, 190, 196, 199, 260, 266, 276, 338, 354

Secret Service 80

Senate 226

Space and Naval Warfare Systems Command (SPAWAR) 325

State Department 69

Supreme Court 5, 276, 355

Veterans Affairs Department 196, 199

White House 103, 170-171

University of California-Berkeley 58, 274, 297, 319

University of California-Irvine 68, 297

University of California-Los Angeles (UCLA) 172-173, 274

University of California-San Diego (UCSD) 104. 112, 114, 115, 134, 151, 180-184, 186, 210, 213, 224, 261, 351, 358

University of Colorado-Boulder 66

University of Illinois, Urbana-Champaign 172

University of Judaism 334, 358-359

University of Maryland 285

University of Pennsylvania 172

University of San Diego (USD) 61, 65, 80, 155, 164, 230

University of Southern California (USC) 67, 171, 173-174, 176

University Towne Centre 77

Unrepresented Nations and Peoples Organization 81

Unsan, Korea 166

-V-

Valentine's Day 226

Vana, Rami 127

Vance, Cyrus 69

Vann, Jim 141

Varga, George 321

Vatican 225

Via Dolorosa 268

Victoria, Manuel 137

Vienna, Austria 48

Vietnam 311-313, 321

Vietnam War 167, 245, 311

Vilicich, Tom 140

Vilna, Lithuania 41
Vitebsk, Belarus 302
Viterbi, Andrew 170-177
Viterbi, Erna 173-174, 176-177
Viterbi Algorithm 170
Viterbi Group 170, 175
Viterbi School of Engineering 171
Vitruvian Man 34
Vizcaino, Sebastian 339
Vlad the Impaler 248
Volkswagen 128
Vons Market 128, 329
V'Shamru 297

-W-

Wakefield, England 305
Wall, Michael 317
Wallace, Sylvia 129
Walmart 254
Walsh, Victor 137-138
Walters, Alice Levine Harrison 152
Walton, Bill 134
Ward, Chris 272
Warden, Barbara 38, 39
Warden, Richard "Dick" 39
Waring Estate 129
Waring Road 129
Warsaw, Poland 158
Washington, George 186
Washington, D.C. 65, 266
Washington Nationals 221

Washington Redskins 95
Watchers, The 307
Water and Sun 135
Waterman, T.T. 122
Wax, Charles 110
Wax family ix
Waxie Sanitary Supply ix
Wayne, Howard 106, 107, 148
Wear, John Robert 275
Weil, Jacob Weinberger 12
Weil, Gay Weinberger 12
Weinberger, Blanche Solomon 10, 356
Weinberger, Henry 10
Weinberger, Jacob ii, 8-14, 354-356
Weinberger, Jacob, Federal Courthouse ii, 7
Weinberger, Jacob, Foundation 9
Weinberger, Richard 13
Weinberger-Breitbard Lodge, B'nai B'rith 10
Weinberger Elementary School 10
Weiser, Betty 100
Weiser, Simcha, Rabbi 94-104
Weizmann Institute 182, 184
Weld, Anita 30
Wellner, Karen 102
Western Hemisphere 159, 251

Western States Jewish History ix, 240
Westminster Synagogue, London 5, 45. 46. 59, 229
Whalen, John J. 132
Whisman, Don 212
Whitworth, Ralph 153
Why Not the Best? 69
Wicuwul 123
Wiesel, Elie 237-238
Wiesenthal, Simon, Center 98
Wikipedia 298
Wilkens, John 321
Williams, Ted 134
Wilson, Doreen 334
Wilson, Pete 44-45
Wilson, Sharon 331-337
Winer, Jack 35
Wineland, David J. 172
Winfield, Dave 134
Winfrey, Oprah 226
Winnipeg, Canada 37
Winslow, Kellen 134
Witkin, Michael 55, 56, 57
Wohlgelernter, David 74
Wohlgelernter, Jeffrey, Rabbi 73-76
Wolof language 67
World Penguin Day 247
World War I 167
World War II 5, 45, 55, 57, 167, 197, 205, 223, 244, 278, 284, 306

Wright, Mickey 134
Wrottenberg, Jonas 243

–X–

Xanadu 188

–Y–

YMCA 242
Yachai, Shimon bar, Rabbi 255-256
Yahadut 100
Yechieli, Amir 211-212
Yedid, Edna 110
Yemen 261
Yeshiva High School (Greater Washington) 96
Yiddish 159
Yifrah, Guy 200

Yom HaShoah 50
Yom Kippur 49, 54, 86
Yom Kippur War 182
York, Maine 263
You Never Call, You Never Write: A History of the Jewish Mother 156
Young, Andrew 69
Young Israel Synagogue 99
Youth With A Mission (Y-WAM) 265
Yulefsky, Yaacov, Rabbi 94

–Z–

Zadok, Shmuel, Rabbi 5
Zajac, Jack 308
Zaks, Gussie 232-238

Zaks, Mike 233-238
Zapf, Lorie 287-288
Zehnwirth, Shimon, Rabbi 83
Zemen, Sheldon 162
Zindel, Paul 155
Zion Avenue 125-131
Zion Avenue Baptist Church 129
Zionists 128
Zohar 255
Zollman, Joellyn 240-246, 277
Zucchet, Michael 105
Zuckerberg, Mark 226
Zuckerman, Arthur, Rabbi 54, 56, 60
Zuniga, Francisco 308
Zuniga Jetty 339

Made in the USA
San Bernardino,
CA